THE ADVENTURES OF THE SONS OF NEPTUNE

"I have the right to go in that Sea. I have a right to clean sea water. I have a right not to be put at risk from infection or pollution and I demand that right!"
- Freddie Drabble, leader of the Sons of Neptune

"The Sons of Neptune are the smallest and most vociferous, serious, environmental pressure group in the world"
Professor Bruce Denness, former Professor of Marine Microbiology, Imperial College, London, and former Professor of Marine Civil engineering, Newcastle University. Published by the Waste Water International Journal, Texas USA 1992.

"We have to thank the Sons of Neptune for their help in achieving clean seas and clean beaches, and improving EC standards against pollution"
- John Napier, Chairman of Yorkshire Water (Keilder Water)

"One of Britain's most remarkable environmental campaigns – I would say most remarkable – owes nothing to Friends of The Earth, Greenpeace, or any other big guns in the environmental game. If you are glad that cleaner seas are on the way, don't thank the Brussels bureaucrats, send a postcard to Scarborough's Sons of Neptune"
- Harry Mead, The Northern Echo, 20/10/1989

"The Sons were right, the final vindication of the stand the Sons of Neptune made over dumping raw untreated sewage in our seas came when two ministers of trade and two colleagues toured the new 30 million sewage works. One of the party was Helen Jackson, a former parliamentary secretary to Mo Mowlam, paid tribute to the persistent campaigners for their works, naming the Sons in particular."
- Mike Jefferson, Scarborough Evening News

"Britain has remained strangely divorced from Green politics, which have taken hold of the rest of Europe and created such heightened environmental awareness. There are signs now of a sea-change, even if it is happening in a typical British way. Gone is the early image of beard and sandals Friends of the Earth, the activists are now sober-suited businessmen or academics rejoicing nevertheless in names like The Sons of Neptune"
- Susannah York, BBC TV programme, Neptune's Children

"It's treated sewerage, of, course, it's not untreated – well it should be treated sewerage that goes out – it should be treated, but still I think you will find it's treated. All of it. Still I think you will find it's treated sewerage."
- Prime Minister Margaret Thatcher to Michael Buerke, on BBC's Nature

"The truth is that water companies all over the country are pumping raw sewage straight into the sea without any treatment whatsoever"
- Michael Buerke, in reply to Margaret Thatcher's statement, BBC Nature

"This is the story of what happened when the might of officialdom was challenged by the schoolmaster, the accountant, the salesman, the solicitor, the bookmaker and the chiropodist, calling themselves the Sons of Neptune, which has developed from their habit of sea bathing in summer and winter. From fun loving eccentrics they developed into a formidable pressure group"
- James Hogg, Newsnight

"Towns such as Scarborough have become role models for other seaside resorts who want to clean up their act. As the Sons of Neptune rather dramatically put it the fight to clean beaches has been worth it, for the seas are the champagne of life, many will toast to that"
- Yorkshire Post Editorial, 08 April 2004

"My concern with the Yorkshire (scheme) is basically the same as any area that is disposing with raw none disinfected sewage via long sea outfalls to coastal areas. There is going to be a long term build-up of pathogenic organisms which would include viruses, bacteria, animal parasites and as a result of this long term build-up there is the potential for these organisms to get back into bathing beaches, into shellfish and into various fin fish that could be consumed by humans. Then if the build-up continues over a long time then we have truly created a health hazard - a microbiological time-bomb"
- Professor Jay Grimes, author of the Congressional report on sewage disposal to the sea, USA 1994, Professor of marine microbiology at Maryland University.

"The Sons of Neptune have done a splendid job. Their campaign was vital in compelling the EU laws in stopping the pollution of the marine environment. Such people are essential for the preservation of our environment"
- Professor Peter Bullock, winner of the Nobel Prize 2007 and adviser to the Sons of Neptune

"As a result of the Sons of Neptune complaint relating to discharges of raw sewage, and in one case, the discharge of industrial effluents, directly into the aquatic environment, the Commission has started action against the United Kingdom for non-compliance with Directive 76/464/EEC - pollution caused by certain dangerous substances discharged into the aquatic environment of the Community."
L. Kramer, Head of Unit, Environment, Nuclear Safety & Civil Protection, European Commission.

"I felt at times as if I was Alice in Wonderland looking on at the mad hatter's tea party [about the Sons of Neptune campaign] At best misinformed opinion and at worst mischievous propaganda"
- Jean Greenan, Mayor of Scarborough - 26 May 1983

"Roman civil engineers two thousand years ago would have been capable of building a more effective system of dealing with the UK's sewage. The Sons of Neptune campaign was a modern-day development of the pioneering work of Sir Joseph Bazalgette in alerting society to the irresponsibility and inherent dangers of unregulated disposal of human waste. Preceding by some seven years the formation of the more-well-known Surfers Against Sewage, the Neptune group were the first pioneers in highlighting this vital international environmental issue."
- Patrick Argent, former editor of the Chartered Society of Designers magazine

THE ADVENTURES OF THE SONS OF NEPTUNE

by Charles White

Printed by McRay Press 01723 370967

A special gratitude to Ann, my wife, whose
threshold of tolerance has been unique.

First printed in paperback in 2011 by McRay Press - Scarborough

Published by The Sons of Neptune Limited

ISBN - 978-0-9512188-0-8

*"Only When The Last Tree
Has Been Cut Down,*

*Only When The Last River
Has Been Poisoned,*

*Only After The Last Fish
Has Been Caught,*

*Only Then, You Will Find That
Money Cannot Be Eaten"*

19th Century Cree Indian Prophecy

The Adventures of The Sons of Neptune

A true story of a fight for clean seas against bureaucratic ignorance, ill-will and greed

CONTENTS

About the Author

Charles White was born in Dublin in 1942. He was educated Summerhill College, Sligo.

He moved to London to study medicine. Settling in Scarborough, North Yorkshire, he ran the first ever course on the history and development of Rock N'Roll at the Scarborough College of Arts & Technology, also opening the first ever museum dedicated to the genre.

This eventually led to establishing a broadcasting career and was dubbed 'Dr. Rock' by the British press. He has presented over 900 radio shows for the BBC network and his television series 'Dr. Rock's Guide To Hollywood' won an Outstanding Award at the New York Film & Television Festival in 1995. He has also written the official biographies of rock 'n roll legends Jerry Lee Lewis and Little Richard. Time Magazine described his Richard book as "the woolliest, the funniest, the funkiest rock memoir ever". The South Bank Show arts programme devoted a whole programme to the book.

He has contributed to The Independent, Sunday Times, The Observer, The Guardian, Rolling Stone magazine, The Tatler and many specialised rock journals.

However, it is his passion for environmental matters that led him to become a founding member of the marine conservation group, The Sons of Neptune whose campaign for clean seas began in 1982, pre-dating the establishment of the more well known Surfers Against Sewage.

In 1989, the Neptune group were involved in the BBC programme 'The North Sea' which won the European Parliament prize at the European Environmental Film Festival Ecovision '89 Film Festival.

This led to a 20 year battle which fundamentally changed EU laws on the dumping of toxic material into the sea which legally safeguard the standards of our beaches and marine environment today.

This book is the first comprehensive in-depth study of the intense campaigning as a pressure group on marine conservation.

Foreword

One day in 1983 I was sitting in my office at Newcastle University when I received a telephone call from professor M B (Warren) Prescod, who was head of the university's then Department of Civil Engineering. Warren had been contacted by the Sons Of Neptune about sewage disposal to the sea at Scarborough: could he check whether the then Yorkshire Water Authority's (YWA) proposal to pump sewage subject to only primary treatment (removal of old bicycles, Tesco trolleys etc and passing the rest through a pea-sized sieve) would be healthy to bathers?

Knowing of my own interests in coastal problems - I was Newcastle's head of Ocean Engineering group at that time - Warren, being already overcommmitted himself, passed the query on to me. And so began my long and happy association with the Sons, six respected professionals and avid bathers whose own experience suggested that swimming around in a brown slick of ground-up faeces would probably not be a good idea.

In the early 1980s theory had it that wave action and sunlight would destroy nearly all the pathogens (bugs dangerous to human health) in sewage discharged to the sea within less than a day. However, in 1985 I came across a paper in *Nature* by an American chap, Jay Grimes pointing out that many nasty bacteria don't actually die for weeks and viruses can live even longer. When they hit the cold water they simply become comatose - wouldn't you? - until swallowed by an unsuspecting bather. Then, once inside a nice warm gut, they are reactivated and get on with their potentially deadly work.

Lillian Evison, a specialist in microbiological health risks at Newcastle's Department of Civil Engineering, subsequently filled in the public health background. At the same time I familiarised myself with the near-shore hydrography off Scarborough and related it to the wider circulation of the North Sea. I was greatly assisted in this by the local knowledge of Captain Syd Smith, the editor of Olsen's Nautical Almanac and a lifetime mariner, a man whose understanding of daily and seasonal variations of the movement of inshore waters around Scarborough was surpassed only by his warmth and sense of humour.

To cut a long story short, buoyed by this growing body of new information the Sons began their decades-long battle to persuade YWA to upgrade its proposed sewage treatment programme. At first they faced the solid resistance of YWA's entrenched view that additional treatment was unnecessary: in those days water authorities were not the enlightened bodies that their cuddly privatised successors have become today. However, persistence - and a high-profile media campaign - eventually paid off to the point that now Yorkshire Water and the Sons of Neptune are working together to achieve the highest standards possible for the whole of the Yorkshire coast.

None of that would have happened were it not for the tenacity of that dogged band of brothers, the Sons of Neptune. I salute them.

Bruce Denness

Independent Environmental Scientist

(former Professor of Ocean Engineering, University of Newcastle Upon Tyne, UK)

March, 2011

Sons of Neptune Introduction

A true story of a mammoth conservation battle.

*I have a right to go in the sea; I have a right to a clean sea;
I have a right not to be put at risk from infection or pollution
– and I demand that right*
- Freddie Drabble, leader of the Sons of Neptune

Our extraordinary story begins in the beautiful town of Scarborough, Britain's first seaside resort. It is a town blessed with an idyllic natural beauty, with a magnificent headland jutting out into the North Sea, crowned by a 12th-century Norman castle and an elegant medieval church, and embellished by two beautiful bays with a splendidly varied hinterland. So much was it admired it became known as the Venice of the North and Queen of the Watering Places. In summer the purple-heathered moors kissed by the honey bees blow sweet breezes down onto the town, where the sea ozone has the quality of freshly-opened champagne.

It is here that a group of friends brought together by their love of nature and their experiences hiking and exploring their environment, started their fight to protect the natural surroundings of their habitat. Their battle to protect the marine environment against the intensive sea-dumping of sewage and toxic waste around the European coast was to lead to the changing of EEC laws in regard to bathing waters.

Charles White, a well-regarded Scarborough chiropodist and expert in twentieth-century music, said: "We never had any intention of becoming a marine conservation group. It just happened. Fate intervened, and led irrevocably to the founding of our group, the Sons of Neptune. Here we were enjoying the gift of life, a group of good friends with a great lifestyle and a flair to take delight in our own way of life. We were apolitical - we lived the life we loved and loved the life we lived.

It happened very strangely. My friend Freddie Drabble, a local solicitor, who was co-founder of the Sons of Neptune and later became the group's leader, had been very impressed with the Laurence Olivier production of the film "Richard III", and, as he knew of the 15th-century king's affinity with Scarborough, organised a committee to stage a Richard III festival on Scarborough's Castle headland.

"This led us to making a trip to London dressed as medieval knights to promote the festival. I am an Irishman, but I ended up dressed as Richard III, England's most maligned king, holding a mock trial outside the Tower of London to claim his innocence. Encouraged by a journalist anxious for a news story, I climbed the railings of the Tower, which made the front page that same day in London's Evening Standard with the headlines:- "Richard III is innocent OK!" and got national publicity for our event. This gave us a perception of the power of the media, and a flair for using it, which was later to prove invaluable in our marine campaign, which lasted nearly two decades and is still active to this day.

"Then we began sea-bathing, which had such an extraordinary impact, physiologically and psychologically, on our lifestyle in general, that we continued to sea-bathe all the year round even in the most extreme weather conditions. I seemed personally to have more energy, better health with no colds or flu, and gained a new vitality, which helped me to write two books. Ever since the joyous impact that rock 'n' roll had on me, since being at boarding-school in Ireland, I had wanted to meet and write the biographies of Little Richard and Jerry Lee Lewis, whose music had inspired me. The empowerment of the sea gave me the spiritual uplift and confidence which propelled me to achieve my life's ambition.

"At first our habit of sea-bathing in all weathers was regarded as frivolous fun by most onlookers, but then the Thatcher government, which had got Britain the reputation as the 'Dirty Old Man of Europe' by the repugnant policy of dumping toxic waste, sewage sludge, and industrial waste into the sea to facilitate the privatisation of the water industry and please the Stock Exchange and shareholders, provoked us into our campaign. We were gaining a greater understanding of the marine environment, its creatures, and its crucial contribution to life on the planet, and because we were going into the sea regularly we saw the effects of what was actually going on. This helped us to acquire an extraordinary spiritual tenacity to fight against the might of government and bureaucracy, and led to us travelling to the US to consult the world's leading scientists on how to combat marine pollution, which was becoming a world-wide concern."

This is a story about the battle for the environment, but it is also a study of the various aspects of the ingrained capability of the human race to engineer the destruction of the planet and of life itself.

The Battle for the Castle Headland

To be an environmentalist in the 1980s was like being a leper in Biblical times.

- Charles White

The foundation of the Sons of Neptune begins in earnest at the end of the 1970s, when we were accustomed to meeting socially as a group of friends on Thursday afternoons to hike around our varied and delightful countryside. Our children frequently walked, cycled, played and rode horses along the disused railway line between Whitby and Scarborough. The line is embellished by stunning scenery with magnificent bays and beaches overlooking the North Sea. These beauteous forms constantly raised our spirits. Unfortunately people had begun to use the track as a dumping ground, especially for old car wrecks which were increasingly becoming an eyesore.

One fine August evening, we hiked from Rocks Lane across the cliffs to Hayburn Wyke, a cosy tavern with excellent cuisine and real ale, which had a history as the haunt of smugglers and pirates. This is a truly outstanding walk with its backdrop and views towards Scarborough castle headland and Filey Brigg and on occasion exposing the depths and nuances of the amazing white cliffs at Bempton. On arriving at the Hayburn Wyke inn we would indulge in some beer and nourishment and make merry while we played dominoes. We heard the bad news that a young girl had fallen and hurt her leg on one of the abandoned rusty car wrecks

"Why don't we remove the car wrecks on the low-loader and take them to the scrap yard next week. It would be a worthwhile gesture to the environment," said Freddie, who had just acquired an old Land-Rover with a low-loader. "Sounds like a good idea" we all agreed.

The following Thursday was a warm, sunny summer's evening. We arranged to meet at Freddie's house and drive up the line where the car wrecks were scattered. Tugging at and lifting the wrecks onto the low-loader proved to be a physical strain and had been just possible for the six of us, and after a few hours we were perspiring heavily. On seeing the inviting blue sea, I suggested that we go for a cool dip in the water. Instantly everyone agreed.

On the way back from the scrap yard, we drove on to the South Bay beach where conditions were ideal for this experience. We leapt out of the jeep and ran across the sands, the waves like frantic white horses seeming to gallop towards us. Our feet hit the sea edge and we all whooped with delight. Plunging into the waves we were all at the zenith point of exhilaration. Swimming, diving and splashing around for the next half an hour, we emerged totally refreshed with a new sense of rejuvenation. "Now for a pint of nectar at the Hayburn Wyke Inn," declared Chris Found. "We've got to do this again next week."

This was to start a regular habit of going sea bathing. So in the next few weeks we continued removing wrecks and going in the sea, then going to the Wyke for beer, dominoes and merriment.

Surprisingly, as the years rolled on and no more rusting hulks replaced the ones we had removed, it was as if we had not just removed these wrecks, but the very idea that this beautiful nature reserve should ever have been a graveyard for old cars was excised.

At the end of August Chris Found said "Why don't we continue going in". At this point we were enjoying the experience so much that we all felt why not? So it continued, and as the cold months of winter approached and as Chris and myself shared the same birthday we said: Why don't we continue until our birthday? Why not?

Soon we were sea bathing all the year round. Naturally our reputation spread on a local level and we were regarded as slightly eccentric. But the experience was rewarding on so many levels. My health seemed to improve, although I wasn't particularly unhealthy. My breathing, perception and general well-being were vastly improved. Freddie was super fit and had acquired a new Labrador called Bo. He would run ten miles with the dog every morning before breakfast. Soon I, too, started running around the Marine Drive, a splendid Victorian construction round the Castle Headland which made you feel as if you were on an ocean liner.

Often whilst running, we would see the fishing trawlers going to sea, porpoises leaping out of the water, seabirds, such as cormorants diving for fish, and auks swimming underwater looking like super Sabre jets. The cloud structure and horizon was always an uplifting sight. There I would meet Freddie for a dip before going to work. In all kinds of weather we would run across the beach into the chilly North Sea. The coldness of the water seemed to give one boundless energy.

Above my chiropody surgery was the newsroom and office of local freelance journalist and photographer Dennis Dobson, who covered local news, conferences and events in the area for both national and regional press, including television. Our activities had produced rich pickings for his agency, as the national press was eager for photographs of colourful behaviour.

It was the beginning of December, Dennis was anxious for news stories. Nothing much was happening in Scarborough. The tide was coming in and going out again and coming in again. Dennis approached me one day asking if we were going in the sea this Thursday lunchtime, as was often the case when local news was scarce. "Of course we are!" I replied

"That's great, as the Daily Mail is interested in doing a piece on you lads. Their angle is a bunch of professional men going in the sea at lunchtime whilst in the cities their counterparts would be hitting restaurants and downing gin and tonics. Can you boys dress up in bowler hats and bring briefcases?"

"Anything for a bit of a laugh," I replied and I rang Freddie and Chris up. "Lets do it, it will good publicity for the town", was the response.

We were aware of the importance of tourism promotion, which benefited all. What could be better than having some fun and doing some good for the community? Chris Found now known as 'El Foundo the Magnificent' because of his gusto on hikes, always racing ahead like his hero El Cid the Spanish knight, who even when dead was strapped erect on his horse to inspire his army when he charged forward.

El Foundo, Freddie and I turned up on the beach for this particular occasion dressed in city gent suits and bowler hats, with umbrellas and briefcases. There we encountered the reporting team from the Daily Mail. They were stunned when we stripped off ready to plunge into the icy North Sea. It had been snowing earlier in the morning but was now a bright, sunny day. The photographer got us to stick our umbrellas in the sand with our briefcases leaning on the side. He then instructed us to walk into the sea, just as an oil tanker was passing by. After taking dozens of shots he finally knelt down on the beach, photographing us through the umbrellas and briefcases walking into the sea.

"That's it. I've got it! What do you call yourselves?" he asked. "The Sons of Neptune" I said.

We had recently been watching a series of Laurel and Hardy films on television and emulated their humour in real life, so we called our group after the film 'The Sons of the Desert'. Like these classic comedians our aim was to get as much fun out of life as possible.

We got great coverage in the Daily Mail and people all over the country were amused and perplexed. Dennis was pleased and tipped off the local TV stations and soon our reputation as a bunch of eccentrics spread.

The winter months as usual brought heavy snowfalls and people were amazed when we continued sea bathing. When one of us had a birthday we would organise an amusing stunt on the beach. On one occasion we surprised one of our number, Cecil Ridley, known as "Cec the Gent" because of his gentle manner and charming way with words. On coming out of the sea, we arranged for him to be met by a French maid in a sexy costume greeting him with a bottle of champagne. Then we toasted him and wished him a happy birthday as the French maid kissed him, quivered, and ran back to her car.

Denis had filmed this hoping to sell it to the local television networks. On this occasion they showed the usual situation when it snows on the M62 with hundreds of cars blocked in the snow. Then they had switched to the scene of the Sons of Neptune coming out of the sea being greeted by the French maid and extolling the health-giving virtues of sea-bathing and boosting Scarborough's image as a resort. In the circumstances this event seemed to be on another planet. We felt that this was good for the tourist image but we were unaware of the hindrance this would later create.

Frankly at the time we couldn't give a damn about what people thought about us, we were having such fun that was beneficial to our health and lifestyle. We continued with our fun and frolics and in the summer months we would bring our kids down for a splash about on the beach. Naturally we became very aware of how dangerous the sea could be. Often there were riptides or strong undercurrents on the turn of the tide. One had to be constantly aware of huge waves as they could pulverise you and the pullback could easily take you under. Generally conditions were excellent. The experience of walking into the sea with seabirds diving in front of us, bringing up sand eels that glistened in the sun was always a delight.

Sometimes we observe a "boiling" which was literally like the surface of the sea boiling. It was caused by huge shoals of fish surfacing. One of my most memorable experiences was watching a huge sea trout shooting up in front of me as I swam out to sea. The more we went into the sea the more we absorbed the atmosphere of the creatures that live in this extraordinary environment.

At this time we were aware of sewage slicks emerging from old Victorian outfall pipes that would, on occasional confluences of tide and weather spew raw sewage into both of the bays. This was repulsive to say the least, but we simply avoided them as we came to know the conditions of the tide and wind which would bring the sewage in. Scarborough's sewage system was built by the Victorians, as were most of the seaside sea outfalls in the UK. They were great builders, and their outfalls discharged the raw sewage far from the beaches, and in normal tide and weather conditions far from the visitors. Scarborough's outfalls were either remote from the town's main beaches or tucked away from public view. It was the latter which exerted the worst impacts.

However, from the early 1900s, when Scarborough began to become famous as a spa town there had been a huge amount of building of both homes and hotels, and the population in summer in 1980 quadrupled the number of people whose waste had to be dealt with. Even as far back as the 1700s the upper class and aristocratic members of society had been encouraged to travel to Scarborough to take the Spa waters, and sea bathing was being recommended for its health-giving properties. Gentlemen would hire boats to take them out in the bay, where they would bathe naked. Ladies, of course, had to be more modest, and would use "bathing machines" – wooden huts on wheels in which they would change into their non-revealing bathing clothes on the beach and then be drawn out, often by a horse, until they were in a satisfactory depth of water. Then they would descend via a trapdoor in the floor and swim. My wife's great-grandfather, James Morrison, a master joiner, came to Scarborough from Edinburgh to make bathing-machines, and later rented them out to visitors. The sea had taken on a major importance in the life of the town since 1845, when the opening of a railway link brought hundreds of thousands of working-class people every summer. By the mid-1900s the Victorian outfalls were no longer adequate for their purpose, and new updated systems were long overdue.

The Victorians, with their flair for the pursuit of excellence, built the architecture of the town, which was the foundation for its style and elegance – particularly the Pavilion Hotel, which stood majestically opposite the railway station, and where guests were treated to faultless service and unrivalled opulence. The Laughton family on acquiring the hotel continued to uphold its reputation. Charles Laughton, who was to become a famous Hollywood actor and director was influenced by his experiences when he lived at the hotel as a youngster. He portrayed Henry VIII in the film of the same title, probably the best-known scene of which is the banquet sequence. In this he attacks a cooked chicken with gluttonous avarice, throwing the gnawed bones over his shoulder. Charles's brother, Tom, who later ran the hotel, told me that Charles had observed this behaviour at the hotel. A regular guest, a steel-mill owner from Sheffield, always insisted on eating a whole chicken – or even two - in this manner on his every visit. The staff supplied a huge bib to cover his clothing, and would spread a sheet behind his chair to protect the carpet and catch the remains of the carcase. Whenever Laughton would visit the hotel on his return to Scarborough he would be greeted by staff, their heads bowed with respect, uttering gently "Mr Charles". The chief housekeeper told me that his bedroom had to be decorated completely with baby ocelot fur. Later, Charles Laughton would be one of the few people to introduce Elvis Presley on national American Tv's "The Ed Sullivan Show".

Scarborough Council in the late 1970s had little interest in the town's history or architecture, and freely gave permission for the Pavilion Hotel's demolition for the erection of a dull concrete slab of shops and offices. It was in this same vandalistic spirit that they allowed the demolition of the beautiful Balmoral Hotel for a similar purpose, and many other pieces of Scarborough's heritage..

One lunchtime, on coming out of the sea, I said glibly "You can bet your life that when you are enjoying something as much as this someone will try and stop it." It was not long before a spectre emerged. One afternoon at the surgery, the phone rang. It was Freddie: "You are not going to believe this – they are going to build a massive sewerage plant directly below the Castle Headland."

"You jest Drastic," I said, knowing his impish sense of humour, I really thought he was joking, but no. There it was in the local paper: Scarborough Council, in conjunction with Yorkshire Water, had chosen this as an ideal site for what was described as a sewage treatment plant to update the town's Victorian system.

That last bit of news we welcomed, but were later shocked to discover that "treatment" simply meant removing the solids - condoms, sanitary towels etc. The human waste, domestic waste, and industrial waste was to go into the sea directly off the Castle headland between the two beautiful bays, astonishingly through a pipe only 600 metres long.

This was in January 1983, and the following night Sir Meredith Whittaker, proprietor of the local paper, wrote a leading article in his Scarborough Evening News confirming this and stating that it was a retrogressive move recalling the days of medieval nightcarts which collected "night soil" from homes. Whilst few locals expressed concern, Freddie was not slow to express the shock and disbelief of the the Sons of Neptune. We soon gained an unlikely ally in Maggie Mainprize MBE, leader of the Fishermen's Wives group, who had a no-nonsense attitude and made a public statement condemning the proposals.

In an attempt to gather support the Fishermen's Wives called a meeting at St. Mary's Parish Hall, at which Town Hall officials gave weak assurances dismissing our concerns about the implementation of the scheme, and which representatives of Yorkshire Water did not even attend. Public concern increased and a general meeting was called at a bigger venue and water officials were requested to attend.

There was a good attendance, and the audience saw a huge map of the Castle Headland placed in the middle of the podium, together with aerial photographs of the area.

Two local councillors exuded an air of self-importance and seemed to form a mutual admiration society with the representative from Yorkshire Water. However the public attending the hall were expressing genuine alarm at the plans, as the headland is regarded as very much the crowning jewel between the natural beauty of the two bays. Councillor Teddy Sulman, who seemed to relish his role in supporting Yorkshire Water, opened the proceedings. "It is my great privilege to introduce the representative from Yorkshire Water who are going to do a marvellous scheme for Scarborough. This is Mr. Taylor whose knowledge is well respected and as you can see from the presentation visuals, we should be very honored that he has taken time to come here", he announced.

Taylor began: "Thank you Mr. Sulman, I represent the YWA and commend to you our plan to build a new £11m sewage treatment plant underneath the Castle Headland and adjacent to the South Toll House . . ." He was interrupted by a member of the audience, who shouted: "You can't build a plant there, it will fall in the sea".

Taylor responded: "Now, now, wait until you see the presentation, the time-lapse sequence of slides shows the progress of the plant underneath the Castle from various angles and the outfall pipe going directly out from the middle prominence of the Castle."

A local citizen rose to his feet before the slide show had finished. "Surely you can't build a sewage plant there as the cliffs are falling down as it is. The whole of the Castle would fall into the sea, not only that but St. Mary's Church would come tumbling in afterwards should you try to build anything under the cliffs - never mind a huge sewage plant."

There was now a collective feeling against the project in the hall, however Mr. Taylor's role was to smooth and soothe the gathering.

"On the contrary. It will stabilise the cliffs and strengthen the foundations, giving more support. We have leading consultants who have performed advanced research on this matter. There is no need to worry," he said.

There was mild applause from a small band of sycophants (mostly local councillors' wives and friends). A fisherman stood up and said he was concerned at the threat to his livelihood. "That long pipe is going to be on our finest lobster beds. You will have to blast right through them to put it there."

Mr Taylor replied "We will do as little damage as possible and we will consult and negotiate if any damage does occur."

An ambitious local councillor called Eileen Harbron, with a loud aggressive voice stood up. "We have looked into this thoroughly and compensation is available from a local government contingency fund," she stated.

Suddenly a voice from the back shouted "You've already sewn this up behind closed doors without consulting the public. The fishermen have already been bought."

"Whats that? Who said that? I'll ignore that," said Councillor Harbron.

The speaker, an elderly, slightly stooping, man in a navy raincoat, slowly rose to his feet, and such movement as it was suppressed the hall to silence. He was unknown to Yorkshire Water, but seemingly very well known to many others in the room. His question was as slow in delivery as it was accurate in its aim. "Excuse me, I am Captain Sydney Smith, a former Deputy Harbourmaster of Scarborough. My question is, if the outfall pipe goes out from the Castle Headland surely the tides will bring the sewage back onto the North and South Bay beaches."

Mr. Taylor replied: "Oh no I can assure you that the tides will carry it out to sea."

"And how will they do that?" asked Captain Syd

"Because the tides run parallel to the shore!" declared Mr Taylor. There was mild applause from the people I had already spotted as sycophants, but the Captain rejoined: "I have sailed all around the world as a sea captain and I know that the tides go in and out, otherwise our bays could not fill up."

The hall became like an undiscovered Egyptian tomb as total silence ensued.

"What kind of roof will it have over this plant?" continued the Captain.

Taylor obviously puzzled, looked to the panel sitting by the table. They whispered and then tittered. "A good roof," said Taylor grinning.

"Aye, it will need to be, as ever since I was a small boy there have been warning notices on the cliffs, 'BEWARE OF FALLING ROCKS'. My family has been sea-faring around this coast since 1602 and I know that if you look at paintings of Scarborough over the last two hundred years, you will see massive erosion of these cliffs caused by huge rock avalanches"

Taylor said "Thank you for that, all these matters will be looked into"

Freddie Drabble stood up "The Sons of Neptune are a group of all year round sea bathers and we of course welcome clean seas, how will this treatment function?"

"I'm glad you asked this question," said Mr Taylor. "The sewage will be pumped through the plant and screened for all solids, condoms etc., then milturated (sic) and pumped far out to sea via the long sea outfall where the seawater, salt and sun will neutralise the effluent completely." There was slight applause.

Freddie then said "But how can that be a treatment?"

"We will continue after a tea break" interrupted Councillor Harbron (who was in later years, as Councillor Eileen Bosomworth to become leader of Scarborough Council). Freddie whispered as the meeting adjourned "Come with me, you've got to meet Captain Syd. I have met him before, he is on our side". He stood out as a man of great dignity and in-depth knowledge. At this stage we knew little about him. He was in fact a master mariner; whose family had been in Scarborough for centuries and were involved with Trinity House. This organization was initially formed to protect sailors, their welfare and families. The captain had been elected as lifetime President of Trinity House and was a war hero who had conducted 12 D-Day landings under heavy fire, for which he received the King's Commendation signed by Sir Winston Churchill.

Most importantly for the present crisis, he was editor of Olsen's Nautical Almanac, the definitive guide for all shipping of annual tidal movements in UK coastal waters - an essential item for every captain of a maritime vessel. Captain Syd was a quiet man who radiated a calm sincerity; in short he was a gentleman. Freddie and I were soon to become aware of his great knowledge of not only the tides and the seas, but also the history concerning all maritime matters.

Freddie introduced me. "I'm glad you are here tonight Captain, it is a great pleasure to meet you," I said.

"Aye" He replied. Then he pointed to the displayed map. "That pipe goes straight out to sea, and the sewage will be washed straight back onto the beaches. The position of that pipe is in the ideal position for getting the maximum amount of sewage back into both bays. There are no scales on any of these drawings, they obviously haven't a clue what they are talking about and cannot have done in-depth studies. The only thing that Yorkshire Water and the Council knows about the sea is that the water is wet!"

Tom, a local fisherman commented: "Looking at these maps,

it looks like this scheme has already been decided upon Captain."

"Aye", said Captain Syd.

Freddie remarked "Just look at this, the YWA have their own private car parks and offices with magnificent sea views. So much for the fat cats. The fishermen have already been taken in, their representative is a bus driver from Leeds. He has not even got to the point where he knows the sea is wet! He recently acquired a hotel overlooking the bay, and he only arrived in town a month ago. His role is to persuade the fishermen to accept this scheme. He knows nowt (nothing) about the town or the industry."

Councillor Bob Stead was listening. He said: "This scheme has been decided upon behind closed doors, the public should have been informed ages ago. I am on the Council and I have only just found out. That Taylor bloke was only working in the coal industry until recently. The YWA have put him in charge of implementing the scheme. He knows nothing about this area or the sea. The Victorians who built the original outfalls kept them as far away as they could from our bays to get the effluent well out to sea."

"Aye Bob, they knew what they were doing. I'm afraid that this scheme would be a disaster for both the town and our visitors," said Captain Syd. "The sewage would wash back into both bays. It is the wrong place to build it."

The reality of this decision began to penetrate our minds like some vile nightmare. How could they perpetrate such a cretinous scheme? They could, of course, because they were in power, the Council backed the YWA and we had been told that ultimately it was the policy of the Thatcher government to privatise the water industry.

Our whole feeling was that this was an exercise in self-destruction and instinctively we knew we had to fight it no matter what. Captain Syd was to become our greatest ally and was soon made an honorary member of the Sons of Neptune. To all of us he became a father figure and advisor. The plans had already been drawn up by YWA and the Council in secret. Those approached to approve the scheme were hand-picked sycophants and establishment grovellers, self-indulgent egotists who had as much interest in the environment and the pursuit of excellence as a decaying lizard in some distant desert.

There were of course some good people in both camps. The job of persuading the council that dilute sewage in it's bathing waters would not damage the towns tourist image was entrusted to it's most highly regarded politician, the Council leader of the time, David Jenkinson. He had become notorious for having praised the town with faint heart during a holiday promotional Tv programme. He told the camera during a live broadcast overlooking the town: "Yes! Of course I would come to Scarborough for my holidays. God has been very kind to us. Just look at this - two beautiful bays, a castle, sunshine! What more do you want? Why go to the Mediterranean? They have nothing more to offer!" Then, turning to the camera, believing he was now off the air, he said cynically: "If you believe that load of bullshit, you'll believe anything!" The camera was still switched on, and the event has been frequently used ever since on out-takes and "blooper" television shows..

We started to object to the scheme. At first we wrote vigorous letters of objection to the local paper, the Scarborough Evening News. Soon the Council turned against us, declaring to the newspaper that we knew nothing about marine matters or civil engineering. This was dangerous ground. We were not engineers, certainly, but we had spent enough time in the sea to have knowledge of the drift of tides and currents to be sure that something at best misguided or at worst criminally negligent was being perpetrated to avoid spending the sort of money which would solve the problem. They also dismissed Captain Syd's extraordinary knowledge with rumours that he was in his dotage – being quite incapable of reflecting that he was little older than was Sir Winston Churchill at the outbreak of the Second World War. We were in limbo as one local group after another gave enthusiastic approval to the YWA scheme. The hotels association led by the new arrival in town, the bus driver from Leeds, who had bought a hotel, had the association members fawning to his every whim. A carpet salesman Frank Tweed, whose knowledge of marine matters and geological structure of the castle headland was negligible at best, was appointed to negotiate with the fishermen.

The majority fishermen took the bait of compensation. They had worked hard for decades on local trawlers and cobles and were always exploited by the fish merchants who creamed off the profits. It was exhausting to watch the fishermen's wives filleting in the fish sheds, they really earned their money doing such work in unsavory conditions. The fishing community were hard working decent folk. However those that ran the industry constantly blamed the Spanish, the French, the EEC, for the decline of their industry. New high-tech sonar and advanced trawling nets could pick up marine life the size of a 5p piece off the sea bed.

Often 90% of a catch was thrown back into the sea because of its lack of commercial value or because a miasma of EEC rules confused the issue. This was destroying the eco-system. Fishermen are natural hunters and are not programmed for conservation. Scientists at this time and even to the present day are ridiculed by their assertions in regard to the decline in fish stocks. The atmosphere was greed - take or die. They had no thought for future generations. One can understand the fishermen's position. They had to survive whilst contending with EC rules (which they perceived as grossly unfair) and the unfair profits made by some fish merchants.

Mr Eammon Gallagher, who, as Minister of Fisheries of the EEC, had stopped the Russian factory ships fishing in the North Sea areas, told me, when I met him in Brussels: "It is almost impossible to communicate with the fishing industry in a reasonable manner."

Meanwhile in Scarborough it had become clear that political and deceptive theatrics had taken place, the so-called public meetings were just a farce, and our objections at first were treated as the utterances of eccentrics.

One of our first meetings with Yorkshire Water was at their Malton branch, where we were invited to see their initial report on the castle headland scheme. Staff were helpful, but seemed condescending as they showed us their complex reports, which they seemed to think would be beyond us. They promised to let us have copies, but Freddie had already got preliminary copies of the reports to look through. He says: "Thankfully with my legal training and Captain Syd's marine knowledge we were able to analyze them, and in no time at all we could see things in there that they did not want us to see, and more interestingly, these reports referred to plans. We were given no plans, so I rang up the YWA and said, 'You have sent us reports but no plans.' They replied 'ooh', as if they hadn't been aware that these reports referred to actual plans. It was just dawning on them at the Malton office. 'Oh is that so, the plans are at Babtie Shaw and Morton, our engineers at Glasgow.' (This was good, they didn't know the significance of the plans!) I politely (in a nice kind of way and playing it slightly thick) asked if they would mind ringing them and ask if they would send me copies and they agreed. When we got the plans, that was it; it was daylight, the full horror of the scheme. The ultimate nightmare was revealed. I am not sure that we would ever have got these plans if Yorkshire Water knew how damaging they were.

"After three weeks they enquired how long it would take us to finish reading them, wanting to know what was our position and what were we going to do. I said to Captain Syd we want a proper meeting at the town hall, we are not just going to show our cards to the YW as they will just go to ground. We will be more open than that. We only show our cards in front of the council, under the gaze of those people who are supposed to be looking after the best interests and welfare of the town - qualified people who will look after our case with fairness and good judgment."

"So a meeting was set up at the Town Hall which would be chaired by the leader of the Council, David Jenkinson and attended by senior Councillors and the Council's Technical Officer. Everyone turned up and we thought everything would be laid bare. Councillor David Jenkinson was at once intensely dismissive before he even heard what we had to say. He opened the meeting saying: "Right. We have come here not to waste time. Let us know what you are here for, and do not waste any of our time." There was no civility, no thanks for the interest in the Town's welfare. Councillor Godfrey Allanson adopted a menacing stance. "We've got our own experts. What do you know? Your like a joke on a box of matches!" (Reference to the infantile quips on the back of Swann's matches) Freddie said: "I can assure you that what I have got to say will not waste your time."

Jenkinson replied curtly "Just get on with it" So we did, and we went through the report. We demonstrated what would happen when the sewage was released at the proposed discharge point, 600m off the Marine Drive, We had their plans. We showed them precisely what would happen. Yorkshire Water's plans showed, their own tests, their own floats, released into the same currents and tidal line as the proposed outfall end, showed that sewage released on the flood tide would enter the South Bay, and on the ebb tide drift into the North Bay, polluting the bathing waters.

Well, having done all this you would expect the reaction to be "shock horror" or "oh my God we never thought it would be this dreadful! This is crazy we cannot believe this! It cannot happen to our town!" Astonishingly there was no reaction at all. Complete silence. All the Councillors and officers sat as if stunned.

Then after a long pause David Jenkinson said: "Well if they don't do this they will spend the money on drains and pipes in Leeds and we will have no scheme." Implying that they accepted the scheme without question.

I said: "It is far better that they do spend the money in Leeds than to destroy our seas and beaches with untreated raw sewage".

They were more shocked that we knew what they were really up to. That we had seen their true position. It seemed they neither understood nor cared about what happened to our precious environment. We left the meeting aghast to think that they were prepared to accept any kind of scheme, that they were not interested, they wanted to close the book, no questions asked.

"At a later public meeting at the Spa every question I asked was shouted down by Councillor Sulman. He shouted 'rubbish' and 'this is ridiculous'. He continued with his ridicule throughout the meeting" At one point in the meeting the Yorkshire Water representative said, "The sewage is going to be screened. It's going to be pulverized. You won't see any nasties floating, no paper, nothing." They used gobbledegook terms like 'comminution' and 'maceration' to confuse and bamboozle the citizens. A person asked: "Is all the sludge going to be pumped out?"

38

"Yes it is" said the YW representative "But it won't be seen. I have two samples to show you, of what difference it will make to the seawater."

"They handed the two bottles around, one with grey water containing the suspended sludge particles, while the other was clear water. Most people were sensibly aghast, but not the councillors. They obviously thought: 'This is fine. It will do for Scarborough. The water might look grey, but there'll be no turds floating about, and disease-bearing germs can't be seen.' "We were all dumbstruck. We thought we were pointing out something crucial to the Town's welfare. Why don't they care? Here we were trying to help the leaders of our Town with something that would save our bathing waters and beaches. We realised then that they had another agenda – which was to get Government money - no matter what we had said they were sold on the scheme without question."

"We were so shocked that they knew what was going to happen. They asked no questions of Yorkshire Water. They completely froze. They wanted to bury what we knew and damn us with ridicule. The only way they could get rid of us was by implying that we were loonies and didn't know what we were talking about. How could we know as much as Yorkshire Water? We were not experts." The ridicule was to continue for over a decade.

Then one day a patient of mine said, in the surgery: "Mr. White, I see you are objecting to the building of the sewage plant underneath the Castle Headland, maybe I can help you. My son is Professor John Dunleavy the geologist who lived in Scarborough for many years and produced his geological thesis on the Castle Headland. He is now in the employment of the South African Government for the National Building Research Institute and Council for Scientific and Industrial Research in Pretoria. He has a doctorate, a BSc. Honours and a Masters degree in geology. His report is that the Castle Headland is a faulted structure and that any construction carried out at the site proposed would certainly cause severe instability in the cliff face."

I was overjoyed! "That is superb news, Mrs Dunleavy," I replied. "Could you please ask him to write in to the local paper and give me his contact details so that the Sons of Neptune can explain the situation". At last we had a scientific contact of world class status. I immediately informed Freddie, who was over the moon.

When we were working, together with Captain Syd and local experts, cobble fisherman, Gordon Fishburn and Bill Sheader (lifeboat Coxswain of 30 years) to find an alternative site. Captain Syd had located a place called Cowlam Hole, a mile north of Scarborough, round the corner from the North Bay, a natural fissure covered by sand on the seabed. This would be the perfect place for the long sea outfall pipe and, as Captain Syd pointed out, would be less expensive in comparison to the horrendous cost and danger to the structure of the Castle Headland and more environmentally suitable. They confirmed that it was the best location for the start of the strongest ebb-tide. Professor Dunleavy supported these observations, but despite being told of this the Council went ahead, giving outline planning consent to Yorkshire Water's Marine Drive raw untreated sewage works. They ignored Professor Dunleavy's report and dismissed Captain Syd's perceptions with arrogance.

Then we had a breakthrough which was to challenge the Council's mocking of our engineering knowledge.

We decided to make a formal complaint to the Ombudsman that Yorkshire Water's decision had been taken without consideration being given to a full treatment scheme. Scarborough Council and Yorkshire Water claimed that they had done exhaustive tests with bottom-drifting ocean drogues, but we became suspicious when a local councillor who was a showman wrote a letter full of scientific data that we doubted he could comprehend. In reality the tests that were done were so ludicrous that they were straight out of an Ealing farce.

Two local fishermen were encouraged by promoters of the scheme to buy six boxes of oranges from the local market and were asked to drop them into the sea about one and half miles off the Castle Headland. Within a couple of hours they began to arrive back on the North and South beaches. Alarmed at this situation the YWA hired a fleet of taxi- drivers from Hull to collect all the oranges at dawn off the beaches before the Town woke up!. Captain Syd was greatly amused to hear of such crass idiocy and we found it supremely hilarious. We then knew we were dealing with blithering incompetence.

At this time another development was taking place. I came together with a local college lecturer, John Daniels, an expert in three-dimensional design and who like myself was a passionate rock n' roll fan. His son Jake, a tornado of youthful zest and energy, had befriended my son Liam, who was cast in the same mould. Since my youth in the west of Ireland my psyche was dominated by music, from Bach to the Burundi tribe, but the prime influences were Little Richard and Jerry Lee Lewis (known as the Killer). Later I would be greatly privileged to write both their official biographies, a task that was a marvellous experience but as traumatic psychologically, physiologically and economically as climbing Mount Everest with a broken leg and descending with two broken legs.

Ever since I was a teenager in my spare time I would seek out record stores no matter where I was for rock n' roll, jazz, cajun, zydeco, blues, world music, movie soundtracks, in other words a full spectrum of all kinds of music. So my collection at this stage was quite extensive. However, it was the rock n' roll explosion of the 1950s that gave me an inexplicable energy which still propels my spirit through life today.

Hearing Little Richard's Long Tall Sally was like getting out of the Bastille after 40 years. FREEDOM, FREEDOM, FREEDOM! JD and I were kindred spirits as were our sons. The more intense, the more humorous, the more bizarre the more we loved it.

A record had to have the same impact on our audio-cortex system as opening the door and letting the Niagara Falls flow through. From my collection I played JD rare rock n' roll ravers, such as Johnny Burnette Trio's 'Train Kept a Rollin'', Ronnie Self's Bop-A-Lena, Screaming Jay Hawkins' Constipation Blues', Little Richard's Get Down with it and a thousand others. JD had mentioned about my musical passion and collection to his head of department at the local art college, resulting in an invitation to do a series of lectures on the development of rock music.

At first I was bemused at the thought of this ever happening, as at that time the Minister for Education, Barbara Castle, was closing down the local teacher training college, so I felt that this was pure fantasy. A letter arrived shortly after this from the Head of Education, Donald Wise, at County Hall inviting me for an interview. I felt that the interview would be worth the experience, but was very sceptical about the outcome. I was shown into the office by Mr. Wise's secretary and as I entered his office he sat down in a huge Gothic chair behind a large mahogany desk. The backdrop was a series of gigantic Carravagio-esque paintings, Michael Angelo statues and Palladian pillars. He peered at me like a hawk over a rabbit. I was supposed to be intimidated. "How important is this rock music?" he enquired. I had recently been to Keele University for an American music conference, so I quoted from one of the prominent speakers. "Well," I said "Professor Charles Ham has stated that rock n' roll music is the most important cultural revolution for over two hundred years. It has given teenagers a stronger role and identity in society."

"Really!" he gasped in disbelief. "How?"

"Well look at The Beatles, how they are bringing millions of pounds into the UK on their music sales and copyrights. Their sales in the US alone are a major contribution to the economy."

We talked a little more, and eventually he said: "Well you have convinced me Mr. White. To be honest I had expected to totally reject the idea of a course on rock n' roll music, but the idea is to attract more people to our evening courses and this seems to be the ideal vehicle to do that." He asked me to prepare my series of lectures and present them to the local college. I structured the course as follows:

The Origins of Rock n' Roll

Gospel, Blues, Jazz, Rhythm & Blues

Great Songwriters

Record Producers

Recording Engineers

TV Rock shows

The Importance of Radio in its Development

Rock n' Roll Movies

The Major Artists

When Dennis Dobson's news agency got the College prospectus, which was always sent to all journalists, Dennis came running down to the surgery. "Are you going to do this?"

"Of course", I replied.

He immediately contacted the Daily Mail, a reporter arrived the following day to get the story and Dennis took photographs of me with my record collection. The headline on the full-page feature was 'Dr. Rock rocks back the clock'. The course ran for 12 weeks, one evening a week, with 36 students signing up to join as well as enquiries from all over the UK. Publicity was inevitable, BBC TV, local and national radio ran the story conducting several interviews. This eventually led to regular appearances on local radio stations, BBC Leeds, Humberside, Tees and best of all BBC Radio London. It was fun and I began to be known as Dr. Rock.

The battle to stop the sewage plant on the Marine Drive was continued but not neglected during the period of the course. We spent the weekends at Freddie's office phoning, faxing and writing to environmental groups, marine specialists, politicians and the media. It would often take the whole weekend. Soon Freddie with his tenacity, had managed to contact Professor Warren Pescod of Newcastle University, a world leading authority in the field of civil engineering. On hearing the proposed plan, he was incredulous. Professor Dunleavy's comments added to his concern. He was familiar with Scarborough's cliffs as he had often visited the Town. Although under tremendous pressure of work by worldwide developments in which he was held in high regard, he came to the town on a Sunday afternoon to see the position for himself. He had tremendous affection for the Marine Drive and was aware of the sewage outfall controversy. However it was the siting of the plant that really concerned him. Freddie and I took him down to the Marine Drive on his arrival. we were walking round and he said "Where are they going to build this thing?"

"Just over there." I pointed to the spot where the 200 foot cliffs were overhanging the site and warning notices 'Beware Falling Rocks". Warren kind of looked at me then looked at the site again, shook his head in disbelief and went back to his car. "I will be in touch after I have given it some thought," he said."

"A couple of weeks went by and I spoke to him on the phone. "Yes, I have given it some thought; as a matter of fact I shall be at a conference in a few weeks' time. One of the partners of Babtie, Shaw and Morton, Yorkshire Water's civil engineers is likely to be there and I will take the opportunity of raising the matter with them - exactly what they are doing in Scarborough!"

Warren asked them and they told him. He just said "WHAT? - Under that unstable cliff?" That comment, it seems, was the depth-charge. "The reason Warren could speak to Baptie, Shaw and Morton was that he had been articled to the company (he had done his apprenticeship with them) so was able to communicate with them. For a short while he had walked with Liam, my son and JD's son Jake who was aged 9 at the time. Jake turned to the Professor and pointed to the headland. "They could not build under these cliffs Mr. Professor. The Castle and the old church would fall into the sea."

"You know young man, you are perfectly right" replied Professor Pescod.

We proceeded to the Harbour Bar and ordered ice creams for the kids. Turning to Freddie and I the Professor said: "As a civil engineer I came here to tell you that which two little boys already knew. Out of the mouths of babes and children, sheer common sense."

For the next few weeks all was quiet except that the Council and local Tory group intensified the ridicule and degradation of our campaign. One local politician re-emerged, changed party colours and become Leader of the Council. She seemed to see the Sons' campaign as an obstacle to her progress. However, our objections to Yorkshire Water's odious project were now getting media coverage because we had the backing of some of the world's leading marine engineers and biologists.

Armed with this knowledge and a new spirit of confidence, we decided we had to meet with Councillor Harbron at a suitable venue. We entered her hotel in an optimistic mood, which led her to be condescending. "What do you lads know about the world of marine engineering?" was the attitude she displayed.

She produced a thick sheaf of documents, extolling the virtues of the scheme. "The Town Hall has given this to me, I am not supposed to show you this," she said, with an air of self-importance as if it was a precious jewel. We suspected that this document would be vacuous and a waste of public money, and showed no interest in seeing it. She had thought she would be able to convince us of the validity of Yorkshire Water's scheme rather than listen to our objections.

The leader of the Council, David Jenkinson, approached us one day as we ran across the beach after our lunchtime dip. "You lads are letting the Town down, we need the Castle Headland scheme. They will spend the money in Leeds and we will miss the boat."

We used his famous television quote back at him. "If you believe that bullshit, you will believe anything." He was not at all amused.

The attitude of the local people was that "you are fighting a losing battle". To be a conservationist during this period was the equivalent of being a leper in Biblical times. An environmental awareness in the country had not become fully developed but it was beginning to be palpable. On our trips around the Marine Drive and dips in the sea, absorbing the stunning scenery, we developed a more intense passion for our environment and creation itself. We felt our energy for the campaign was coming from the sea, Neptune's domain.

There was now silence for several months, but we suspected

that Yorkshire Water's plans had been severely torpedoed. The Council was still doing everything to suppress our cause.

Then, suddenly and remarkably, Yorkshire Water announced in the national media the cancellation of the Castle Headland scheme.

Freddie had made contact with Professor Bruce Denness, Professor of Ocean Engineering at Newcastle-upon-Tyne University. He immediately condemned the Castle Headland scheme and considered that dumping raw untreated sewage in the sea was no longer acceptable. Britain had gained justifiably the reputation as the 'dirty old man of Europe' for this odious practice. Our investigations indicated that the EEC laws demanded proper treatment of effluent discharging into estuarine waters

We later learned that this idiotic scheme had been stopped at the highest government level.

We celebrated on the beach, toasting the Sons with champagne as Captain Syd held Neptune's trident high!

We had won the battle of the Castle Headland but the sewage war was to continue . . .

We returned to our enjoyment of the sea

On 17th January, my birthday, it was a cold and dull winters' day. I was awakened by the doorbell at 07:30 am, the bed seemed so warm and cozy I did not want to leave. However I knew that we had to go for our daily dip as I shared a birthday with El Foundo the Magnificent (Chris Found) and this had been arranged for the event. I also knew that Freddie and the Sons would pull a couple of practical jokes, as this was the usual custom on our birthdays. I got dressed, grabbed my towel and togs, opened the front door, the boys were there with a bottle of whisky. An imitation English Heritage blue plaque had been placed above my door proclaiming "Charles White: Author Lived Here". My car was fully decorated as a birthday cake with a huge candle on top of the roof and prominent lettering printed on the sides "Gasp! It's Doctor Rock's birthday". El Foundo said "You drive your car down we will meet you on the South Bay slipway". On the way there the heaters soon emitted a foul fishy stench which got worse as I got to the slipway. The boys had planted kippers on the sides of the engine. On pulling up at the slipway I was anxious to get the swim over and get on with the birthday celebrations, as the temperature was very low. I felt secure that this was the end of the pranks. On getting out of the car I started to change into my swimming trunks, Freddie and Chris approached me wearing dressing gowns and insisted I wore one as well. As we walked onto the beach there was a group of people dressed in period costumes. Jennie, Freddie's secretary, was dressed as a Victorian nanny and there were several other voluptuous and beautiful girls dressed in nightgowns, surrounding what appeared to be a huge bathroom suite sitting incongruously on the beach, complete with bath, wardrobe, mirrors and plants. They immersed me into the bathtub, which was full of very hot water brimming over with bubbles and started to lather my hair with shampoo whilst offering me drinks of champagne and rum. Now I was really disorientated, compounded by soap in my eyes, the alcohol, the cold, and the whole situation. Everyone was having a good laugh but I was beginning to worry because the bath water was extremely hot and my upper body was freezing cold (later I learned that our friend Heather Nunn, who worked at St Thomas's Hospital, on the seafront, had given them access to their hot water system). The shampooing seemed to go on for an eternity and more alcohol was offered to me, now I was dreading going into the cold in case I suffered an aneurism.

"It's time for the dip!" shouted the boys as they lifted me out of the bath. The run to wards the sea was quite daunting. As I entered the sea more friends came rushing over offering yet more champagne and congratulations, the disorientation was acute, I felt as if this was some extraordinary dream. They were encouraging me to enter the sea and were edging me into the water; naturally I felt the shock of the cold sea.

At the same time about 30 yards away I noticed a huge dorsal fin emerge from the water, and I froze, shocked and horrified. The movie Jaws had high impact on the public imagination at this time and so when I saw this incredible sight I was bewildered, with a mixture of awesome terror and disbelief. Then this huge fin turned and came directly towards me. The boys shouted "Run for it!" as the fin approached menacingly. The shark, as I was convinced it was, then turned away and I breathed a sigh of relief. Relief turned into bewilderment and terror once more as it slowly turned again and headed straight for us. I could almost hear the now famous Jaws theme song by John Williams. The situation was so unreal I could not believe it was actuality. The shark fin looked very real and when it was about 20 feet away still coming towards us, I resigned my fate to the Gods. By now crowds were gathering on the seafront and I could hear their alarmed cries. Then, as the fin came right up to us I looked down into the water and saw something bright blue. It stood up. It was a diver from the local sub aqua club complete with air bottles and a three-foot-long fin attached to his back. Several emotions weakened my being, horror, extreme disorientation; then an unbelievable feeling of relief. He took off his oxygen mask and gasped "Happy Birthday! Is there still hot water in that bath I am bloody frozen!" as he laughed hysterically. It was my diver pal Steve Davison, I realised, when the culprit was unmasked. He ran to the bath and plunged into the warm water. Meanwhile the crowd's anxious cries had changed into fits of laughter, and now everyone was joining in the fun. We had a quick plunge into the cold sea and then ran back towards the bath. Steve the diver said "We have been rehearsing this for months, every inch of my movement was choreographed by Pete Lassey and the divers at the sub-aqua club"

Chris Found said : "That is why we had to keep shampooing you in the bath, so you couldn't observe what was going on in the sea before we got you in." Freddie had come up with the idea and, as usual, was very thorough in the prank's execution, leaving nothing to chance - it was like a David Lean production. That is why his nickname is 'Drastic Drabble'. He gets things done, no matter what."

Now that was one birthday I will never forget! Spielberg would have been proud!

Freddie Drabble, leader of the Sons of Neptune – his tenacity, spirituality, and energy created by sea bathing led the EEC to pass laws protecting our bathing waters.

First publicity shot of the Sons. A midwinter dip - while City gents are sipping lunchtime gin and tonics the Sons of Neptune are off for a swim in the icy North Sea.

A birthday surprise – Charles White is treated to a hot bath and shampoo with champagne and rum by glamorous girls, prior to the daily ritual of immersion in the icy North Sea . . . but that was not to be the only shock!

Directed like a Steven Spielberg production, a Jaws type shark's fin approaches the bathers, and is then revealed as a scuba diver dressed for the part.

Freddie's birthday continuing to celebrate life on the beach with lots of fun. Cecil Ridley, Chris Found, Charles White, Freddie Drabble and Bryan Dew.

The Sons of Neptune celebrate the victory of the Castle Headland. Left to right: Bryan Dew, Capt Sydney Smith, Freddie Drabble, Geoff Nunn, Charles White, Cecil Ridley, Chris Found.

Richard III – the origin of the Sons

The story of the Sons of Neptune began when a group of friends got together in 1976 to show the beauty of the town of Scarborough and organise a medieval festival. Freddie Drabble, a solicitor, had attended a re-enactment of a historic battle in the Castle grounds by The Sealed Knot, a group that toured ancient monuments and battlefields to recreate conflicts of the past at their original sites, which had left a significant impression on him. The setting was the Castle Headland, which juts out between Scarborough's two beautiful bays adorned by the 12th century Norman castle, which looks over the North Sea, protected by walls on the south side, enclosing a delightful green pasture which gives way to steep rocky cliffs on the seaward side. Encircled by the Marine Drive, this combined work of man and the natural beauty of Mother Nature's own sculptural creation is a jewel of continuous fascination. This landscape, no matter the weather or light conditions, is always strikingly dramatic. Sometimes with light variations, it is a doorway to emotion that raises one's spirit to a dignified platform that is the key to an elated joy of existence itself.

In the 1970s Scarborough's main industry was tourism, ideal for family holidays, two beautiful sandy bays divided by the Castle Headland. Each had an array of smart hotels overlooking the sea. Each hotel was intent on presenting its best frontage, freshly painted for the summer season, an indication of the town's desire for excellence.

The two main theatres, the Futurist and the Floral Hall presented shows of the highest calibre, featuring such comic greats as Tommy Cooper, Ken Dodd, Norman Wisdom, Des O'Connor, Harry Worth and Morecambe & Wise. Other artists throughout the seasons included Cilla Black, Mike Yarwood, The Bachelors, The Carry On Team and one-night stands from international stars such as The Everly Brothers, Johnny Mathis, Woody Herman, Stan Kenton, Howard Keel, James Last, and Shirley Bassey and rock bands like The Beatles and the Rolling Stones and other major icons of the Sixties. The Spa also catered for the classical set and for many years Max Jaffa and the Spa Orchestra attracted huge audiences. The Black & White Minstrel Show was created in Scarborough in the early Sixties and became an international success. This of course attracted media attention resulting in frequent radio and television broadcasts from the Town.

It was through one of these that I got my first media break. I had just finished work one Friday afternoon when a friend, David 'The Meatcleaver' Myers, a local solicitor who acquired the name for his swift disposal of witnesses in court, came to the surgery and offered me a spare ticket to the BBC's "Any Questions" recording at the Grand Hotel. I answered: "I'd love to see how radio is recorded."

The Grand Hotel, just a short walk from my surgery, is a huge, imposing and impressive building, which was for many years the largest hotel in Europe, a tribute to the Victorians who made Scarborough Britain's first and most successful seaside resort. `

It looks like a huge ocean liner, is believed it to have been modeled on such a vessel, and was built on the site of a house where Anne Bronte was staying when she died.

During the Second World War, the hotel was used as a base for the RAF and visited by Sir Winston Churchill during the conflict. It is said that Hitler declared that he would use it as his HQ when he eventually conquered Britain.

The programme was to be broadcast live from the hotel's elegant ballroom where 300 chairs were laid out for the audience. David Jacobs, a stalwart of BBC radio was the host, it was quite a thrill for me to see the microphones and the large table for the panel. Enoch Powell and the liberal peer Joe Grimond were among the panelists.

Our seats were at the back of the room. It was election time, so most of the questions pertained to the political situation. The BBC staff passed out forms for the audience to contribute questions. At the time my interest in politics was remote, added to this I had had a heavy day at work and I just wanted to sit there and enjoy the event, but "You must fill in your form," said the BBC lady, staring intensely. I thought of, and scribbled, Alexander Pope's line about politicians "Some truth there was - but brewed and bathed in lies to please the fools and puzzle all the wise," to which I added the question "Why do politicians insult the public's intelligence?"

As preparations for the show began, I sat there chatting away to Dave Myers having forgotten about this. Soon there was an announcement that certain people had been called to the front. Six names followed and I was chatting and joking with people around me. Suddenly a hand tapped me on the shoulder. "Mr White, please go to the front."

I was terrified. Enoch Powell was an awesome figure, a giant in the political realm. How could I face him? I was very relieved when the BBC lady said there might not be time for my question.

Soon the red light went on and a countdown to being live on air followed. I could feel the excitement. Live radio was the delight of my teenage years but this was serious stuff.

Every question was answered by each member of the panel, and beads of perspiration began to develop on my forehead as they rapidly got through the questions. Then I heard: "Mr White, your question". Remembering my mother's advice that the English people speak clearly, like Robert Donat and George Sanders (both of whom I later discovered were actually Polish), I delivered my question with great gusto. David Jacobs prompting: "Enoch Powell what do you say?"

Powell, who was a superb orator, a great scholar, and a noted intellectual of his time, then proceeded with excellent dialogue to justify the great work that politicians did for society. Other members of the panel were not so powerful. Jacobs concluded: "Well Mr White, what do you say to the panel?" I regained my composure and replied "It is obvious that they are going to continue to insult the public's intelligence," receiving rapturous applause. David Jacobs looked down from the stage: "Good question Mr. White". I felt a gleeful zing. What a relief. The programme had made a huge impression on me. The power of radio and the miracle of sound! It was amazing to think that this could be heard by millions of people all over the UK. I was totally fascinated by the whole experience.

"How does one get into radio," I asked Jacobs later, and he replied: "It is preferable to specialize in a subject and to approach your local radio station. Radio Leeds is your best one from here."

On returning home my wife, Annie, said that she had been impressed and had recorded it. Playing it back seemed like magic; there I was on radio – amazing. One day maybe! At the weekend the programme was repeated. My Uncle Jim, in the west of Ireland, picked it up and so did friends in London and Dublin. It brought home to me how powerful a media source it was. I continued to meet people for some weeks afterwards who were impressed by me having only a few seconds on air.

Soon I would encounter a man who would become a life-long friend as a result of this happening. A friend of my wife's, Jill, and her husband, David, had a cocktail party in Scarborough, at which a pleasant group of friendly people gathered together for drinks in a relaxed atmosphere. One chap stood out, dressed a sharp suit, and bubbling with vitality, humour, and a zest for life. It was Freddie Drabble, a Scarborough lawyer.

"Well done on your broadcast," he said. I was naturally delighted. We immediately got on and became instant and, as it would develop, lifelong friends. The following week I was invited to go on a hike with a bunch Freddie's friends called The Twirls. This group were to become my closest friends, and that meeting would lead to the most extraordinary adventures. Our hiking expeditions took us all over the UK, France and Spain.

The first friends my wife and I had in Scarborough were Geoff and Heather Nunn who were just completing their first year as hoteliers and had had a record-breaking season at their hotel The Suncrest. As a result they had decided to hold a party. Heather was a cookery lecturer at the local technical college, and was among the first teachers in the UK to establish a vegetarian cookery course. One of her pupils was a dancer called Sarah Brown, who had spent the summer season appearing at the Floral Hall and was a very charming lady who hardly knew the difference between a kidney bean and a cabbage on arrival in Scarborough. After attending Heather's course she opened a vegetarian restaurant. It was not long before a BBC producer after visiting her restaurant, approached her to present her own BBC2 series. This was followed by a collection of books on the subject.

The timing was perfect as the public were now becoming more aware about the importance of diet and food. Geoff was a master at the local public school. My first impression on meeting him was that he was a marvellous fellow – the image of Sir Lancelot Spratt, as portrayed by James Robertson Justice in the hospital comedy film "Doctor in the House". Geoff is a uniquely strong individual and a no-nonsense man with a passion for music, red wine and humour. He and Heather were superb hosts. Along with their usual flair for magnificent, magnanimity they held a party at the Suncrest Hotel to celebrate hotel's success. Geoff was in charge of the film shows at his school and could order any film available. We were allowed to choose our favourite films for an evening. Our three choices were – "Richard III", (Laurence Olivier), "Sons of the Desert " (Laurel & Hardy), and "The Plank" (Tommy Cooper). After a wonderful evening of merriment and superb food, the movie shows started. "Sons of the Desert" and "The Plank" gave an air of elation at the party, but it was "Richard III" that pulverised us all with the power and intensity of Laurence Olivier's performance – his perception of Shakespeare's analysis of the various characters reached into the soul of humanity. So much so, that Freddie having recently been very impressed by a re-enactment of a battle by the Sealed Knot, was now fired up with enthusiasm, and suggested: "Why don't we have a Richard III battle re-enactment at the Castle?" Most of those present agreed that it would be a fun thing to do. It was now 2am, and we were all caressing the shores of inebriation. To most of us, it seemed like the whiskey talking and that it was just a transient remark.

Not so Freddie, soon to be known by us as 'Drastic Drabble', because once he makes up his mind to do something he becomes as tenacious as a barnacle on the bottom of the Titanic. Within a few weeks Freddie was organising a committee to present a Richard III festival at Scarborough Castle. At this stage I never thought it would take off as Richard was seen as a subject of ridicule at the time. Monty Python's Flying Circus would regularly have a Richard III Loony Ward on their TV series. Nevertheless I was delighted to be asked to join the committee organising the event.

I had an eclectic record collection, which comprised everything from African tribal and South American music to medieval, classical, 20th century American recordings and the whole spectrum of rock.

Out of the blue, and as a result of my music connections, Freddie's committee, formed to organize the festival and later to become Scarborough Pageants Ltd, immediately put me in charge of music production, I was flattered of course, but still thought that this wouldn't take off.

Freddie's energy and determination seemed boundless and soon began to set my fires of enthusiasm alight. The inspiration was sealed by the almost fanatical in-depth knowledge of local historian Marie Belfitt. She had information that Richard III held his navy in Scarborough in 1483 to protect the English fishing fleet on their trips to Iceland. He gave the town its own charter in 1483 and he and his wife had a residence in the town. At this time the Icelandic Cod Wars were raging, so I was amazed to hear these facts.

Seduced, I was consumed with a new found passion, further inspired to support this project when local up-and-coming playwright Alan Ayckbourn (now regarded as Britain's leading playwright) encouraged the leading actor in his company, Chris Godwin to volunteer to help us with weaponry and battle techniques. Soon there were various medieval soldiers, pikemen, and even a 14th century siege machine parading around the town. Alan would later say: "I woke up to the unusual sight of these medieval pikemen parading past my house. The play I was writing at the time concerned a committee member and his impact on group. The festival committee was the ideal basis for this play."

Ayckbourn was a cultural jewel in the town, putting on marvellous productions to raise our spirits and fire up our imaginations, at his now world famous Theatre in the Round. His play "Ten Times Table" would later be inspired by the shenanigans created by these events.

At the first meeting of the Richard III committee, which was held at Freddie's offices, various appointments were organised. Marie Belfitt and Kate Hampshire who were both members of the official national Richard III Society of the White Boar had done an in-depth study of the monarch for the society's magazine, the Ricardian, with precise observations of Richard III's life and times. Much to our delight there was also a magazine called The Blanc Sanglier (White Boar) for members of the Yorkshire Richard III Society. It emerged that there were actually branches of the society all over the world.

Kate was given the title "Lady Katharine" because of her dignity and knowledge and belief in Richard's role as a great king for the good of the people and for his historic significance - not the evil corrupt murderer as portrayed by Shakespeare. This, together with Laurence Olivier's impressive interpretation of Shakespeare's misrepresentation of the real facts, has tainted Richard's image in the minds of ordinary people now and in the previous centuries.

These discoveries further propelled our desire to stage this festival. At first we called ourselves the Castle Committee; this was soon sub-divided when the ladies committee was created, Marie and Kate made delightful medieval costumes for the event. Marie Belfitt was further given the title of Historical Research Director because of her fervour for Richard and her incredible knowledge of local history. The Castle Committee underwent further changes until – acknowledging the risks of battle - it assumed limited company status.

Support for the idea of the festival spread like wildfire - so much so that which started as a week's festival expanded to ten days in October, plus extra battles to warm up in July and August. This was a titanic task, which took 18 months to prepare and organise. The battles were choreographed by Chris Godwin, who was chosen to play Richard III, and Alan Ayckbourn and his company was to do a series of medieval playlets.

During the next year the chiropody practice was as demanding as ever, my social life was dominated by playing squash, hiking, and family life, but soon the festival was to begin to control my life.

The squash club was extraordinary. It was still a private club. The Yorkshire Lawn Tennis and Squash Club was the title and it held a strong snobbish taint from its former glory. Great tennis legends such as Ken Rosewall, Virginia Wade, Pancho Gonzales, Lew Hoad and Little Mo had brought global attention with them when they played there. The tennis circuit was deeply embroidered in the town's pride. Here, for a reasonable fee you could enjoy the luxury facilities; superb courts, a lounge with a bar, stewarded restaurant and excellent service.

Jonathan Smith was the champion squash player at the club at this time. His personal friend was Jonah Barrington who was world champion, and had given a whole chapter of his book on squash over to Jonathan's serve. "He would walk slowly forward to the service spot. The ball, when struck would fly in a perfect semi-circle high above his opponent before hitting the wall, where it would immediately drop straight to the floor along the wall like a dead bird. It was almost impossible to return."

I played Jonathan on several occasions and he would appear nonchalantly on court in a tracksuit and plimsols that looked as if they had been found on an archaeological dig.

We would play squash or tennis for several hours of a Sunday, have a shower, enjoy a beer and play poker. It was about this time that one member, Joe Gordon - later to become known as 'Explosive Corrosive Joseph" (for reasons that will become apparent) began to show signs of the unusual.

Joe arrived late one Sunday afternoon, riding bareback on a large white Cleveland mare and looking like an Apache warrior, with a squash racquet sticking out of a bag and a rope around the mare's neck, which he tied to the Palladian pillar outside the club. Rushing to the club bar, he approached a pint of beer with fist clenched, knowing it belonged to his friend, Len Berry, who was standing at the bar, and dropped a sheep's eye into the clear glass of beer. It looked like an octopus, with its various tentacles and bloody bits. "Tell Len I kept an eye on his beer," he chuckled.

An hour later, he came to join us for poker. All went well until I put 30p in coppers on the table. "I can't stand coppers", he cried. "This is a serious game chaps". With that he knocked the table into the air, with glasses, cards and coins flying, as if released from the force of gravity.

It was about this time that we collectively, although not professors of psychology; realised that there was something not quite right about Joe's behaviour.

One night he invited myself and Bill Ellis, an estate agent and keen squash-player, back to his hotel to have a late drink and listen to his new Russian hi-fi system. All was pleasant and relaxing until Joe put on an LP of Tchaikovsky's 1812 overture. The sleeve notes on the album must have been over-enthusiastic, as Joe proceeded to read them aloud and to imagine what it must have been like as a Muscovite with Napoleon's army approaching ready to rape and pillage. He became paranoid and opened a cupboard, taking out one of the three shotguns it contained. At the climax of the overture, as the cannons began firing, Joe shouted "Get back you French bastards!" and let go both barrels of the shotgun through the window, which shattered. The record stopped and there was silence. Bill and I were frozen with shock - it was past midnight and the only sound was of the needle in the groove. Three of the hotel guests appeared timidly in the hall, partly dressed and curious. "What's happening?" enquired one, in a state of mild terror. "Its all right, go back to bed, don't worry!" said Joe, in a sudden flip from raging psychopath to smooth hotelier.

Meanwhile Scarborough Pageants was erupting in an effervescence of activity. I was now elected as media promotions man, a role which I really enjoyed, as interest in the forthcoming festival was amazing, the region's media seemed to devour any snippets of news about it, and as a result we were sending out a constant flow of press releases. We decided to have a preview event before the main festival, which was to take place on 25th September – 3rd October. By now the ladies committee had produced splendid medieval costumes, exact replicas of the period. Chris Godwin was ready to play Richard III. Other key members of the pageant were Chris Found, Cecil Ridley (Cec the Gent), Geoff Nunn, Dave Robson, explosive corrosive Joseph, and Nigel Ironside, whose role was to acquire cannons for the battles.

Corrosive was fired up by the idea of the battles. His respected family firm made turbines for factory plants, and Corrosive, bored with the ponderous monotony of production, had formed an explosives division to the company. This was certainly going to add zest to both the firm and the festival. Some time later a figure entered Freddie's office, badly burnt at the edges, and bandaged like an Egyptian mummy. It was, of course, Corrosive who had inevitably misjudged the power of explosives in his experiments. His unbounded enthusiasm in his explosive role was emphasised when the new owners of a former garage site called him in to help. They wanted a huge tank, which had contained petrol, removed from a deep concrete bunker. Corrosive packed too much explosive either side of the tank and, standing 100 yards away, he detonated it. The tank was blown about 100ft into the air, both ends blown off like flying saucers. One of these, hot and spinning as it landed on the ground, raced towards Corrosive. As he ran and turned out of its trajectory it turned - then zap! It struck him down. Appearing later bandaged in Freddie's office on crutches, with toes and legs akimbo he had seemed to be chastened, and resolved to abandon his explosives career. But some time later he confided in the group that he had found the answer to demolition with what he described as his "magic wand". It was a thermal lance which could reach temperatures of 2,000 degrees! His first job with this new technique was to demolish an old factory wall, but he unfortunately failed to examine the other side of the wall, and on penetration the thermal lance unleashed a river of pig slurry onto the factory floor. Corrosive had his first, or perhaps second, inkling that maybe - just maybe - demolition was not his forte.

Freddie's love of horses meant that getting local riding schools involved was essential, and he was supported by El Foundo, plus the charm and dignity of Ces the Gent, who also had a love of horses and had many contacts in the equestrian world. Had he ever joined the diplomatic corps, the world would undoubtedly be at peace. Freddie with his obvious flair for getting things done, and known as Drastic Drabble. Geoff Nunn was often working hard at his teaching job, as was Bryan Dew, who was a rep for Pilkington Glass, so they could not always give full commitment, though they assisted whenever able. Many others joined in to help with the battles and parades.

Norman Murphy actually built a full size replica of a medieval siege machine and took great delight in parading it about town with his pikemen. In fact he would appear at any event to display the *trebuchet* at the drop of a hat. He was fascinated by historical events but occasionally got his centuries mixed up – some time after the event, he was still showing the 14th-century siege machine at Civil War events. Many more were now keen to enrol. Tony Austin was a respected and successful sales manager, but the idea of being a medieval knight on horseback in battle also appealed to him. He needed an occasional escape route from the high pressure life of the sales force.

Company director with the same firm, Chris Coole observed: "Tony had done some horse-riding and had also managed to walk the greasy pole over the lake at one of the many shows put on at the local Open-Air Theatre. On the morning of the first battle at the Castle Tony, who was convinced he was an accomplished equestrian, and had recently seen the film "The Magnificent Seven", went to collect his horse from the nearby village of Burniston, where the farmer had said he would leave it out on the morning before the battle. Dressed in all the regalia of a medieval knight he walked to the field only to find his steed was at the far end. He managed to coax it a little nearer and eventually the horse stood, puzzled at the sight of Tony in all his regalia. As he reached it the horse shot off to the top end of the hill. He spent the next couple of hours unsuccessfully and sweatily trying to catch the terrified creature, still in his regalia. Eventually he got hold of the horse and made several unsuccessful attempts to mount it before finally, in frustration, deciding to lead it all the four miles from Burniston to the Castle. Said Chris: "He reached the tournament just in time, but he was so knackered he had to rest before he joined in the last battle session. His dream of being as effective as the Black Prince at Agincourt dashed, he rode the horse back to the field like a rejected Don Quixote." He said: "Who would have thought that the former champion of the Open-Air Theatre's greasy pole event would be reduced to this!"

Freddie recalled the first training routines: "We took the horses to Northfield Farm, to a lady who was an expert horsewoman and had told me: "Bring the horses here, we have a good yard with loads of room". We were going up there to familiarise the horses with explosive devices, so they would get used to them in battle. I had kept the explosives intention from her, for obvious reasons, because horses and explosives these days don't really go together. So when we arrived and I finally confessed to her what our plan was. She was alarmed and exclaimed: "Well, you are not doing it here! No, I am not having it! I've got some young stock here, and I *don't want any loud noises!*. I can't believe you are coming here to do this. You are not doing it!"

Freddie's went to work with his immense charm, and eventually persuaded her to agree. He said: "I knew what I was doing and I managed, after reams of dialogue, to convince her, God knows how, I persuaded her that battles did indeed take place with horses, with cannons going off and that they did get used to it. It had to start somewhere, and this was the ideal place. She eventually seemed to be calm about it, so then Cecil and I got on our horses, and Joe let a thunder flash off in the distance, then moved closer and the bangs became louder. Amazing. The horses were not at all startled. In fact they didn't seem remotely bothered. It was a good job, as we had riders from Les Dickinson's riding school, and among them were some elderly ladies, who were his best clients. In their costumes, chainmail, etcetera, they really did look like medieval knights."

Freddie had spotted Cecil as a likely candidate to take part in the battles because of his love of horses, which went far beyond his role as a bookie. Said Cecil: "Freddie came to my house and tried to persuade me to join the Richard III committee, and at first I refused, as I felt I wouldn't have enough time. However he left his file behind, and came back for it and used a bit more persuasion, and I finally agreed to be the character Sir Thomas Sage, Master of the King's Horses."

We also made contacts with other people who staged re-enactments. One such outing to acquire swords for the battles took us on a trip to West Yorkshire. Chris Godwin joined us in Freddie's Volvo and we drove to the small village of Wurston where we visited this antique shop of Murgatroyd Beamish, a tall bearded man with staring eyes. It was a dark, dank winter's night. He invited us in, and we followed him down a long winding stairway. On arriving at a large cellar door, he opened it with a huge key, and we continued down the steps into a deep underground cellar. We all shuddered as we looked around in this eerie atmosphere with goats' heads and chains hanging from the pillars. Chris Godwin's eyes were on stalks, and terrified he whispered to us: "Devil worship! That's what's going on here!" Murgatroyd disappeared into the gloomy darkness and we followed, quaking. He said: "There are some swords here. You lot, get hold of them," As he paused to look at us the whites of his eyes seem to increase in size. "Would you like to see the suit of armour that Richard III wore, I've got it here. It was found in an old farm barn near Ashby de la Zouch, near Bosworth Field, Leicestershire, where Richard was defeated in battle."

There was a silent pause. "I'm afraid we have to dash back," said Chris Godwin, sensing the weird and strange vibes, and we scrambled up the stairs with the swords, loading them into the Volvo even though they were very heavy.

We felt a sense of relief when we got into the car. But it wouldn't start. Through the pouring rain and darkness came Beamish, with a huge broadsword. He looked terrifying, and we thought we were going to become human sacrifices. Freddie wound the window down still desperately trying to start the car. "Here is the sword that Richard III used in battle," said Beamish.

We took it in via the window. "Thank you," said Freddie. "I will take it to the Battle of Scarborough". The car started, and we drove out of that car-park like a bat out of hell.

Chris Godwin had trained a group of local lads in the use of pikes and swords. Nigel Taylor had forged real cannons at his steel factory. These weapons would fire balloons which were filled with a highly explosive mix of gases. Freddie had these balloons in the back of his mother's old Ford Cortina while casually driving around town. These cannons were made of the strongest steel, but a fracture developed in the barrel of one of them. Corrosive had been too generous with the explosive gas. We imagined what would have happened if one of these over-loaded balloons had exploded whilst driving around town, the whole place would have been blown away and we would have been protein for the seagulls.

We were now promoting the festival to boost and prolong Scarborough's end-of-season tourist industry, and we were hoping to get a contribution from the local council. We had now registered ourselves as a company in London as Scarborough Pageants Ltd. The company now established individual roles, Freddie Drabble was appointed Chairman

Historical Research, Marie Belfitt and Kate Hampshire Period Costumes, Ian Morrison, Uniform & Armour, Chris Godwin, Army Composition and Battle Strategy, Charles White, Public Relations and Music Production, Cecil Ridley Equestrian Organiser, Brian Shipley, Scarborough Fayre Programmes.

Our first publicity stunt was to contact Lord Olivier, then we sent a delegation to meet him and his wife, Joan Plowright . Then came our first press release, Olivier, one of the great cultural figures of our time offered his "warmest and best wishes for the success of your splendid enterprise" which he considered "a marvellous idea" in a telegram.

Olivier's support was a great coup and thanks were due to to Alan Ayckbourn for his influence and connections.

Through Marie Belfitt's research, we had found that Scarborough had been granted a Royal Town Charter in 1483. We sent the press release to BBC North TV, who responded instantly. Just before the first event we managed to get the charter out of the Town Hall.

The publicity machine was off to a superb start. On the Sunday morning the day we were to rehearse, my role was to see that lady bank clerks were at their ticket booths and to ensure that the Nottingham Jousting Company were accommodated with stabling facilities, as well as supplying stands for their armouries. These were disciplined, well-trained, passionate medieval jousters who took battle re-enactments as a serious commitment.

The smell of horses and the clang of steel swords were awesome. The Black Knight looked ferocious, as active as Tarzan in overdrive, leaping on to his horse with broadsword in hand, with gracious ease. He looked terrifying as his sword swished through the air, with black armour and unshaven face it made him the perfect baddie. "The apparel doth proclaim the man". It was still early morning, the view across the castle grounds over the sea towards Filey Brigg, Bempton Cliffs and Flamborough Head was magnificent. The blue sea and the green grass seemed to have a divine touch. On the edge of the hill the ladies committee dressed in their colourful medieval costumes were the picture of elegance as they seemed to glide towards me. "Charles", declared Marie Belfitt, "Chris Godwin is unable to play the part of the king today, he has got to go to BBC Manchester for Alan Ayckbourn's play as the actor Richard Briers has been taken ill. We've decided that you will play King Richard! There's no-one else, you'll have to do it.""

I was horrified, and said: "No not me, my role is public relations, sorry folks." As Marie continued to insist I protested:. "Look, I am an Irishman. It is no time for an Irishman to be playing England's most notorious king" (At this time the IRA's armed campaign on the mainland for a united Ireland was at its zenith. Lord Mountbatten was blown up whilst fishing off County Sligo and British soldiers were being shot in the Six Counties).

"That has nothing to do with this," insisted Marie. "We have only an hour and a half to the opening ceremony at St. Mary's Church, you have got to do it" .They swarmed around me like a pride of predatory lions. "Follow us to the changing-room," said Marie forcefully. Bewildered, I felt I had no choice. I was dressed up as King Richard and went hopping around the room doing a mock imitation of Lord Olivier's performance. "Stop it Charles," commanded the ladies. I was very nervous about the idea. It started to rain with dark clouds overhead, the last thing we needed on the first day of the Festival. The Queen was played by a local girl Christine Mortimer. We were both apprehensive as we entered the church. The local vicar, the Rev. Keys Fraser, was to bless the company and wish the festival success. There was a dramatic moment, when the sun shone through the stained-glass window of the church. It was a glorious feeling - an announcement of good weather from the man upstairs.

The opening event was a success but made us very much aware that we needed to do a huge amount of work for the two-week festival ahead. Over the next two months we had to use all our guile to get the support of the local people, who now realised we were out to make a success of the festival for the benefit of the Town.

Cecil recalls: "There was a gipsy horseman who had volunteered to help, and when he saw the morning's bad weather he was about to leave. Then, as the sun broke through he came back with several horses, which he proposed to use to give children a ride round the festival site – for 15 per cent of the takings. During the event he had a constant stream of customers, and queues formed, but at the end I asked him how he had done . he said 'Terrible, terrible. – I didn't make a penny!' - and rapidly left the Castle with his horses.

As Cecil enthused: "During the battle the pikemen went forward, and we knights on horses charged. We were all very close to each other, and one of the elderly ladies fell off her horse between Freddie and I. I pulled up my horse, thinking 'Oh God, she's a goner' as she didn't move. Then she perked up, smiled, and said 'This is fun!' and got back on again. A falconer had been active before and after the battle giving displays to add to the atmosphere, and after the battle he told me that one of his falcons was missing. He had to go back to Nottingham, so he asked us to go up before sunset and see if the falcon had returned. He gave us a piece of string with hook attached, on which he hung a chunk of meat. "Just swing it round your head and shout 'Woo-hoo, woo-hoo", he said, and it'll come to you. However we knew the seagulls had driven it away, and it wouldn't be seen again.

The Friday before the main festival BBC televisionhad given us fantastic publicity, filming the ladies in their costumes followed by Christine and myself as the royal couple, descending down the Castle steps surrounded by pikemen and soldiers-at-arms.

Then Freddie, Cecil and I were interviewed with the Charter, I described Richard as a great King and plugged the festival as much as possible. Cecil read out Laurence Olivier's statement of support.

The BBC "Look North" programme opened their main six

o'clock news with the legendary clip of Lord Olivier 'Now is the winter of our discontent etc.', then presenter Jeremy Thompson said to camera "That is Shakespeare's image of him, but here we have the real Richard III. You are not like the king that Shakespeare portrayed," he said to me.

I burst into my dialogue about Richard being a great warrior and King for the common good of the people and could not have leapt onto a horse with a broadsword with a withered arm and a hunchback. That was just Tudor propaganda - Richard was the last great Plantagenet King of England.

A close friend of mine Dave 'Meatcleaver' Myers after a hard day at the office was served his evening meal by his mother and on seeing me on television jumped out of his chair. "Bloody Hell, look at this mum" he exclaimed, as he spilt his dinner all over the floor. "It's that bloody Chalky White, dressed up as Richard III". For weeks afterwards, I was astounded by how many people had watched this. I then realised what a really powerful media television was. Our publicity was working better than expected; we even got the front page of the Yorkshire Post.

Marie had gathered evidence to prove that Richard was innocent of the murder of the two princes in the Tower, so we decided it would be a good idea for me as King together with my loyal knights, to hold a mock trial outside the Tower of London to prove his innocence. Full of determination, with Freddie and my brother-in-law John Standidge, and others all dressed as knights in armour and myself in full attire as Richard, we set out for London after the following morning's rush hour after staying at my sister's home in Beckenham.

As we crossed Tower Bridge we were disorientated, so we pulled up beside three Cockney workmen at the roadside. "Could you please tell us the way to the Tower of London," said I in my kingly robes surrounded by loyal knights crammed into Freddie's car. "Who the bleedin' hell do you think you are, Richard III?" they said as they reeled in hysteria. "Well actually I am," said I. Further hysteria ensued 'A bleedin' Irishman, the King of England? Wait until I tell my mates in the pub tonight, they won't swallow this one! The Tower's just a quarter of a mile to the right, watch out or they will have your head off, Paddy!" We drove away, leaving them helpless with laughter.

At the Tower hundreds of tourists were milling about, as we pulled into the entrance I was bursting for the loo, having a bladder the size of a peanut, I rushed to the nearest gents, forgetting that I was wearing tights, in my haste to relieve myself. A series of wolf-whistles and remarks followed, in shocked response to my gaudy regalia. "You better not bend down in here mate," chuckled one man.

As I came out of the toilet, two tourist buses full of Japanese tourists pulled up in front of me and seeing me dressed in kingly costume rushed excitedly forward, wanting to have their photo taken with me and some to sign their brochures. However the mock trial was due to begin so I had little time to indulge them. We had already picked a spot outside the Tower for the trial.

The Beefeaters, who were former army and SAS officers, were aware of our arrival and purpose and forbade us to enter the Tower. A group of about a dozen media people had gathered there already. I was approached by one reporter, Helen Minsky, together with a photographer, and told: "Climb up the railings and proclaim your innocence." This I duly did. After a brief reading of the mock trial and some radio interviews, a few photographers snapped us. We decided to set off for a pub lunch at my favourite West-End pub ,The Salisbury in St. Martin's Lane. After a few beers and a sumptuous lunch, we walked towards Leicester Square and zap! The Evening Standard's billboards announced "Richard III is innocent OK", supported by a fine piece by Helen.

Magnificent publicity for our festival! We had come to London from little Scarborough and hit the big publicity fan, resulting in amazing coverage that began to spread through local radio all throughout the north of England. BBC local Radio Sheffield, Humberside, Leeds etc, front page of the Yorkshire Post etc. The publicity even reached Ireland where the national newspaper The Irish Independent had a photograph of myself and Queen Anne with the headline 'Irishman King of England.' The family was praying that the IRA hadn't bought a copy.

The festival opened on the Saturday 25th September 1976 with a procession through town followed by a cornucopia of events over the next few weeks. On Saturday a medieval banquet was organised at the Castle. Early English music and dancing were performed by the Leeds Consort with dances of the time.

The menu included dishes, pate on granary bread, smoked mackerel, cutlet of roast boar, roast stag, syllabub, cheese, and consommé. Real ale, mead, cider, wine and liquors were served.

The local technology college catering department had the task of preparing the food. The Mayor and Mayoress were to be guests of honour. On the afternoon of the event, we suddenly realised that the marquee firm had overlooked lighting! A tidal wave of neurosis engulfed us. Fortunately Freddie's close friend Chris Coole, known as 'Coolie', came to the rescue as his firm supplied generators.

Could they install them in time for the banquet? We were on the edge of despair for at least two hours. Coolie had managed to get some lights but was unsure if he could get them installed in time. My duty was to wait at the Castle entrance to greet the Mayor and Mayoress with the uncertainty of the lights still hanging over us.

Tom Young, the Mayor and the Mayoress arrived by limousine. The Mayor was a tax inspector specialising in Customs and Excise. He was a rigidly serious man with an expression of impending doom. His wife, Doreen, was full of fun and humour, who oozed with a charming sexuality, whilst her husband had the expression of a gargoyle on the face of Notre Dame in Paris.

Soon the crowds started to build up and the medieval musicians Christopher Mountford and Van de Loop who played the lyre anxiously whispered in my ear "There are no EFFING lights!"

"Not my problem, I am the EFFING KING!!" I whispered.

How could I explain this to the mayor? What would happen to all the food? Would we have to give the people their money back? Would the whole venture collapse after all our hard work?, it was a nightmare!

Then relief came, Coolie got the lights going.

Our main concern was to prolong Scarborough's holiday season and improve the town's image as a class resort in contrast to the Kiss-me quick persona of Blackpool.

The royal table was to host the Mayor and Mayoress and on entering the tent the flowers, and medieval music created a suitable ambience. It was great to see everybody in costume, an atmosphere of past graciousness and nobility. The heraldry group, part of the Richard III Society, heightened the colour of the event with their heraldic imagery.

Drinks were presented in goblets by the banquet master and the squire announced that food would be served. A group of six knaves came forward and bowed with a dozen smoked mackerel on poles in front of the royal table accompanied by musicians of the period. The food was served on bread as there were no plates in this period, with just a dagger to cut the food.

All was quite salubrious until Freddie stood up to welcome everyone as an overture to the Mayor's speech. Then a group of idiots from the local Round Table who were already well inebriated started heckling with remarks such as 'Sit down get on with it" Then they started to throw bread-buns soaked in wine at the royal table. Those that fell short of Freddie found the Mayor in easy range. After a well-aimed bun hit him on the nose, our Mayor's expression went from glum to fuming, and, gritting his teeth he said in a forceful voice "I'm not going to give a speech to this rabble!"

I stood up and tried to defuse the situation but I soon realised it was impossible. Fortunately the jousters arrived just in time to give a demonstration of their vigorous sword-fighting and antics. Their appearance soon quelled the rabble into silence

Soon the Black Knight was in full flight, he came to our table in swash-buckling mood.

Suddenly his sword cut through the lighted candles, they remained intact. Then with a cheeky grin he blew out the candles just as they fell to the table – just like in the movies. The Mayoress gave a squeak of delight. The Mayor remained grim-faced. Ignoring him the Black Knight continued to talk to the Queen as the Mayor continued to talk to Freddie. The Black Knight with ultimate audacity whilst standing on the royal table grabbed hold of the mayoress, pulling her up out of her seat with one hand, he gave her a long, passionate kiss. The mayoress just cooed and giggled. Hell, if the mayor had noticed that it would have been the end of our festival and all of our hard work would have been in vain.

The banquet continued, ale and mead were drunk in large quantities and most of the folks were caressing the shores of inebriation. The mayor even began to smile as we escorted him back to his car. He thanked us for a splendid evening and the mayoress just giggled all the way back to the limousine. The displays and exhibitions over the next few days supported by the local townspeople proved that an end of season festival could be a success. This success enhanced our credibility as a group. At this stage the Town Hall were reluctant to recognise our organisational abilities and innovation and this perhaps created a level of envy which would continue due to their incompetence.

The ramifications of the festival continued for some time afterwards. The White Boar Society, a branch of the Richard III presented me with a statue of a boar and thanked me for my role and promoting his reputation. I was appointed as Chairman of the North-East branch of the Richard III Society.

My first invitation was to the Sheffield University to a medieval tapestry and heraldic function accompanied by Marie Belfitt, Lady Katharine, and other ladies in medieval costume, we drove to Sheffield. It was a marvellous occasion with displays of authentic tapestries and heraldic emblems which were very impressive, created by this team who were obsessed by this historic period. Once again mead and ale flowed with authentic food of the time presented with flair and style. The ladies looked beautiful with their tall hats and flowing veils, add to this superbly-designed dresses that showed off many a fine figure. These people obviously loved their craft. We were soon merry with mead and elated with ale. The next day, I met the girls. They said: "We don't know how we got home." I had to admit: "Neither do I." They elaborated: "At one stage you went round a roundabout the wrong way, several times and another time you were trying to replace a cassette tape which fell on the car floor and you continued to look for it whilst still driving." My final comment was: "His Majesty thanks the Lord for driving us home safely that evening."

Another event occurred at the Merchant Taylor's Hall, in York, which was taken over by the Richard III Society for their annual banquet. This is a superb ancient building dating back to the 14th century. with the authentic atmosphere to match. King Richard was Duke of York.

On arrival at the beautiful old hall, we were impressed by the ornate, authentically reproduced costumes of the period. Everyone there looked as though they were from the 14th century. Outstanding were two cardinals dressed in red silk doublets. I felt honored to be amongst these people and admired their passion for Richard and their belief in this historic significance. After I gave a short speech, I was approached by these "cardinals", who said I was requested to attend a meeting. I followed them upstairs and on entering this spacious room found a large group of approximately 24 people sat round a large table which was dominated by an imposing lady at the top of the table looking most elegant and imperious. One of the cardinals instructed: "Stand still".

The group stared at me intently, I felt uneasy. The lady at the head of the table stood up and declared with authority: "Yes. He is Richard'. With that everyone stood up and bowed towards me as they uttered to me "Your Grace". I was perplexed, but thought: "This is fun!" Then the two cardinals turned to me and said "Your Grace, do you mind if we anoint you with sacred oils?" "Not at all" I said, "as long as I can first have a pint of beer."

Many other events followed but these are the most memorable. As chairman of the Richard III Society I got a great insight into how strong the organisation was and its intent to prove Richard's historic importance. However, busy in my practice some months later, a phone call from the local evening paper. "Are you chairman of the Richard III Society?" I answered: "Yes, but I am very busy at the moment."

"I am sure that you are aware that there is conflict in the

society over the White Boar emblem representing Richard?" said the reporter. "Not really, as far as I am concerned they can call themselves the Pink Elephants," I said with feeling.

It was on the front page the next day. A slow news day indeed!

The most important result from the Richard III experience is that it cemented our initial friendships and was to lead to members of the committee and The Twirls hiking group uniting together in a lifelong friendship. Family life and work at the chiropody surgery continued. In retrospect the energy required to play Richard III and run a full-time practice could only have been possible with an understanding wife who had an amazing threshold of tolerance. Eventually this event would lead to the formation of the extraordinary conservation group The Sons of Neptune.

Poster advertising the Richard III Festival, 1976.

SCARBOROUGH PAGEANTS LTD. PRESENT

KING RICHARD III
Festival at Scarborough

Saturday
25th Sept.
1976

Sunday
3rd Oct.
1976

SCARBOROUGH PAGEANTS LIMITED (formerly Scarborough Castle Committee) is
responsible for the organisation of the Festival.
Scarborough Castle was built in Norman England and was a strategic stronghold in the
reign of King Richard III. The Company (Scarborough Pageants Limited) was established
to focus attention on the history of Scarborough by arrangement of Tournaments, Pageants
and other activities. Its members are local people and any profits are utilised and any
any profits are utilised and...

The "Court" at Scarborough Castle.

The "trial" at the Tower of
London to prove the innocence
of Richard III.

Charles White as King Richard.

Captain Thomas Sydney Smith MBE

"I never lost a ship and I never lost a man. Everyone who sailed with me came back with me."

To walk across the Scarborough sand at 7am just as the sun is rising is an awe-inspiring experience, which always makes me feel as though I am at the very heart of creation. As I gradually proceed into the sea, the waves crash towards me like galloping horses at speed. At the moment I dive into an oncoming wave, a shock of cold and powerful exhilaration vibrates through my body. It is as though I have been shot out of a huge bottle of freshly-uncorked champagne, leaving chilled bubbles bouncing all over my body. Surfacing to see the sun greeting me over a delightful cloud structure on the horizon enhances this indescribable sense of exaltation. The dawn's reflection on the wide sea and the breaking waves makes me feel at one with the cosmos.

Sea bathing boosts the immune system; the sense of well-being it gives can be almost overwhelming. A quick run back across the beach will take the edge off the euphoria, but leaves one relaxed, clear-headed, and with enough energy to accomplish anything. All things seem to take on a greater significance. The sheer physical enjoyment of being in the sea is enhanced by the joy of observing the life and the creatures in the sea. The life, joy and vitality that is naturally there rubs off onto those in it.

At least, this was the situation up to 1983, before which the question of pollution and sewage outfalls never entered our simple minds. We were like youngsters reborn chasing in and out of the sea. By going in the sea we discovered and experienced a new heightening of the senses and an improvement in our health and perception. We were better able to cope with everyday work and problems and it seemed to generally improve the mind, body and soul.

After our morning dip, we would often drive up to see Captain Sydney Smith, who had become our mentor and father figure. He had been at sea since he was a boy, seen pretty much everything the planet had to offer and captained several merchant ships during the Second World War. With a smile that told you it had made his life feel worthwhile, he would say: "I never lost a ship, never lost a man."

When you got to know him, you would hear a few stories that indicated this very nearly wasn't the case. In the Battle of the Atlantic, for instance, Syd was at the bridge for hours, months on end looking out for bombers and steering his ship out of the way of the falling bombs. Many times they would miss the ship by only a few feet.

One day we called and Syd had all his many medals out for a polish. There were also personal letters of thanks from King George and Winston Churchill, for his twelve D-Day landings. It was an impressive sight, and Captain Syd was an impressive man.

When well into his eighties, Syd would still sometimes row five or six of us across the bay without experiencing so much as shortness of breath. He would shoot up and down the quayside ladders like a squirrel and never seemed to feel the cold. We would often call at his house at 7.30am as he raised the red ensign at the side of his garden shed. Inviting us in, he would uncork the whisky bottle for his favourite toast – "Confusion to our enemies", then "Cheers". This became a ritual we followed when we had victories to celebrate in our long-running battles for the environment.

Syd initiated the ritual in late 1983, just as our campaign was in full flight. The threat of the sewage plant had only appeared in the last two years and we still had trouble taking seriously the idea that this crazy scheme would get anywhere. We gradually realized what an extraordinary man of exceptional dignity and experience he was - literally a hero.

Captain Syd was born in Cooks Row, in the Old Town of Scarborough, Yorkshire, in 1907 into a seafaring family, and the Town remained his home, although his adventures took him to every corner of every continent.

Let him tell it:

"Our family at sea goes back to the Spanish Armada. After that every man Jack of us went to sea – there was nothing else to do in those days in Scarborough. The sea was our life. Some Scarborough seamen fought the Armada and that led to Scarborough's connection with Trinity House.

After the Armada, the men were not paid by Queen Elizabeth, and most were left to go back to sea, beg or starve. The following year, there was only about a quarter of them alive. The Scarborough ship owners and sea traders got together to help these men. They opened a subscription fund and got the blessing and money of Trinity House, London, which strengthened the relationship as an organisation.

Thomas Smith, who was my ancestor - my second name is after him - was a founder and subscriber, from that time all my ancestors were seafaring men. My great-great-grandfather, Matthew Smith, was a ship owner and master of Trinity House up to 1801. Christopher Smith, his son, built Scarborough's first-ever lifeboat in 1801.

His son Matthew and his brother Thomas were ship owners and in the winter of 1860, coming in from Cuba with a cargo load of sugar, they lost the mainmast in a storm off Kinsale, south west Ireland. There was no air-and-sea rescue in those days, so they collected the wreckage together and managed to put a jury rig (improvised sail) on her, and eventually managed to sail into Milford Haven. Before Captain Matthew Smith left Milford Haven, he got himself married to Mary Inon, a Welsh lady who could hardly speak any English – just enough to get herself married.

"My auntie Margaret, my Auntie Lisa, Uncle Will and my father could all sing Welsh songs in Welsh, but they couldn't understand what they were singing about. The funny part of it was that when I was serving my time as an apprentice sailor I got shanghaied to a ship in Cardiff and for several years spent nearly all my time in the Bristol Channel."

The family moved round the corner to Albion Place soon after Syd's birth. His father was an open-boat fisherman in a coble and the family lived on fish and shellfish. Life was tough for young Syd. At the age of seven he was rowing visitors around Scarborough's South Bay for a few pence a time. His father helped with the tunny fish bonanza, which gave an extra income to the family. First memories date back to the morning of 16 December 1914, when the German battlecruisers Derfflinger and the Von Der Tann shelled the town. This was an indiscriminate attack on a civilian population and homes, unheard of before in warfare, which outraged the entire country. This incident led to the design of the recruitment poster "Remember Scarborough" which became one of the most famous images of enlistment advertising during the Great War – second only to Kitchener pointing out: "I Want You".

Renowned in later life for his extraordinarily detailed memory, Captain Syd would often relate stories such as this:

"German U-boats twice attacked Scarborough after the initial bombardment in WWI. One U-boat commander even boasted he used to enter Scarborough's South Bay and lie on the bottom to listen to concerts at the Spa in the evening, even coming ashore to attend! After the war, he wrote to the council to complain that the orchestra had played a wrong stanza in one recital!"

Educated at Scarborough's Friarage Primary School and the Graham Sea Training School, he followed his father, a local fisherman, into a career at sea, initially on herring boats and then aged sixteen, entering a four-year apprenticeship in the Merchant Navy with a Cardiff-based cargo-ship.

Quick to learn the necessary skills and knowledge, he rose consistently through the ranks, eventually taking his Master's exam at Newcastle in 1936.

For the next few years, Syd criss-crossed the world, and sailed merchant vessels to every corner of virtually every continent. My son Liam returned from travels around Indonesia in 1996, and was visibly astonished to see Syd's memory burst into life when he mentioned this to him at Christmas dinner two years later. He regaled us with tales of his experiences of the archipelago nearly six decades gone, and his recall of its complex topography and bizarre wildlife, in particular, left us pretty speechless.

He had sailed across the world so many times that he seemed to have an extraordinary intimacy with the oceans of the world, and he would often pepper his conversations with the jewels of his knowledge. For example, he would recall that as a youth there was no electricity in the Harbour, but "the phosphorus in the sea would light the keels of the boats, so we could see our way to them". With regard to pollution of the seas, while sailing in the Atlantic by the Canary Islands in the 1960s and 70s he remembers noticing the increasing pollution spreading to that area from the North Sea.

He was a devoutly Christian man, certainly not one for "holding court" - but his tales, when they came out, were always the high points of an evening's conversation. By this time Syd was losing his sight, but he would become so animated, you could think he was almost half his age, never mind unable to see you properly. He was so sharp and aware of his surroundings that his rapidly encroaching blindness made no difference. Founded on experience at sea, his knowledge was the equivalent of a Masters degree, and he was qualified to sail and land any ship of any size – up to and including the QE2. He could also navigate by the stars if need be, and became one of the world's leading authorities on tidal movements. However it was not until the Second World War that his incredible seamanship would face its greatest challenges.

Syd recalled: "On September 3rd 1939, I was mid-way across the Atlantic, delivering manganese ore from West Africa to Norfolk, Virginia. The radio operator entered the cabin with a message, saying that a state of hostility now existed between the British Empire and Germany. Orders were to make to the nearest Allied or neutral port.

"So we continued to Norfolk and discharged our cargo – it was about three thousand miles, but it was as near as anywhere else. The next order was to go to the Vancouver grain silos to pick up ten thousand tons of Manitoba number one grade wheat. We delivered this to Port Royal, Jamaica, and topped up our fuel bunkers."

Syd continued to make transatlantic deliveries with his crew on the ship Empire Trent. A couple of years later, the theatre of war had spread, and the battle of the Atlantic was approaching its height. An extraordinary event took place on his return journey from Chicago to Cardiff, loaded with explosives, when he joined a military convoy, which sailed into an area peppered with U-boats and minefields. The Empire Trent developed engine trouble and had to slow down. A heavy mist fell, but as Syd and his crew began to lag, a ship came out of the fog with "a bone in its teeth". This means that at speed, as the ship parts the water into white waves, it looks like a dog with a bone in its mouth.

With the Empire Trent loaded with high explosives, and only one gun on board, Syd called his men to alert and held a cool stance, expecting an attack. Out of the mist, came a voice: "What the hell are you doing Syd?"

"Aye, is that you Percy Pickles?" cried Syd. "We're having engine trouble; we've had to slow down."

"Bet you thought we were Germans," replied Percy, "We turned around to meet you, thought you might have been sunk, good to see you're all right, lad. Make your own way home Syd, we've got to get on."

Commander Pickles happened to be from Scarborough and the two were old friends, neither remarked on the chance of the encounter.

On 30th June 1943, 55 miles north of Cape Finisterre – which is near the French-Spanish border - the Captain had his most gruelling experience of the war.

"The ship was just about on its last legs, lack of maintenance and pushing it hard had us even unable to pump water out. Everything was over-stretched because shipping was at such a premium. They would just say get out of it, get on with whatever mission you're on. We were just about north of Cape Finisterre – right on their doorstep - when we had a combined attack by Fokker Wulf bombers and U-boats. One particular Fokker Wulf bomber came out on reconnaissance and had a go at my ship. I only had one gun, a Bofors. My gunner let fire and he scarpered quickly. I said to the gunner, "He's just getting the range of the gun, He's got it now." I told him to keep an eye out and not wait for orders to fire, just let him have it, I'll handle the ship.

"I knew the Bofors gun had a range of twenty thousand feet, and sure enough, so did the German pilot as he returned with a vengeance. I stood outside on the bridge with my binoculars and saw his bomb doors open. I realised I had to put myself in his place as a huge cluster of bombs were released. I knew that I was in control – fortunately the ship was loaded to starboard and she was quick on the helm.

The bombs came so close to us you could have touched them. Aye, then they exploded and lifted the ship – loaded with nine thousand tons of iron ore – about three feet out of the sea. It blew out her dynamo and that was the end of our de-gaussing mechanism, which was to protect us against magnetic mines. It also broke all our bilge lines, so we couldn't pump out water if we got any leaks. But we were all still in one piece.

The plane went off for another load of bombs, and came back to attack us again - four times. We didn't get much sleep. But the gunner was a good lad, from Lucas, in Fife, only fifteen years old, but already a veteran of three trips across the Atlantic as a gunner. I recommended him for an award."

This action led Syd to be awarded the King's Commendation for bravery, presented to him by Sir Winston Churchill.

Captain Syd's adventures continued as he acted as a vital link in a wartime organisation called "The Pipeline", which smuggled escaped prisoners of war from occupied Europe. Operating his ship between the port of Huelva in south-eastern Spain, and Gibraltar, ostensibly carrying coal, Captain Syd often risked capture in daring missions to rescue escapees. Having volunteered for special operations, Captain Syd was involved in four Allied invasions, the first being in North Africa in 1942.

On one occasion, the captain sailed into Algiers and unloaded coal, then went on to Dorme to pick up manganese ore. At this time, there was a high alert on as Captain Syd's sister ship had been sunk only a dozen or so miles down the coast after leaving the port. The port's pilot refused to take Syd through the normal route and would not venture more than a mile from the coast. Syd was under strict orders to follow the same route as his sister ship, but using his own instinct, clung as close to the coast as possible all the way to Malta. He arrived a week late, and heard about the many ships that had been lost since he was last in port. Syd was called before the Admiralty to answer for his disobedience of a direct order. He said, "Well, the ship's here, the cargo is here, the men are here and I'm here while you've lost most of the other ships you were hoping to have here by now."

A noted event in which Captain Syd was involved also occurred in Huelva, not far from the mouth of the River Guadalajara. As a tidal expert, he knew these waters intimately and was involved in Operation Mincemeat, a deception plan to mislead the German High Command into believing that the Allies would invade Greece and Sardinia instead of Sicily. This involved using a corpse dressed as a major in the British Army carrying false "Top Secret" documents giving false details of Allied war plans. It was planned to float the body to wash up on the beach in Punta Umbria, near Huelva, Spain, as though it was a drowning victim following an air crash, though in fact the corpse was that of a Welsh tramp who had died following rat poisoning. Documentation on the corpse confirming his rank and social activities, including love life, was backed up by MI5. The original plan was hatched by Ian Fleming, creator post-war of the James Bond stories. Captain Syd remarked: "A local fisherman saw the body floating, and I was on the beach when it was landed."

All went well with the plan, as the Spanish, though neutral, eventually informed the Germans, who took the bait, dispatching 19,000 troops to Greece, leaving the beaches at Sardinia comparatively free for the British landing. This has been regarded as the most deceptive flanker since the Trojan Horse.

In command of the Canadian-built ship the Fort Finlay, he took a leading role in the ferrying of troops and equipment for the D-Day landings in June 1945. He made eleven trips from Tilbury docks to the Juno beach Normandy. Under heavy bombardment from land and air, and with the constant threat of mines, often in total darkness, Syd carried a total of 600 Welsh guards, 140 Churchill tanks and all the attendant ammunition.

He was later to take the eighth army "Desert Rats" up the Adriatic to Ancona, being the first vessel into the Italian port after it was captured. Behind the hills above the town, the battle was still raging though the town itself was completely deserted. Syd was loaded to the gunwhales with high explosives, and enemy shells were still flying over the hills towards the harbour.

Syd stayed away out to sea for safety's sake until things calmed down a little, and then docked. Almost immediately, the shelling started again, and a jeep full of Green Howards came racing up to him. The captain of this group of fellow Yorkshiremen immediately took him away and instructed the crew to scatter. Later a destroyer turned up and began to shell the entrenched enemy positions, and some hours later the battle was over. Syd's crew, however had scattered and since they were needed to unload the ship, a search was mounted. Eventually one of the Green Howards heard singing, and found the crew in a cellar full of bottles of marsala wine, all of them completely clattered.

After D-day, Syd was posted to Madras and was assigned to ferrying Indian troops and tanks up the coast for the invasions of Burma and Malaya.

This was a big job, as the Japanese army had very nearly broken into the subcontinent through the crucial Himalayan bottleneck of Burma. The volunteer army of the subcontinent was the largest in the war, comprising over two and a half million men. He later received the Burma Star for his efforts.

It was a great honour and compliment to the Sons that the Captain supported us. His intimate knowledge of the seas around Scarborough and his superfast recall of vital information made fools of our enemies countless times.

After the war Sydney opted for a quieter life and more time at home with his wife Gladys. He edited Olsen's Nautical Almanac – the bible of the tides around the British Isles, giving lectures and acting as a consultant on tidal matters around the UK. He was made an honorary elder brother of Trinity House London – the oldest nautical society in the world – and elected lifetime President of Trinity House Scarborough.

He was also a trustee of Wilson's Mariners Home. Herbert Temple, who worked with Captain Syd at Wilson's and Trinity

House, said of him, "My first and lasting impression of Captain Syd was that he was an absolute gentleman. I never heard him raise his voice to anybody. He was saintly. He may have had to bawl and shout at his men, but such was his personality that he could persuade people to do his bidding without having to resort to this. Colleagues told me that during the war, he remained cool and analytical in the most intense situations. He was exactly the same gentlemanly fellow all the time. Even in his last few years, any applications for his help would be dealt with straight away. He had tremendous recall of local events. Marvellous. You couldn't pull the wool over his eyes at all. It would have been appropriate to have made him a freeman of the town, but because he showed up the Town Hall's so-called experts as buffoons, they resented his authority on all maritime matters. He would often say the only thing Scarborough Borough Council know about the sea is that it is wet. He was always to the fore, and when visiting dignitaries came to town, they would be entranced by him, as he was for many years Scarborough's Deputy Harbourmaster."

The Captain of the Endeavour, an exact replica of Captain Cook's ship, which when docked at Whitby Harbour had an initial queue of several thousand people – was so entranced by Syd's tales that he spent two hours listening to his anecdotes. He was so fascinated by his knowledge that many VIPs were kept waiting while he conversed with Syd.

At his home, Syd's library comprised virtually a museum of shipping history. Such was his knowledge that he could identify a ship of any type or shipping line, of any period, by photograph, drawing or painting.

By the time the Sons met Syd, he was seventy. We fully realised the honour of his company, made him an honorary member of the group immediately, and were relieved and honoured when he accepted. Despite his age, from our first meeting Syd's youthful vigour often amazed us. He would often insist on rowing us – up to half a dozen men four decades junior to him - across Scarborough's bays or further up the coast. He was probably right to think he would make the best job of it - but too polite to make the point. Captain Syd, although a man of geniality, was really angry that Yorkshire Water and Scarborough Council gave the go ahead for the Scalby Mills sewage system and their refusal to listen to professional qualified advice, given free of charge, on the outfall system. The sea was in his blood and in his psyche, and he was hoping that laws would be passed forbidding the dumping of any suspect substances into the sea. To show his passion, when asked if he had millions to spend and how he would spend it, he would say: "Scarborough has one thousand years of maritime history so I would like to spend it on the harbour, to bring it back to what suits it best. That is the fishing industry when it was the premier fishing port from the Humber to the Tyne, thereby making many all round the year jobs instead of seasonal work."

He enjoyed a drink of whisky, and his most precious possession was his sextant, which he bought in 1929, but the sea was his life and few had his vast knowledge and passion for the marine environment. He was crucial to our battle to protect the marine environment. With his extraordinary knowledge and perception of life, our campaign now had firm foundations. He was proud indeed to say that he never lost a ship or a man. Few knew that he was a non-swimmer.

Captain Syd Smith MBE becomes an honorary member of the Sons of Neptune.

Capt Syd discusses adventures at sea with (L to R) Charles White, Capt Chris Blake, of the HM Bark Endeavour, and Ann White.

Captain Syd with the Sons at a ceremony appointing him President of Trinity House.

Portraits (and overleaf) of Capt Syd by Doug Gray, of Scarborough

We Fought Them on The Beaches

With our victory over the Castle Headland scheme, one battle was over, but the war still continued. Yorkshire Water and, of course, the Council, were still committed to sea-dumping of raw untreated sewage and were now searching for another site for an outfall pipe. We commissioned architect Lord Deramore, of Pickering, to design a scale impression in watercolors of a screening plant building at Cowlam Hole, a natural inlet several miles north of the castle headland and away from both bays.

Freddie and Captain Smith, together with local fishermen, and their intimate knowledge of coastal inlets, had found what we believed was the ideal place for the long sea outfall there.

Freddie had not been able to believe it when he and Captain Syd sailed in Maurice Harwood's small fishing-coble into the inlet known locally as Cowlam Hole. Whenever the swell subsided razor-sharp rocks appeared on both sides of the boat, and Freddie's sense of danger was enhanced when the boat bounced on the sea-bed. "As I was looking at rocks on both sides," said Freddie, "I naturally assumed that we had hit them. Instead of that we had just the answer we wanted – SAND! A sandy inlet ideal for an outfall pipe."

Captain Syd said "This is a unique and ideal place for the outfall pipe as the currents here will actually take the discharge far out to sea and away from our bathing waters, you would think it was put here for that purpose."

The Marine Drive/Castle Headland scheme was cancelled in September 1984, and little was heard of any Yorkshire Water plans for about a year. Then came a revelation near the end of 1985, when we discovered to our relief that they had costed a scheme for Cowlam Hole. But we were later devastated to learn that they had also costed a plan to build their sewerage plant at Scalby Mills, at the north end of the North Bay and its popular beach. Lord Deramore's plans showed a well-designed farmhouse with gardens and landscaping to accommodate plants and wildlife.

Our proposal as a conservation group would be to promote the natural history, scenic beauty and appeal of the area for the benefit of local people and tourists. We had found the proposed building by Yorkshire Water more suitable for a horror movie than one that would complement our fabulous natural scenery. But that was nothing new - environmental awareness and conservation of the area were remote to the true agenda of Scarborough Council and Yorkshire Water, who continued to ridicule us as irresponsible troublemakers.

Professor Pescod, who had helped us win the battle of the Castle Headland, could no longer help us publicly, as he had been appointed to the board of Northumbrian Water, but he handed us an Excalibur by putting us in touch with Professor Bruce Denness. Professor Bruce said: "I first met Freddie in 1984, when a colleague at Newcastle University, Professor M. B. "Warren" Pescod, Head of the Civil and Environmental Engineering Department, passed me Freddie's request for help in dealing with sewage disposal in Scarborough. I was the Professor of Ocean Engineering specialising particularly in the inshore environment and welcomed the prospect of investigating Yorkshire Water's proposal to dispose of sewage through a so-called long sea outfall at the end of a bathing beach after only preliminary and primary treatment. Yorkshire Water were relying on the widely held theory of the day (the T90 theory) that tidal and wave action, together with dilution and salinity and the ultra-violet rays of the sun destroyed 90 per cent of pathogenic bacteria within a prescribed number of hours, based on the tidal regime at the point of discharge, so that the ground-up sewage – effectively raw with only large items, such as assorted rubber-ware and old Tesco trolleys filtered out – was not a danger to health. Freddie suspected otherwise.

Freddie and his intrepid band of fellow all-year-round swimmers, who called themselves the Sons of Neptune, knew from first-hand experience that the resulting brown slick emanating from the outfall looked neither healthy nor attractive – apart from the ever-present flock of seagulls that appeared to relish its entrained nutrients. I studied the way that the slick would move after leaving the outfall and discovered, as had Yorkshire Water's consultants, that it would not return to the beach for at least 10 hours. So, according to their 10-hour T90 theory they could discharge the effluent from the outfall without any health risk.

"So we appeared to have drawn a blank. That is, until 1985, when I noticed a paper in Nature magazine [the world's leading scientific journal], by an American, Professor Jay Grimes, of New Hampshire University, who showed that dangerous bacteria could survive in sea water for weeks, due to being able to enter a state of dormancy until they were able to enter the body of an unsuspecting bather, when they could then become virulent again. This meant that after several days, or even weeks, from discharge these potentially dangerous bugs would infest Scarborough's bathing waters and wash up on the beaches able to cause serious infection.

It was a stroke of luck Bruce finding the Nature article about the survival of disease-transmitting bugs in the sea. It was really the most valuable breakthrough in our whole campaign for clean seas, coastal waters and beaches. If the Sons could demonstrate that more than 10 per cent of the bugs could live longer than 10 hours it would disprove the T.90 theory that most disease-bearing bugs could survive for no more than 10 hours in Scarborough's tidal regime.

Freddie contacted Professor Grimes whose research with Professor Rita Colwell led to the production of a Congressional report. Unfortunately the T.90 theory was still accepted in the UK, although no proper research had been done since the findings of the Medical Research Study published in 1959.

Freddie said: "When I spoke to Professor Grimes he realised straight away that anything like the so-called long sea outfall schemes pursued by the UK Government were redundant - the whole of the US was moving towards full treatment and Canada was already advanced in this practice. If the UK Government was to continue with this it would spread the contamination further along and out into our coastal waters. He believed that this was his chance to help save the UK from a policy that microbiologically would destroy the marine environment, and he thought that through our group his discovery would help the British Government to take measures which would be effective to avoid pollution of coastal waters.

"Some of the information in his US Congressional report was so interesting and revealing. For example, in hospital discharges when this kind of effluent is put into the sea pathogenic bugs can transfer such resistance levels in the sea to those which have resistance. In other words, they can empower their disadvantaged fellow bugs. It is like a chap coming into a pub and buying pints all-round." The reality was that Yorkshire Water's scheme was good for breeding super-bugs, rather than killing ordinary bugs - unbelievable!

Professor Bruce said: "The Sons of Neptune were obviously a bunch of characters, but without guys like them, nothing would be achieved. Freddie was a man with incredible drive, he was the main engine. He certainly was. The Government wanted to update the water systems, but they did not want the huge expenditure before floating it on the Stock Exchange. The event that changed the policy of primary treatment to secondary treatment was actually when the Fylde & Lancashire County Council in July 1988 had interpreted the Sons report and the Sons had negotiations with the leader Louise Ellman and sympathetic protest groups. My work and Professor Jay's work, published at their own expense by the Sons, was presented to Parliament, proving that the Fylde scheme was flawed because the prescribedT90 die-off period of 40 hours for their scheme was no longer credible. Subsequently North-West Water backed out of their proposals to dump raw, untreated sewage on their coastline, and as a result that sounded the alarm for every other resort."

The Congressional Report had been handed over to the Sons because of our tenacity in fighting the UK authorities. We knew from this Report that it was not only the Scarborough scheme that was obsolete, but that similar schemes planned for other coastal towns were similarly flawed. We commissioned Professor Denness to apply his expertise in ocean engineering and the latest microbiological discoveries in the United States to prove that the Scarborough scheme was not only a danger to human and marine life but a total waste of money. Bruce's contacts in this field and his esteemed knowledge attracted support from leading world scientists to contribute to this Report.

Bruce's report, entitled "Sewage Disposal to the Sea", was launched by us in London on May 14 1987. Freddie stated at the launch: "We thank the people of Scarborough for their huge interest and concern in the group's long campaign against Yorkshire Water and the Government's out-dated policy. We had become publishers by compulsion. We are really more happy to be in the sea at Scarborough, where we are not prepared to see our marine environment turned into a poisonous mire. We also condemn the so-called experts who were brought to our beautiful Town from other areas, who knew little about the vagaries of local conditions so far as the tides and currents are concerned, and had neither perception of, nor affection for, the Town. The huge resources of the sea would encourage the development of germs that would be a direct threat to mankind. We as Sons of Neptune are speaking for those in the sea and say that this must stop now before a terrible chain reaction of infection is unleashed amongst sea life and eventually back to us." [At the beginning of the 21st century the folly of not treating sewage properly gave rise to "superbugs" such as c.difficile and MRSA, which are the plague of modern hospitals].

The Scarborough Evening News May 14th 1987 reported: "Sea Campaign Bid for world re-think on long sea outfalls - No alternative to disinfection". A copy of the Denness report was sent to all 49 members of Scarborough Council at the cost of several hundred pounds. Only THREE replied and gave the Sons their support - forrmer policeman Bob Stead (Ind), Jean Green (Con), and Brian O'Flynn (SDP). They were then routinely attacked by other councillors.

Meanwhile several things were happening. BBC Tv screened a "Newsnight Special" devoted to the Sons campaign on 23 June 1987, and included interviews with Bruce Denness, Professor Grimes, and various Sons, including Captain Syd, whose authoritative knowledge made Yorkshire Water's insistence that the scheme was right, look like infantile nonsense. The YWA's area manager, John Taylor said: "We have done a massive amount of survey work, done current metering, and sea-bed surveys, we've run the most sophisticated mathematical models, and they quite conclusively prove that the sewage will not return to the shore." Captain Syd, in reply, said: "Yorkshire Water put in the sea some bacteria-laden drifters that float along the bottom of the ocean floor with the tidal movements. They put them in where the end of the outfall will be. They all finished up on the shore. Scarborough Borough Council spend a fortune every year carrying away the seaweed that's washed up on the beaches from outlying rocks – not only in winter, but all the year round. The sea has seasons too. The seaweed is torn off the rocks, the tidal inset brings it in and scatters it along the north shore, and it comes up to such a height that they have to clear it away, so anything they put in the sea here will come back to the shore, including sewage – and dead bodies as well."

In July of that year, the European Commission registered the Sons' formal complaints that the Scarborough scheme would be unable to comply with the EC's Bathing Water Directive and would be a danger to human health and the marine environment.

In August the Prince of Wales expressed his interest in the issue and asked to be kept informed. Although the Prince, like the Sons of Neptune, has been ridiculed over the years, he has recently been acclaimed by Time magazine and Vanity Fair as a champion of the environment. This acclaim was supported by the world's leading scientists and conservationists.

On 3 December a Tyne-Tees Tv documentary, "A Suitable Case for Treatment", with a soundtrack featuring the Beach Boys record "Don't Go Near The Water", examined the issues in depth.

Bob Stead was particularly supportive: "As a child visiting Scarborough from York with my parents, my brothers, sister and I always ended up on the beach followed by a paddle in the sea, despite my mother saying 'Don't go in the sea, it's dirty'. We soon found out why when learning to swim and having to push toilet paper, floating stools and other garbage out of the way. At that age the word sewage did not mean a lot to us. Later in life we taught our children to swim in the swimming baths, not the sea. Upon coming to live in Scarborough. it was obvious, seeing the broken short sewage outfall pipes in the North Bay, that something had to be done to clean up the sea and our beaches. It had been done in other places so why not Scarborough? Who was interested in doing something about it? Who would take on the Council and the Water

Authorities? Thank heavens along came a group of Scarborough men who would do just that. They called themselves the Sons of Neptune. These men of Scarborough fought for ALL the people of the town and for the thousands of visitors to Scarborough, to give us a clean sea and clean beaches. They had many trials and tribulations along the way but due to their concerted efforts we have ALL benefited. In a future of Scarborough I hope these men are not forgotten, but will be remembered as the Sons of Neptune. If someone says "what did they do" just reply "Go for a swim in the sea and find out".

Scarborough Borough Council completely ignored our research that the new plant should be at Cowlam Hole and with contemptuous disregard or, as many perceived, pure spite, declared that the new plant and outfall pipe would go ahead at Scalby Mills - smack dab in the North Bay, a salubrious residential area overlooking the classic golf course and magnificent sea views. Both the Council and Yorkshire Water had secret meetings and refused to take input from those who actually used the sea and had daily contact with its environment. At the same time they ignored our scientific report with the inane comment "whilst bacteria in the sea might live longer in seawater elsewhere they do not do so in the North Sea at Scarborough" – totally dismissing the findings of the world's leading scientists! It reminded us of the film "Jaws", in which the mayor of a small seaside town refused to inform the sea-bathers that there was a Great White shark in the bay "in case it affected the town's economy". At the same time the local evening newspaper had carried a piece about the latest epidemic to affect human beings all over the world. We learned that the AIDS virus had survived 38 hours in our temperate seas.

However Scarborough Council and Yorkshire Water ignored the reports and continued to insist on the pre-medieval Viking settlement plan. A BBC Newsnight crew arrived in Scarborough to film the Sons campaign. They spent a week in town, interviewing those involved in the issue. At this time we were being attacked by the local establishment, and condemned by the Department of Health, the Council and local politicians. Many believed that we were attracting bad publicity for the Town and that we were scaremongering. We were then offered a major television documentary for Channel 4 but Freddie refused as he felt that the Sons had had sufficient publicity recently, and the opportunity was taken by the newly-formed group Surfers Against Sewage, formed some 8 years after the Sons.

It was a delicate threshold; we did not dare comment on the AIDS situation as even Scarborough Hotels Association was vigorously and vociferously opposed to our campaign, as were those individuals who were fawning to the establishment. This produced some extraordinary public outbursts.

Dr. Jean Greenan, the Mayor of Scarborough, stated in her valedictory speech that "she felt like Alice In Wonderland at the Mad Hatter's Tea Party when she heard of the Son's activities, spreading their impish propaganda". She proceeded to condemn our campaign via arrogant letters in the local paper. However we knew that local detractors were ineffectual, ignorant and completely misinformed. Other coastal authorities were contacting us and we also had great support from senior consultants in the local medical profession. Scarborough Hospital's Professor John McFie, a consultant surgeon, praised our campaign on first arriving in Scarborough and so, too, did Mr. Piers Percival, one of the world's leading eye specialists, plus general surgeon George Smith, as well as GP Doctor Tony Chico, so we disregarded local dissent from self-deceiving individuals.

Opposition to the Sons came, perhaps most surprisingly, from a recently retired local marine scientist Dr Jack Lewis, who at one stage had looked after the oceanic laboratory in Robin Hood's Bay and was regarded as an authority on a particular species of New Zealand shellfish. He fully supported the dumping of raw, untreated sewage as did Dr Greenan. Both still believed the outdated theory that salinity and sunlight would kill off most dangerous bacteria.

Peter Lassey, a college lecturer and diver, noted that Doctor Lewis regularly stated during lectures that the sea was one big antiseptic tank. In letters to the Scarborough Evening News he stated "He compares it favorably with dumping chemicals at sea – claiming that sewage in the sea poses fewer problems because it is organic and easily decomposed."

In reply I stated: "Doctor Lewis is a Doctor of Philosophy. Philosophy is concerned with two things, trivial questions that are soluble and crucial questions that are insoluble." The Robin Hood's Bay marine laboratory was closed down at this crucial point in history, when the North Sea was at its most polluted, sealife was dying, and toxic waste was pulverising it daily. The Marine Conservation Society, who had previously supported long sea outfalls, now backed our campaign and demanded secondary treatment. Freddie was asked to present our research to Cornwall County Council. He flew down to Truro and they were grateful for his presentation and detailed explanations. However, another member of the local medical profession, Dr. George McIntyre, a local councillor, who at one stage was Chairman of Scarborough's Department of Tourism, ridiculed our campaign for full treatment, saying: "Sewage disposal to the sea – ecologically, Yorkshire Water's proposals would cause no problems and could prove a positive benefit." This viewpoint, expressed by a doctor of medicine, was a serious setback to much of the good work that Freddie was doing to save the Cornish bathing waters from pollution.

Freddie stated: "If they had taken our advice there and then it would have saved them millions and improved the reputation of their beautiful coastline and bathing beaches."

Later, Scarborough's newly elected Mayor, hotelier Harry Dixon, who vigorously supported the raw untreated sewage scheme, viciously attacked the Sons of Neptune in the local press, urging the public "do not support these people, boycott their businesses" and naming Freddie Drabble, Cec Ridley and Charles White. Our own Tory MP Sir Michael Shaw, dubbed by the national press as a "Thatcher Poodle", was safely entrenched in Westminster representing the Town, as Scarborough was a stronghold for the Tory party. The old Tories had been great in their business acumen and in promoting the pursuit of excellence for the Town and its future and they did a fine job. Unfortunately those in charge now were party men and in our observations were more in the self-interest vein and party policy than that of the town's welfare.

Sir Michael Shaw wrote to us: "I have always taken the view that, subject to full consideration of the facts, the YWA long sea outfall scheme should be proceeded with just as fast as possible, in the interests of everyone. You informed me that you had additional expert evidence that would rule out the present proposals and favour your own Cowlam Hole proposals. I pressed your group to make it available to the Council and I ensured a copy was sent to the Department of the Environment."

But in the Yorkshire Post, 19th December 1988 Sir Michael slammed the Sons. He said the scheme was vital because Scarborough's beaches needed urgent action to bring them up to safe EEC bathing standards. "It was wrong for the pressure group to attack the project because it would be to Scarborough's benefit as a leading holiday resort."

I responded in a letter as follows.

Dear Sir Michael,

Incredibly you still support the YWA long sea outfall system which intensifies the dumping of the Town's raw untreated sewage into our North bay. The present situation is intolerable but it has been for many decades and you have never done anything about it. You must surely be aware by now that this obnoxious practice has been condemned by the United Nations, the EEC and by our own Committee on beach pollution. The fact that pathogenic viruses and bacteria can survive in sea water obliterates any arguments to continue this vile practice, the main reason that the YWA scheme will make matters worse in Scarborough is that it dumps all the towns untreated sewage directly into our North Bay insuring that pathogenic material will have a greater survival rate. Please do not quote the YWA to us as they no longer possess a threshold of credibility in this field. They lied to the people of Yorkshire by saying the Bridlington scheme had worked – it has failed many, many times and in fact did not even pass the EEC preliminary tests. (We can supply the scientific evidence to prove this). Other outfall schemes have not only failed but have made conditions worse. Great Yarmouth has made conditions worse and at Southend, six children were paralyzed when the new outfall scheme was opened. The Thames Water Authority denied that it was their fault; they claimed it was from "a previous contamination" but an independent inquiry stated that the viruses that caused the paralysis were present in the sewage which came from the new outfall. Southend and Essex County Council have since called for full treatment.

The YWA of course have done no virological tests yet you expect not only the residents of this resort but visitors and their children to bathe in these disease ridden and dangerously filthy bays.

We sent you a copy of our specially commissioned report with contributions from the worlds leading marine scientists and marine engineering experts which totally condemned the YWA's scheme (outfall) and indicated incompetence in its structure and purpose. Our report by Professor Bruce Denness "Sewage Disposal to the sea" was based on a multi-national and multi billion dollar report to the U.S Congress by Professor Jay Grimes. We also flew to the USA to see first hand up to date sewage systems and their function and application in a progressive society, over the past decade our group consisting of local business and professional men with the town's best interest at heart with our own money and time have pursued excellence in this matter.

We have already proved the YWA's total incompetence in this field by exposing their disastrous fiasco for the castle headland. We have always informed you of our progress to which you have responded superficially with phrases such as "in the meantime greatly improved conditions could be enjoyed"

Your continuous support for everything the YWA states is not in the best interest of the community. The abuse of public trust and of public funds by the YWA is alarming. We notice that post privatization they have been given immunity against sewage flows into our rivers and our domestic water. As guardians of our water (the single most important ingredient in our lives) they have behaved worse than criminals, by their continuous contamination of our rivers and seas with toxins such as lead, aluminium, nitrates, sewage sludge, hospital waste etc, etc (see "Britains Poisoned Waters" published by Penguin). We would remind you that eventually this material flows into our North Sea whose floor is already covered with sewage sludge and industrial toxic material which is destroying life forms and the food chain. Our government has failed to cease this obnoxious habit. In 1990, at the North Sea Conference, the Danish Prime Minister condemned the UK. "The British Government should stop playing with our lives" she stated. Yet you still support these criminal acts against this community I say criminal because it endangers human life – destroys marine life and our environment. Why do you still support the YWA? Are you a shareholder of theirs?

It seems that you are prepared to support the YWA's outdated destructive outfall rather than the quality of our seas and beaches in Scarborough. The House of Commons Beach Pollution Committee has confirmed that raw untreated sewage is a "health hazard". As formerly loyal Tory voters most members of this group are disgusted by your laissez-faire attitude to this matter which portrays to us an MP who could not give a damn about our town or its future. Should this vile outfall go ahead, on the day that 300,000 tonnes of the town's raw untreated human waste begins to pour into the North Bay with its lethal cocktail of disease bearing viruses and bacteria will you and Lady Shaw be the first to plunge into it as you wish our visitors and their families, their children and themselves to do? I think not, hypocrisy will rule. Remember your children and grandchildren if they pick up AIDS, salmonella, poliomyelitis, aseptic meningitis, infectious hepatitis and 111 other possible diseases, are we to sympathize with the Shaw family or say they deserve to smolder in their own putridity like Sir Michael, who wanted our beaches to be contaminated by untreated sewage.

Please demonstrate you really understand this problem by giving an in depth reply. We assume you remain as usual sitting on the fence. This is a cowardly betrayal of the Town's interests that you are prepared to support an ideology that poisons and pollutes for profit rather than promote the quality of life.

Should you continue to support the YWA's outfall our group will make sure that the public become aware of your role and that even the blue rinse set comatose with Tory apathy will be made aware of what exactly is happening. We will also field our own candidate in the next election. We sincerely hope wisdom will be your guide, that you will now condemn the YWA scheme and demand full treatment of our sewage. So that every man, woman and child may enter our sea without fear of disease or pollution.

Unless you demand the immediate suspension of this raw untreated sewage scheme in its entirety, for a new proper scheme incorporating full and effective treatment of sewage before its discharge into the sea, history will show that you are guilty of dereliction of duty in this matter. You must demand a dignified solution to this problem

Yours sincerely

Charles White

The impact of our report was powerful and its ramifications were to change the EU laws on bathing directives. The Australian and Brazilian governments ordered copies of the report. A German TV crew also arrived in the town, and the BBC produced a major TV series on the North Sea which was shown in most European countries. The section featuring the Sons as Neptune's Children, won a major award, the European Parliament Prize, at the European Film Festival, "Ecovision'89", specifically presented to a project dealing with European-wide ecological issues. On 23rd June 1988, the programme went out nationally as well as being beamed into Europe, and there was reaction to it from several countries.

Our contact in the USA, Professor J. Grimes, when asked by reporter James Hogg about outfall plans he replied "It has been my position for a number of years now that it is neither scientifically nor environmentally sound to dispose of raw untreated sewage into our seas and certainly not into coastal zones and estuaries. This would build up in the long term and add to the burden of pollutants in the sea and certainly would be a danger to both human health and marine life."

In reply YWA's chief micro-biologist Dr. Gary O'Neil said defiantly: "I believe that the ocean is the biggest and best sewage works, this type of solution is used throughout the world and is the best solution for the disposal of raw untreated sewage"

Roy Ayrton, Scarborough's environmental health officer, who

had been sent a copy of our report, made this comment: "The sea is an extremely hostile environment for sewage bacteria. Sewage released well out to sea ... a clean and simple operation"

Tide, the International Marine and Maritime Journal (Volume 1 No 2), gave the following review extract by Peter Christie:

"A local group of just six conservationists/swimmers, marvellously named the Sons of Neptune, got together to fight this scheme and press for a much better form of sewage disposal. Derided and ridiculed they stuck to their guns and commissioned Professor Denness (late Professor of Ocean Engineering at Newcastle-upon-Tyne University and now freelance) to argue their case via this report. They won!"

"With the recent ludicrous decision by the British Government to identify only 27 (yes, 27) beaches as "marine bathing beaches" in Britain both this battle and its outcome has set an important precedent to all of us who love the coastline and respect the ecology of the sea. If you wish to do something practical about cleaning up the sea then buy this booklet, read it carefully, and then act." A similar review appeared in Nature magazine.

Nevertheless, and in the face of such concerns from leading scientists, the YWA proceeded to augment their proposals by building a visitors centre at Scalby Mills to promote their scheme with a display featuring artists displays and plans lauding how wonderful the development would be.

At this time we received the good news that the Fylde scheme for Blackpool and coastline was now cancelled, thanks to the Sons' report by Prof Denness.

The YWA general manager, Mr. John Taylor, made the following statement: "I have had a lot of dealings with the Sons of Neptune, on several occasions, and there have even been referrals to the Ombudsman and they have accusing us of maladministration. The Ombudsman rejected their claims; they are totally misinformed and are basing their views on emotion, not on hard scientific fact."

He made this statement even though our Report was produced by the world's leading scientists in the field. I was not surprised by the YWA reaction, but felt that the Ombudsman, the neutral arbitrator in our democratic system, had failed us after such a damning report against the YWA and the Government's policy. The YWA still continued to insist that the Scalby Mills long sea outfall would take all the effluent away from our bays and beaches.

Captain Syd, in his role as editor of Olsen's Nautical Almanac, wrote: "They are doomed to failure because they are running a pipeline at a place where the tides are wrong. The outfall is going out on Scalby Ness, and when the tide comes in it is compressed between the Scalby Mills rock shaft and the Mascus rocks, and where it is compressed it accelerates, the speed of it comes in like a millrace and spreads along the North Beach sands. Anything in that tide's way will spread along the North Bay and north shore sands. It's bound to. Besides, anything that is put in off our shores is washed back."

We received great praise and sincere thanks from the Leader of Lancashire County Council, Louise Ellman, and their support groups for our scientific contributions. Our campaign attracted attention from groups across the country. One such group, called WaterWatch, was instigated by our activities and protests. Meanwhile Scarborough Council continued to criticise our cause, and John Trebble, Chief Executive of Scarborough Council stated:

We have faced a very aggressive campaign from the Sons of Neptune in particular. They have received wide media coverage. Frankly I believe the water authorities have not got their message across as well as the Sons of Neptune has. The Council's attitude is that we are very much in favour of the water authority's scheme. We have a very unsatisfactory situation here in Scarborough at the present moment. The entire town's sewage is discharged through four short sea outfalls without any prior treatment whatsoever. That means that all the raw sewage together with the debris is going straight into the sea. The short sea outfalls are no longer than the low water level. What the water authority are proposing to do is to take all the town's sewage to one discharge point which will be at Scalby Mills, where it will be screened in a properly designed plant, which will take the discharge, which is water.

The water will only then contain bacteria in fine particles to a long sea outfall 1,400 metres out under the sea and then discharge it. That will get rid of all the pollution as far as we are concerned and meet the EEC criteria for bathing waters. In fact we will be well within that criteria.

The reason that Yorkshire Water was unable to counteract the Sons and their scientists was simply that they had fallen behind the times and that they had developed a laissez-faire attitude. They had also recruited management from other industries for example the local regional manager Mr. John Taylor, we were told, had previously been in the coal mining industry and lacked in-depth knowledge of the marine environment

As for Mr. Trebble's statement, it was misleading as it failed to make clear that screening did nothing more than remove bio-nondegradables. It had no initial impact of reducing disease, which would require full treatment.

It did not remove the body's waste fluids, or the disease-causing bacteria and viruses and could not possibly pass the required EEC criteria, which demanded full treatment.

I made this statement: "The proposal to dump thousands of tons of raw untreated human waste into the sea without proper treatment when the leading scientists in the world in micro-biology stated that it will activate the viruses and bacteria and go on to intensify their disease-causing abilities is a crime against the community. For a tourist town to do that and then invite people with their families on to our beaches and to swim in a polluted sea is despicable. It is like a lethal vile enemy arriving in the town and imposing this upon us against the will of 95% of the townspeople."

Freddie Drabble stated "As it is now we go in the sea all year round. What is going to happen if this new scheme happens and conditions are worse? Sometimes there are good times and others not so good under present conditions when sewage can be seen bathers stay out of the water. But if the YWA scheme goes ahead there will be no more good times. as sewage may be present but cannot be seen. Our research indicates at the moment that the YWA scheme cannot work, as we have removed the foundation stone for it. We have a £24 milion pound scheme proposed for

Scarborough that is pure nonsense. It is nonsense because it relies on the scientific misunderstanding that microbes in the sea die off within four hours, and this has been proven to be false."

Our next hurdle was to prove that the T90 die-off time was discredited, and that both bacteria and viruses could survive for far longer periods in our temperate seas than once believed. In fact in some cases they became more virulent.

Through our scientific contacts we got in touch with Dr. David Wheeler, of the Robens Institute, to come to Scarborough to prove that our scientific findings were correct. We were forced to do this, as the microbiological contributor to the Denness Report, Dr. Lillian Evison, a virologist from the Dept of Civil Engineering at Newcastle University, who was a colleague and friend of Professor Bruce Denness, had subsequently made a statement withdrawing her original support for one of the most important findings confirmed by other scientists.

She said: "Some of the conclusions of Professor Denness's are correct and I agree with most of his conclusions, but I do have reservations, in fact I disagree with one of his conclusions which was all sewage discharged into the sea should be disinfected before being discharged into the sea. I think that this is not necessary and in most situations it is perfectly satisfactory to discharge sewage to the sea by long-sea outfalls."

Professor Denness commented: "Lillian is a very good and world-renowned micro-biologist. My contention is that the Scarborough outfall is not properly designed. Lillian Evison says it is. I have some standing as an ocean engineer. My conclusion is based on all the local currents at Scarborough. It is that whatever you put through a long sea outfall at Scarborough will come back on the shore."

As Dr Evison had backed away from the full support she had given in the Denness Report, we were now on our own to prove that the U.S. research on the survival of sewage bacteria in the sea was correct, and that it was happening in Scarborough. The Sons were determined to disprove conclusively the YWA argument that survival time of sewage bacteria was much longer in the U.S. sea than in British waters.

The group contacted Dr. David Wheeler, a microbiologist at the Robens Institute, of Surrey University.

Together with the Robens Institute, and scientist Pat Gowen, of Friends of the Earth, the Sons set up The Neptune Project using Maurice Harwood's coble equipped with plastic chambers to collect seawater bacteria samples, which were maintained in these chambers in the sea over a period of 24 hours. This was to prove that the bacteria did not die quickly enough to enable the scheme to comply with EC safety laws. These samples were tested hourly to calculate the die-off rate.

As we set out from Scarborough Harbour we were joined by Captain Syd and David Lazenby, as well as Dr. Wheelers girlfriend. On reaching Scalby Ness we grounded the plastic chambers in shallow water off the Ness towards the shore, always ensuring they were fully submerged. Then we spent all night on the shore ensuring the chambers of seawater and the bacteria they contained were fully submerged in the receding tide. Freddie remembers the search for driftwood to keep our fire going on the beach to give us some warmth overnight. Dr Wheeler was the soul of vigilance. Every hour during the night samples were taken by long syringe from the submerged chambers to be placed on incubation. Fish and chips were dropped off for us on that remote shore about 9.30pm, and then we were on our own with the sea, the syringe, and the bugs.

These were the extra miles we had to travel to prove beyond any doubt that the T90 theory might be suitable for a Viking settlement, but not for the present state of the sea.

Later Dr Wheeler, in a report to the House of Commons all-Party Environmental Committee's enquiry into sea and beach pollution was able to state that bacteria could survive in the sea for over 100 hours, whereas the YWA scheme was based on misinformed calculations that 90% of harmful bacteria would die within 10 hours – a fatal mistake.

Further tests around the UK proved that dangerous viruses

from sewage could also survive for months, if not longer, in coastal waters. Dr. Wheeler also told MPs that they had not been given the full picture and pointed out that the Environmental Department and the National Rivers Authority had played down the risk of infection, maintaining that there was little or no conclusive evidence that serious diseases could be caught from seawater. But well-researched and documented cases of infectious diseases and outbreaks from sewage-polluted water in the USA, Africa, Hong Kong etc. had shown that people who swam in the sea contaminated by sewage were more likely to fall ill than those who had not done so.

The Neptune Project conducted by the Sons and Dr. Wheeler blew a hole in the water authorities' and the Government's privatisation plans, as there was no provision for proper sewage treatment with the outfalls. The sun and sea-water theory was now literally dead in the water.

Freddie said: "Professor Jay Grimes and Rita Colwell had already in their research for the US, Japanese and other governments discovered that dangerous bacteria and viruses in all old dumping sites, even in remote oceans, still survived".

Rita Colwell, Professor of Marine Microbiology, University of Maryland, had declared: "EEC standards are inadequate, as they do not test for hepatitis and other enteric viruses. Technology is now available to do these tests".

Terry Max Hazen, Professor of Microbiology at Puerto Rico University, USA, and resident microbiologist at the Savannah River laboratory says:"EEC standards are useless. We now have the technology to look at and enumerate specific pathogens (disease-causing microbes). We have evidence of the accumulation of harmful pathogens in the sea and build-up in the food chain. I would not swim in Scarborough's waters, even if they did comply only with EEC standards, or advise my friends to swim there."

Professor Jay Grimes "Theories of dilution and dispersion are not borne out for the Scarborough scheme. They do not disperse and move around in cores and settle on the seabed. Strong correlation in the US tests between coastal pollution and gastroenteritis insists that sewage must be treated i.e. Sludge removed and effluent disinfected. Professor Jay also stated that he would not swim in the Scarborough sea even if the new scheme complied with EEC standards. He would have reservations about even going in to take samples.

Ken Collins, Scottish Euro MP and five-year chairman of the EEC committee, said we should not be dumping sewage sludge in the North Sea as it is a partly-closed system and he expected the EC to review and tighten standards as the state of knowledge was growing. Ken Collins, in his communications with Freddie Drabble, was vigorous in his fight to stop the outdated outfall system and sludge and waste dumping in the North Sea, and helped the campaign to outlaw this practice.

Then, on 2nd May 1988, Lillian Evison, again changed her stance by saying that the T-90 criteria on which the Scarborough system was based, along with many other similar schemes in the UK were inadequate.

The Denness report had an enormous effect on marine groups across the country and our experiment with the Robens Institute at Scarborough, brought us into contact with the Fylde Coast groups. This is an area covering Morecambe Bay, Blackpool and the Lancashire coast. After extensive correspondence with Louise Ellman, Labour leader of Lancashire County Council, we were eventually invited to a public meeting at Rivington Hall, a gift to the Lancashire people by industrialists the Lever Brothers.

Freddie, Captain-Smith, and the Sons arrived and were warmly greeted by Louise Ellman, Group Capt. Harry King, of the Fleetwood Save our Bay campaign, as well as Graham Cook, of the Fylde Boat Angling Club, and Commodore M. Chapman of the Fleetwood Windsurfing Club. The Sons had their work cut out, as did Lancashire County Council, because North West Water and the Government were still determined to go ahead with raw sewage and sludge dumping even though Blackpool had, at this stage, a terrible reputation for pollution. But the Denness report together with the Neptune Project gave Louise Ellman the means to prevent North West Water going ahead without a public enquiry. Although we were thanked for our support, the Sons were disappointed that she had not invited Freddie to speak to the audience.

This goes back to the betrayal of Labour Councillor Mavis Don in Scarborough and the Fabian Society meeting at the Delmont Hotel where the voice and opinions of the Sons were suppressed.

Barry Hampshire, life-long member of the Labour Party " I had known Mavis Don and her family and had worked with her husband Eddie at the Evening News and being in the hotel business I was well informed of the Sons of Neptune campaign, she was leader of the Council. I knew this would be a marvellous opportunity for Labour to take the moral high ground over the outfall fiasco, so I approached her at a Labour Party Executive Committee meeting and explained that it would be a substantial coup over the local Tories who vigorously supported the YWA. Mavis turned on me and instantly dismissed my suggestion to support the Sons saying: 'These matters have already been decided upon. Nothing can be done'. I also attended the Fabian Society meeting at the Delmont Hotel where the Sons were deliberately being prevented from presenting their case, as they were being labelled by the Town Hall as troublemakers."

Councillor Harbron, who had changed her name by marriage to Bosomworth and was the current Mayor of Scarborough, stated on the Tyne Tees TV special programme, "A Suitable Case for Treatment" (broadcast 3rd December 1987): 'I think that recently the Sons of Neptune have done us great disfavour and they have done it nationally and I resent that because I have the interest of Scarborough at heart as well as them. They are not doing Scarborough any favours. The people of Scarborough have been the victims of misinformation and I think when this scheme is put into action, people will see that this is what we need in Scarborough."

When asked by the television interviewer if she had heard the Sons position that this scheme would make matters worse because it intensified the contamination, she responded: "Nothing surprises me now about the Sons of Neptune, and this is another example of their irresponsible behaviour".

To escape from the pressures of continuous concentration on our battle for clean seas, our hiking group would have long weekend breaks to break the monotony when fatigue was about to set in.

One such invitation arrived just in time, it was an invitation to the Sons of the Deserts tents, a society dedicated to the celebration of the comedy duo Laurel & Hardy. We had during one of our many treks to the Lake District a situation where travelling from Newby Bridge over various peaks we got disorientated and wound up in Ulverston after an exhausting 20 miles over hills and dales. We were due to have pub lunch at 1pm, but did not arrive in the small town until 3pm. It was a quiet afternoon and the pubs were shut so we sought refuge in the Laurel & Hardy Museum - Stan Laurel was actually born in Ulverston (as was the mother of Bill Haley, who was the first true rock n' roll idol).

We were greeted by a charming, friendly and humorous chap called Bill Cubin, who had founded the museum which was full of memorabilia and had a small cinema which showed the duo's films non-stop thrpugh the day. He was also the Mayor of Ulverston and had recently appeared on the cover of the glossy magazine Cumbrian Life with HM The Queen . He was a great character.

We told him of our plight and within a few minutes he produced flagons of beer and sandwiches. We spent the rest of the afternoon caressing the shores of inebriation and laughing hysterically at the wonderful comedy of Laurel & Hardy. We were so delighted we joined the appreciation society 'The Sons of The Desert' after which the Sons of Neptune were called. We formed our own tent and continued to celebrate the comic genius of the duo.

Many months later we received an invitation to the AGM of the Sons of the Desert Tents, which was to be held at the weekend at the beginning of February at a Trust House Forte 4-star hotel on the shores of Lake Windermere. It proved it a great winter tonic.

We set off from Scarborough and by the time we reached the M6 an intense blizzard had started. We felt we might not get there as there were reports on the radio of two climbers being frozen to death on Helvellyn. Miraculously we arrived at the hotel only an hour late. On entering it was another world where we were immediately aware of the warmth and atmosphere of joyous frivolity that exuded from everyone there who were dressed as either Laurel or Hardy. This included the full spectrum of lifestyles from physicists to coalminers and dustbinmen, from dress designers to dairymaids.

TheTv's in our rooms were constantly showing Laurel & Hardy movies, and even the staff were dressed up as characters from their films. There was so much glorious gladness and madness happening that we could not assimilate anything except the fact that we were now firmly in Laurel & Hardy land.

Bill Cubin presented a talk on memorabilia, and Stan's daughter, Lois, told of what life was like in Hollywood with the greatest comedians of the 20th century. It was such a different atmosphere that we totally indulged in the fun.

This allowed for a variety of costumes – Scottish gear, British colonial army gear – and included a banquet in a "Sultan's palace". The menu was presented as the names of Laurel & Hardy films, Toad in the Hole served with Laughing Gravy. Hog Wild with Any Old Port, Supper Nuts for starters. Before we were piped into the banquet by a Scottish piper, we were all in a merry state. Suddenly the main hall door opened, a gust of cold wind and a flurry of snow blew into the lobby, and there stood two Indian doctors, bewildered and perplexed with the shock of seeing nearly two hundred Laurels & Hardys. We helped them with their luggage and invited them to join in the merriment, but the look of puzzlement on their faces indicated that they hadn't quite absorbed reality of the situation. They had been recommended to come to this "nice quiet" hotel after becoming mentally exhausted dealing with an influenza epidemic at home!

We invited them to join us for the souvenir photograph of the occasion and they looked as out of place as one-legged polar bear in the Sahara desert.

The climax of the dinner was the traditional Laurel & Hardy act of throwing meringue pies. A BBC crew had arrived from the "Holiday" programme and BBC Radio 4, and its presenter, Susan Marling who had the old imperious air of the BBC. She was quick enough to interview Freddie at the end of the dinner after he had been zapped by a pie. "What's it like to get a meringue pie in the face?" She asked in her posh BBC voice. Freddie grabbed a pie and popped it in her face. To us this was hilarious but to her it was – unexpected! On her recovery she enquired: "I understand that you chaps are called the Sons of Neptune and that you swim in the cold North Sea all year round, and we were wondering if you would have a dip in Lake Windemere in the morning". We agreed to do it, saying we had brought our swimmimg trunks. There was a look of glee on her face as she imagined us frozen in the lake.

The next morning the Sons marched down to the water, the countryside was in the grip of a deep frost and the lake was frozen over. We had to be wary as we crossed over slippery rocks, followed by a reluctant BBC crew. With a sense of gusto we broke the ice and plunged into the water. There was a look of incredulity on the face of the crew as we came back towards them.

"Have you ever swum in anything colder than this?" enquired Susan Marling.

We replied: "Actually we found it a lot warmer than the North Sea at this time of the year".

"You all look all rather jolly and healthy," said Marling.

"Yes," we replied, "and there is no Max Factor involved."

Scarborough beach protest (L to R) Captain Syd, The Thatcherloo, Steve Mallalieu, Stuart Carlisle, Chris Found, Dave Lazenby, Bryan Dew, Charles White, and Freddie Drabble.

Protest near the Houses of Parliament, London, against the floating of the water companies on the Stock Exchange.

More trouble for Yorkshire Water – Sons protest at the YWA annual meeting in Harrogate, August 1992. Where the Sons frustrated by the incompetence on the board attempt to replace two members with two Sons as directors.

Sons continue to protest against the intensification of the dumping of raw sewage sludge toxic waste and chemicals into the North Sea supported by the Thatcher government in 1989.

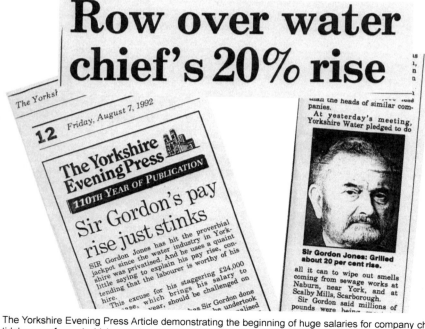

Row over water chief's 20% rise

The Yorksh

The Yorkshire Evening Press
110TH YEAR OF PUBLICATION

12 Friday, August 7, 1992

Sir Gordon's pay rise just stinks

SIR Gordon Jones has hit the proverbial jackpot since the water industry in York-shire was privatised. And he uses a quaint little saying to explain his pay rise, con-tending that the labourer is worthy of his hire.

This excuse for his staggering £24,000 rise, which brings his salary to ...ase, which should be challenged on ...year, should be challenged on ...as Sir Gordon done ...he undertook ...alised

...an the heads of similar com-panies.

At yesterday's meeting, Yorkshire Water pledged to do

Sir Gordon Jones: Grilled about 20 per cent rise.

all it can to wipe out smells coming from sewage works at Naburn, near York, and at Scalby Mills, Scarborough.

Sir Gordon said millions of pounds were bein...

The Yorkshire Evening Press Article demonstrating the beginning of huge salaries for company chiefs, a tidal wave of greed which awarded the incompetent and supported the destruction of the environment.

USA to the rescue!

Towards the end of 1987 we had accomplished a major feat; we had obtained from the US scientist Professor Jay Grimes, an advance copy of his Congressional Report, involving not only the US government but Japanese and Canadian marine scientists, and research centres throughout the world.

This report was a damning indictment of the dumping of raw sewage and other pollutants into our oceans and estuaries. Professor Jay summed up the complex scientific report by saying the practice was "a danger to human and marine life and would create a microbiological time-bomb" (in other words superbugs). Professor Jay was compared by us to the US cavalry coming to the rescue of a beleaguered fort. He gave the Sons the ammunition to prove that the proposed scheme for Scarborough and other resorts throughout the UK was more suitable for a Viking settlement than a modern community on an island which was then known as "The Dirty Old Man of Europe" because of its pollution of the sea and air.

The official presentation of more highly important scientific papers was to be held in Williamsburg, Virginia, in November 1987. Professor Jay had kept us updated with the progress, Freddie and I decided that we had to attend this vital conference and also meet with Professor Jay Grimes personally, as he was the man whose role was so significant in our fight against pollution in our seas.

Now armed with the Professor's research, supported by his colleagues, the leading scientists in this field, this gave us a sense of exhilaration and achievement, as we set off for the USA. We landed at New York to be greeted by Freddie's old school pal Peter Mole, known as "Pew". We flew to East Hampton, where, we thought, Pew was going to put us up for the night, and still under this impression, after a meal at a local restaurant and several beers, we were surprised when Pew suddenly stopped outside a hotel and said: "You are staying here tonight boys". The next morning he called to pick us up, but feeling it was appropriate, being the Sons of Neptune, we insisted on going for a swim in the sea. Pew naturally looked aghast - it was November, and thousands of Canadian geese had flown south to the local lakes. The ocean seemed chilly, but after all, we explained, we went swimming in the North Sea at all times of the year and that was very chilly too, so we casually changed into our togs and ran towards the sea. "You will probably die," exclaimed Pew with an air of cynicism. It was cold but we did our usual strokes. As we came out Pew said: "You didn't stay in there very long," and laughed as if he was disappointed that we hadn't expired.

Pew, who sold classic English cars to the Americans and was very much the refined Englishman, if a little reserved, dropped us off at the edge of a wooded area and pointed in the direction of his impressive house, saying: "Doreen will look after you." We walked up to the house and rang the bell. The door was opened by a petite lady dressed all in white. "Ah, It's Freddie and Charles," she said, "stay there a minute". We were puzzled. She came back with a vacuum cleaner. "Now take off your shoes," she demanded. Freddie and I obeyed looking perplexedly at each other. Doreen gave us a good hoovering down. We thought are we in a Woody Allen movie? Is this really happening? It was indeed! As we entered the house we noticed everything was white, the carpet, the TV, the walls, salt and pepper pots, and even the cat! Pew followed us nonchalantly a few minutes later, saying, "Doreen is working on a promotional campaign at the moment." I turned to Freddie privately and said "We have called at the White house - not THE White House but this white house!" Phew was taking us into New York to see the sights after breakfast as he had an apartment in the city. By now Doreen had gone up to her white office and we went up the white stairs to say goodbye. She bade us farewell with the question: "You guys want something to take home? This is a wonderful product, have you got cats at home?" "Yes", we replied hesitantly. "Well that's just great, you can give them this, the latest craze, dehydrated cat food." She handed us two sealed plastic bags of white material that resembled dried mushrooms. "I really believe this product is wonderful," she said with religious zeal. As we left I said to Freddie: "Yes, we are in a Woody Allen movie!" We arrived in New York in time for lunch, and I took Freddie to Sardis restaurant, renowned for being used by Broadway set.

The next day after seeing some of the sights in New York

with Pew, whose flat was next to the UN building, we agreed that we should take him out to dinner at one of his favourite local restaurants, Sparks, where the rich and famous dined. The restaurant was peppered with autographed portraits of legends such as Grace Kelly, John F Kennedy, James Stewart and many more. As a carnivore I was delighted to see the finest joints of beef displayed prominently. I took a wine list as a souvenir for our wine expert, El Foundo the Magnificent. For a moment I got that "Is this really happening?" feeling, Hey I was really living it up in New York! Pew had done a fine job, we indulged in the finest beers and wines, I had my American Express ready but Freddie insisted on settling the bill. We expected it to be about 60 dollars; it was a staggering 240 dollars. Pew said nothing. We did a swift tour of NYC, the United Nations building, Sardis, and the Empire State Building etc. One of the reasons we had chosen to stay in New York was for me to meet a lady called Lucy Kroll, a Broadway agent, whom I had contacted with help from Alan and Heather Ayckbourn. This was to discuss the possibility of doing a movie based on my biography "The Life and Times of Little Richard". In the afternoon I had an appointment with Lucy at her apartment on Broadway. On our way we stopped at a truckers café and had our best ever bowl of French onion soup, great value at a dollar fifty for the two of us and a contrast to Sparks at 240 dollars.

Lucy's apartment was incredible. The entrance was festooned with posters of musical shows from various theatres world wide. She was an elegant lady of a certain age, with an air of feminine dignity. Her Puerto Rican maid, Marie, confirmed her status as a person of achievement. On entering her living room, we were immediately dominated by huge rock sculptures, which looked as if they had erupted from a volcano. Lucy said that was exactly where they had come from. "My sculptor extracts the rocks from the edge of a volcano and then shapes them – it costs $300,000 dollars to do that," said Lucy nonchalantly. After pleasant introductions Freddie told her about our main purpose on our visit to the US, which was to stop the dumping of pollutants into our seas. He burst into an enthusiastic tidal wave of dialogue about sewerage and Lucy Kroll was entranced with him. She also enquired, and was fascinated to hear about, his work as a lawyer.

When Freddie told her that I was a chiropodist/podiatrist, like a lot of people who were informed of my profession, she immediately pointed to one of her feet saying: "I am having trouble with one of my toes, it is very painful". I told her I would be glad to diagnose it, and she took her shoe off. It was quite simple, a painful corn. I told her I could easily treat it, but I hadn't got my instruments" "What do you need?" She said. I told her a scalpel, sterile blade, some antiseptic and a dressing would do the trick. "If I send Marie out to the drug store to get these could you treat me?" I said "Of course. I already had a great theatrical agent called Peggy Ramsay as a patient". "She's a friend of mine!" exclaimed Lucy. Peggy is renowned through the world of theatre and literary agents. Lucy then began to tell us about her work, how she bought the rights to the musical Oklahoma from an Indian farmer and was agent for Sweet Charity and many more musicals. Among her closest friends were Katherine Hepburn, Rodgers and Hammerstein, and even Marilyn Monroe, who was photographed in her apartment.

She then asked me about how I came to write Little Richard's life story. "Little Richard is constantly in a state of outrageousness throughout his life," I told her, "and the latest episode is that he was asked to present the American Music Merit Awards, attended by such luminaries as Celine Dion, Mariah Carey and a host of other celebrities. He launched into a passionate diatribe about how HE should have won an award after all these years, saying: "I've been singing all my life! Stand to your feet if you think it's time for me to win! Stand up! Stand up! Let me see you!" He got a standing ovation." Lucy looked bemused by this, she looked through my portfolio and files on Little Richard and was impressed by his imagery, then after a general dialogue about the prospect of a movie, Freddie and I bade her farewell and proceeded to La Guardia airport from where we had a flight to Richmond, to attend the 23rd Joint Conference sponsored by the United States-Japan Cooperative Medical Science Program. The reality of the serious purpose of our visit kept flashing across our minds as we thought about our beloved Scarborough and the fact that the powers at be were still supporting the outdated scheme. To us, it seemed like insanity, not only would it be a waste of public money but that it would destroy the image of the town as Britain's first seaside resort.

We also felt it was criminal as it would have to be updated to EC standards, and this would cost millions more. But the privatisation of the water industry was priority - money was more important than people's lifestyle and the environment. We travelled to Williamsburg in a rage as we recalled the UK scientist on the BBC "Newsnight" program who had ridiculed the US research.

La Guardia was a fascinating place from where the famous Catalina luxury planes flew across the Atlantic to Portugal and Ireland. Our flight to Richmond, Virginia, the conference venue, was scheduled for early evening. It was a small plane and everyone was exceptionally friendly. We got chatting to a group of fashion designers from Richmond who were promoting their products in the Big Apple. When Freddie and I mentioned that we were in the US to get a report on sewage they were in hysterics. The flight across New York on the early November evening was like flying over a sea of diamonds; however later into the flight the pilot seemed to be avoiding imaginary missile fire, every few minutes we seemed to drop hundreds of feet and zoom back into the clouds with amazing frequency. The Virginians, who were familiar with this, confided "Don't worry, he's a Vietnam vet, enjoy the ride."

We stayed in Richmond overnight and the next day we traveled by bus to Williamsburg. We arrived to be greeted by people dressed as early English settlers when they first came to Virginia. They had created a historic village, which was very realistic, with carpenters building houses of the period, blacksmiths shoeing horses and people going about their daily lives in costumes of the period. Most impressive of all was the fact that they spoke to us in the language of the time, as though it was still the 1780s. This was the town's tourist attraction and it was delightful. Returning to our hotel in Richmond, Freddie could not wait to check out the conference venue, as scientists from all over the world flocked into the town. Professor Jay Grimes had the greatest regard for Professor Rita Colwell, who would be presenting the keynote speech on the survival of human gut bacteria in the sea. It was a delicate threshold because we felt that the US scientists, did not want to embarrass some of their UK colleagues who had supported the Thatcher toxic seas policy. Freddie as usual went for his morning run and spotted a lady jogging, who was pointed out by a scientist that we had met at the hotel as Rita Colwell. Although we would have been delighted to have met Professor Colwell we had to remain incognito, as we were concerned that she might decline to reveal the results of her latest research if she knew we were there.

The morning of the conference was electrifying. It seemed that hundreds of scientists entered the hall from all over the world, and we were overwhelmed with the friendliness of those that we met, they seemed to want to help us with our wants and requests. We had heard about the great work that the Canadian government had done in the treatment of effluent discharged into estuarial waters. The US scientists at the conference were extraordinary in their efforts to help, they actually arranged for us to visit a chicken factory at nearby Chesapeake Bay, to see the most up to date technology in dealing with its effluent problem. This factory had in the past been threatened with closure by the U.S. Government for the pollution with its effluent of a river. Highly toxic because of its high nitrate content. It had the sewage flow equivalent to a town of 12,000 population.

The US environmental agency demanded that they restore the river to its former state and that it did full treatment of all waste disposed of into the water or the plant would be shut down. As we entered the factory to observe the work that had been done the first display showed a horrific totally toxic river devoid of life in all forms - plants, fish and insect life were nonexistent. Actual samples of the water and the destroyed vegetation were displayed, and this reminded me of the River Aire in Yorkshire where water scientist Dr Tony Ward had had the audacity to say its quality was improving, when it was quite obvious to any ordinary person that it was poisoned. The other display showed the miraculous cleanup done on this river as a result of using the latest technology. It was no longer a putrid mire but a clean river with fish, frogs, birds, insects and embellished by flora bursting with the joy of mother nature in full flow. Then came the most important part of the tour, the key to full treatment was the final touch to kill off residual bacteria and viruses, so that pure water would be flowing into the river rather than disease-causing germs. The water had gone through primary and secondary treatment, and then after that a series of large ultraviolet lamps radiated the water to drinking-water purity.

Then we suddenly thought why hasn't Yorkshire Water or the UK Government sent some representatives to this conference. Why should we have to do this at our own time and expense? We were resigned to the conclusion that they simply did not care.

Back at the conference, the scientific reports arrived, and Freddie with his legal-eagle abilities leafed through the immense concentration of scientific dialogue. He stopped. "Eureka!" he declared. "Here it is, the evidence that we required, the results of the report state that disease- causing germs can survive in the sea. They might be asleep but they are not dead. It's now imperative that we demand full treatment in the UK".

For the rest of the conference we mingled with the scientists and felt content with our experiences. As we were to meet Professor Jay at the University of New Hampshire, we were to call at Washington first. We casually mentioned this to a scientist at the conference, Dr Jones (a microbiologist) he announced: "Fellers I am going to Washington and you can gladly have a lift with me". Our contact in Washington DC was Harry Reilly, from Scarborough, who was seconded from the EEC as a diplomat with the EC trade mission, right-hand man to the British ambassador. Harry is a man of flair and style, oozing with self confidence and a no-nonsense approach to life. During the part of his life he spent in Brussels he showed a remarkable ability to communicate and celebrate the best things in life. We had met him through Barry Hampshire, an old friend of the Sons of Neptune, who had put us in touch with Harry in the US. His family had always returned to Scarborough for Christmas, and Harry would join in with us for festive drinks and fun. We were lucky to leave Williamsburg with the scientist, Dr Jones, who knew Washington well and would drop us off at Harry's home. Dr Jones, a rather intense person, remarked how much he loved fresh air. "Keeps you healthy," he quipped. We agreed with him - as it was November there was lots of fresh air about. We were not prepared for him to leave the window open on his side of the car, though! At first it did not seem so bad, but as we got half-way into the four hour drive to Washington walls of snow had built up on either side of the highway. Freddie, very much a healthy outdoor person who loves fresh air, was in the back of the car and began feeling very much like an iceberg. Every hint that the window might be closed fell on deaf ears. But at last we arrived at Harry's house in Washington. We thanked Dr Jones hesitantly and he sped off, opening the other window! We both felt that we had climbed Mt Everest with both legs broken, Freddie more than I, as he had experienced the most of the blasts of cold air. Harry and his grand wife Sue had prepared a meal for us and Harry immediately placed a glass of beer in our hands with enthusiastic hospitality. If ever there was a rehearsal to go from hell to heaven then this had been it. Harry was bursting with his usual vitality and humour and Sue served excellent food. Pictures on the mantelpiece of our beloved Scarborough with various sea views made us feel even more at home, more importantly these reminded us why we were in the USA, to protect and preserve our beloved bays. Harry continued to pour out the gargle, and as we approached 2am we were certainly caressing the shores of inebriation. It was nearly dawn when we crawled into our beds and we went out like a light, instantly. We had consumed vast amounts of different ales.

Then, as though we had had just a few minutes sleep, the bedroom door burst open and there stood Harry, dressed immaculately and looking like an advert for a Moss Bros businessman complete with briefcase in hand, looking as fit as Tarzan "We are off in a few minutes," he enthused. Freddie and I had eyes like cherries in buttermilk after the night's merriment and moved at a snails pace. "How come you are so fresh?" I asked Harry, who worked as a diplomat with the EEC trade delegation. "Part of the job. If you work for Sir James, you have to be able to consume a bottle of brandy at lunch and proceed at full speed afterwards," he said with complete confidence. We had breakfast at a small café near the embassy and bade farewell to Harry. We then hired a car, set off to the University of New Hampshire at Durham, to meet Professor Jay and to inform him about the information gained at the conference.

Professor Jay became director of marine science at the University of New Hampshire, but started his career at Colorado State University where he gained a BA, and an MA in marine sciences from Drake University, and a PhD in microbiology. Thankfully for the Sons his Congressional Report gave us a very wide insight into marine pollution beyond our shores and confirmed our own belief and experience that this was a serious problem for all mankind. We drove from Washington through Pennsylvania, via Boston, to New Brunswick, passing through the colourful remains of the Fall, where the trees, even though it was November, still wore most of their autumnal elegance. Arriving at the Institute of Marine Science and Ocean Engineering, at Durham, we were warmly greeted by Professor Jay, a gentleman whose quiet demeanour belied his brimming in-depth intelligence. We took him and his secretary for dinner, and it was not long before the conversation turned to sea pollution. He told of the immense progress of the Canadian and US governments, who were the leading the field in full treatment of waste disposal to the sea. He said he was amazed that signs of human pollution, even e.coli, were now found in the remote depths of the Pacific Ocean. As for Yorkshire Water's proposed scheme in Scarborough he said: "My main concern is the same as it would be for any area that is disposing of raw non-disinfected sewage via long sea outfalls into coastal areas. "There's going to be a long-term build-up of very pathogenic micro-organisms which will include viruses, bacteria, and animal parasites, and as a result of this long-term build-up there is the potential for these organisms to get back onto bathing beaches, and into shellfish that could be consumed by humans, into various types of fin-fish that could be consumed by humans. If this could happen over a long period of time then we will have truly created a health hazard. A microbiological time-bomb. He was emphatic that full treatment all over the world was the answer. And it was imperative that ultraviolet radiation was used to kill off any residual pathogens.

This helped coastal towns all over the UK, Europe and the world. He later stated: "I am glad that Professor Rita Colwell and I were able to help you".

In 2009, when visiting an aquarium in Nevada, US, I was informed that 78 per cent of the world's fish stocks were depleted, and fish farms, which had been regarded as the saviour of the fishing industry, were now decimating the ocean's eco-systems and causing new disease levels among wild fish. Ocean fishing, especially in Europe, is attempted to be controlled by the quota system, which has led to a miasma of confusion.

Britain's rivers and lakes are contaminated by domestic detergents and, more recently, by the effects of prescription drugs which have entered this environment via effluent systems. For example, contraceptive drugs have affected the fish, which have ingested the action that changes the hormones of the fish, and subsequently the birds which eat the fish. This is largely due to the fact that the water companies are not spending enough on proper treatment.

Prof Bruce Denness, marine microbiology expert, professor of Ocean Engineering at Newcastle University, and Principal Scientific Officer at the Imperial College of Science, London University.

Prof Jay Grimes, of Maryland University, author of the US Congressional report, which was the key scientific evidence that raw sewage dumping would build up a microbiological time-bomb affecting human and oceanic life-forms.

Prof Bruce Denness and the Sons at the London launch of the crucial Denness Report published by the Sons in 1987.

Professor Jay Grimes discussing his Congressional report on the effects of ocean disposal of toxic materials and its effect on the environment. With Charles White and Freddie Drabble, USA 1987.

Visiting the most effective treatment for killing dangerous viruses in Chesapeake Bay with final ultra-violet impact – a scheme which the Sons were fighting to be accepted for the UK.

Professor Peter Bullock, Nobel Prizewinner 2008, who advised the Sons. (image The Times)

THE POISONOUS SEAS

If you destroy the sea you destroy yourselves
– Jacques Cousteau

In the period from 1983 to 1996, a heightened awareness of the importance of the environment and its conservation became more prominent in the consciousness of the British public, due to the increased coverage by the media and excellent documentaries on all aspects of Nature and the marvels of our planet. It was during this period that we regarded our campaigning as inspired by our sea bathing, and with a sense of self-mockery we would declare that "Neptune and the man upstairs were on our side".

The Government and the YWA claimed that the new raw untreated sewage scheme down the coast at Bridlington had passed the EC bathing water quality tests. We also knew that the Thatcher government was a powerful political machine. We also had a formidable battle ahead and at this stage were warned that our campaign could jeopardise many multi-million pound schemes. The Government and the water authorities were fully committed to opening long sea outfalls all over the UK, and there was no doubt that hundreds of millions of pounds worth of contracts had been signed.

"You lads could wind up in the concrete of one of those outfalls," a senior marine engineer told us. We were not in the least concerned at this, as the urgency of our goal of clean seas ruled our minds ultimately.

The system had hurled us a maze of bamboozling gobbledegook over the years, most of it to distract from their ultimate aim – a low-cost privatisation of the water authorities. Our threshold of credibility was gaining ground thanks to Neptune's influence and Captain Sydney's in-depth knowledge of the sea. We already had complained to the ombudsman about the water authorities not consulting interested parties – in our case sea bathers. We were after all, the ones who went in the sea. The ombudsman rejected our complaint. However, our complaint to the EC about the Scarborough scheme was treated favourably. We were supported by Professor Bruce Denness, Capt Sydney Smith, and Professor Jay Grimes of Maryland University US.

The BBC program "Newsnight" on 23 June 1987 did a 20-minute report on the new scientific research proving the danger to health of raw sewage disposal to the sea. The program prompted communication from Euro MPs, especially Scarborough's MEP, Edward Macmillan-Scott. In conjunction with the Robens Institute, we conducted the Neptune project under the guidance of marine biologist Dr David Wheeler. We proved that the bacteria did not die quickly enough in the sea to comply with the EC safety laws. We were already helping Lancashire with our research, which led to a successful campaign to avoid a raw untreated sewage scheme at Blackpool, and we were in touch with similar groups all over the UK, including the Cornish campaigns, Tyneside, Whitby, Bridlington, Filey, Sandsend, Robin Hood's Bay ,and upcoming schemes in Scotland and Ireland. The BBC then launched a major six-part series on the North Sea which was shown in the six countries featured in the series. The Sons were featured generally, and one particular episode – Neptune's Children – was named after our group.

The series, which was narrated and presented by Susannah York, was powerful and had immense impact, showing that countries all over Europe were destroying the North Sea and marine life with sewage sludge, industrial and chemical waste, just dumped into the sea without any treatment whatsoever. The rapid decline in fish stocks and marine life such as dolphins and porpoises – and seals in their thousands – were not only the results of over-fishing, but also of this practice. The coastline of the UK had an alarming increase in ulcerated and deformed fish, as well as contaminated shellfish. In Norway, acid rain from UK power stations had poisoned lakes and devastated forests, and huge toxic blooms of killer algae had disseminated and virtually annihilated all natural sea life to a depth of ten meters.

Professional diver and former college lecturer Arthur Godfrey gave me a most sensible take on the decline of the fishing industry when he said: "The quota system doesn't work, and it's been proven over and over. The boats catch huge netfuls of fish, then have to throw any which exceed their quota back into the sea – dead. It's absolute lunacy. The only answer, and I have talked to fishermen, and they agree, is to permanently close off to everybody the areas where the fish breed – they know where they are. No fishing there, ever. The reason they won't do it? I have been told that, for instance, an area off the Danish coast where sand eels, the main food for cod, breed is where the Danes use suction dredgers to catch the sand eels and turn them into fish-meal, so they won't allow a ban. The answer to conserving fish stocks is to close the breeding grounds to fishermen and state that no-one can fish there – ever."

Arthur Godfrey had shown his awareness of and sensitivity to, the problems of sewage sea pollution during his time as a professional diver, when he refused to dive anywhere near raw-sewage outfalls.

Meanwhile the UK was continuing its practice of dumping 33 billion tons of sewage a year into the sea without treatment, and over half of the beaches around the UK failed the basic preliminary tests for health standards. However, the Government continued to play the ostrich, by continuing to open long sea outfalls. The Minister of the Environment, Michael Howard, opening a new outfall at Hyde in Kent, in 1987 declared: "I know that many people are suspicious about long sea outfalls. May I say that my understanding is that all that happens in inland treatment works is an attempt to reproduce artificially what the sun and the sea do naturally - far out, where this long sea outfall will be discharging into the sea."

At this time, the Thatcher government were still extolling the virtues of this Viking settlement-era theory. The T-90 test was the only indicator test used by the UK, but there was now far more realistic evidence to reconsider this practice. The reality was that viruses survive in our waters for as long as seventeen months, and that they also carry lethal diseases. The alarming AIDS virus could survive for at least thirty-eight hours it had been proved by initial tests, and poliomyelitis and hepatitis were well known to survive in coastal waters. The Government evaded the reality of scientific progress by the use of political theatrics. Critics in environmental groups began to point out that the Government was deliberately putting off proper coastal sewage treatment because it might discourage potential investors in water privatisation, meaning less revenue for the Government and failure of the policy.

Yorkshire Water Authority's new PR people were still floundering in their development, and sometimes looked quite silly – not for the first time. In the run-up to the opening of the Scarborough outfall, Yorkshire Water's spokesman appeared on TV showing a computer graphic model which indicated that the tides would take the sewage away from the new sewage outfall plant, and that it would be impossible to locate any bugs along the coast near the plant. Computers were still perceived as the infallible new gods of knowledge. Captain Syd's comments were as short and swift as a sword swipe decapitating its victim. He said: "No amount of computers can change the way the tides act. They still go in and out, and I know the water authorities say that they run parallel to the shore, but this is not so."

Freddie Drabble, questioned on BBC TV, said, "They might as well use a child's toy. The tides do not change, even for computers."

Tom Jackson, when appointed as a non-executive Yorkshire Water Board member, who had an excellent CV, but in a PR press release they emphasised that he was an expert on 'Rupert The Bear'!

Trevor Newton, who was Managing Director of Yorkshire Water in 1995 when a severe drought hit Yorkshire. Stand pipes were the order of the day with people queueing up for water in the streets. Newton appeared on T.V. showing people how to wash in a cup of water. A few days later it was discovered that he was travelling to his Mother-in-law's house to bathe in a jacuzzi giving the impression that he was living the high life.

A few months before the official opening of the Scarborough outfall samples were taken by Dr Pat Gowen of Friends of the Earth and Greenpeace, and Dr David Wheeler of the Robens Institute indicated that there were large deposits of sewage sludge and virulent pathogenic bacteria on the beach near the outfall. Scarborough was condemned as a sea of shame. We knew they were determined to open the outfall in spite of all our efforts to get the best for Scarborough, but we were well prepared, as three years before we had taken several samples of the sand where the proposed outfall was going to be. These were kept in sealed jars and stored in a safe in a local bank, as our own environmental health department had blocked our efforts to get samples of seawater from our bays analysed by local laboratories. The local council did not consider any of our local protests, they just bulldozed over all aspects of the ramifications of the effects of raw untreated sewage on human health and the marine environment. The YWA did their own tests and thanks to Dr Gowen taking samples all along the coast, which he taught Freddie to do, it was proved that the bacterial contamination was well in excess of the EU guidelines. But testing of the air near the pumping station produced blank slides under the microscope. This was because the Company was blowing toxic air into the sewage works through powerful acids to try to kill off foul smells which were affecting the health of local residents. The Chimney venting the works was just a few yards from the outfall. This problem was a factor in delaying the privatisation of the water industry.

So determined was the Thatcher government to misrepresent the clean seas and beaches that they allowed the Keep Britain Tidy group to have their own Blue Flag award for merely putting wastebins for litter and dog-waste on beaches. While we admired and supported this group, the award of a Blue Flag misled the public as the EEC Blue Flag is the most important indication of clean seas and beaches while the Keep Britain Tidy flag did not inform the public that there were health hazards in the sea due to untreated sewage. For example, dog-owners would often take their dog waste home and flush it down their toilet, which waste, explained Captain Syd, would be brought back by tidal conditions onto the beach. A supporter of the Sons' campaign commented: "They should change their name to the Keep Britain Turdy group."

I appeared on a BBC 4 radio proramme "Costing the Earth", with water authority chairman Sir Gordon Jones, who declared that Bridlington's new outfall had passed the EEC test, and I pointed out that this was impossible as the plant had no treatment of toxic material whatsoever. On his insistence that he was right I declared:

"Historically you will smoulder in your own putridity."

The chemicals used included hydrogen peroxide, bleach, sulphuric acid and peracetic acid. We were amused and alarmed to see the water authority laboratory technicians wearing biological protection suits, like astronauts crossed with Daleks as they trod our beaches for samples to prove the seawater was safe. Over the years we had noticed a decline in sea creatures and the marine life around the bays. In the summer we missed the diamond-like reflections of sunlight on the sand eels, through shoals of which we would dive regularly. We were really alarmed to discover a vast increase in the number of dead seabirds being washed up on the beaches as well as mammals such as porpoises. Reports from Bempton Cliffs, a major breeding-ground for seabirds in the UK, indicated that thousands of kittiwakesand guillemots were dying. The reason for this became clear when the sewage dumping produced toxic algae which drove the sand eels further out to sea. So far out in fact that the parent birds which brought the sand eels back to feed their young in the nests could no longer do so, because the eels had become absorbed so deeply into their digestive systems, that they could no be regurgitated. As a result of this hundreds of thousands of baby kittiwakes died.

(In May 2009 we revisited the Bempton Cliffs bird sanctuary with our friend Derek McNearny, who now lived in Alberta, Canada. He had never seen the incredible sight of the myriad variety of birds nesting on these awesome cliffs. On the way to the cliffs we quoted to him Shelley's Ode to the Skylark, as we had to each other on previous hikes to this part of the coat, when we had been captivated by dozens of skylarks soaring out of the meadows into the sky with their joyous birdsong. :

Teach me half the gladness
That thy brain must know,
Such harmonious madness
From my lips would flow,
The world should listen then, as I am listening now.

On our visit we noticed that there were no longer as many skylarks as before. "Never mind," I said to Derek. "Soon you will be surrounded by delightful puffins – you will feel as though

you were in a Walt Disney movie as they fly around your head."
Sadly there were no puffins to be seen, due to over fishing and
pollution.)

Fired up by this, the Sons decided to take a trip to London
to protest against the flotation of the water industry on the Stock
Exchange. We prepared our protest by producing T-shirts which
showed a seal with blood dripping from its eyes with the slogan
"Don't buy a share in Death". This was launched at the local Sixth
Form College where the students enthusiastically supportive of our
cause, as they had become, unlike the Water Authority and the
Council, fully aware of how precious the environment was. The
demo received good coverage in the local media with the students
sporting the T-shirts. The local Tory MEP, Edward McMillan Scott,
however, supported the Sons and criticised Yorkshire Water and
other authorities about the out-dated scheme, saying: "I believe
a duty rests with the water authorities to anticipate the results
of new scientific evidence and new European standards which,
in all likelihood, will be more stringent. The Department of the
Environment should be protecting the environment, not its own
reputation. There is no place for such secrecy in today's Britain."
We admired McMillan Scott but knew that as a Tory he was treading
on thin ice - the Sons were seen as anti-Tory in a Tory heartland,
and he did not wish to appear in our favour. Poet Alexander Pope
sprang to mind "Damned with faint praise, assent with civil leer,
and without sneering taught the rest to sneer".

Tony Robinson, a Brussels based spokesman for the Socialist
group in the European Parliament stated: "This further evidence
will underline the need to proceed with enforcement action against
British seaside resorts in breach of the bathing water directive. In
terms of domestic British politics, these findings cast further doubts
over privatisation, with the prospect of water authorities having to
pay out sooner rather than later for a civilised method of dealing
with sewage,"

Freddie's passionate energy levels had reached ultissimo
heights and so had mine, when we saw the insane abuse of
our beautiful Town and the pollutants that were supposed to be
treatments, destroying our magnificent bays. At the end of each

working day, we would walk the cliffs from Rocks Lane to Cloughton Wyke to discuss the latest developments and strategies in our campaign.

At the weekends we would spend hours at Freddie's office, contacting the Press Association and other media with our latest information. We also contacted various scientific bodies for more information and sent out press cuttings to resorts and marine conservation groups with similar problems. We spent much time communicating with politicians who supported our scientific arguments against sea pollution and even more time to those who opposed our campaign.

However we had our fun times too. Freddie had instigated many practical japes and surprises for friend's birthdays and with his 50th birthday approaching we had to instigate an exceptional surprise for this unique occasion. Our group fortunately enlisted the help of Freddie's very efficient secretary, Jennie, who was very attractive, with a great sense of humour, and was an ideal ally. It was decided by the group that I should not be involved with the initial plans as I was seeing Freddie on a daily basis and he would pick up on the nuance that something was afoot.

Eventually two plans were put into action, Jennie was booked for a holiday in Florida with her husband, Geoff, and two daughters, Victoria and Louisa, on the week of Freddie's birthday.

At first this seemed to dampen enthusiasm. However this was overcome by an ingenious idea. Jennie's brother Chris Coole was a director of Dale Electric, an electrical manufacturing company, and was up to date with the latest technology especially satellite communications. The plan was to surprise Freddie at his home on the evening of his birthday celebration.

Local hotel the Palm Court had just been refurbished with superb décor and a delightful swimming pool. Before Jennie's family set out on holiday, Chris arranged to film the family at the edge of the swimming pool surrounded by palm trees and tropical plants supplied by local florists. This was to give the impression that they were actually in Florida, disguising any hint that the film was shot in Scarborough, as it was to be delivered as a birthday surprise "via satellite".

Freddie was always proud of the fact that he never failed to complete a client's will before they expired, and Jennie was more than familiar with Freddie's perceived triumph in this field. The group realised that this was his Achilles' heel.

As his 50th birthday approached, and during our usual intense discussions about the Sons' campaign, he started to mention a client that he went to visit at a local nursing home, in order to arrange his will. The client, an Australian, was, he said, a really nice man suffering from AIDS. This was unusual, as Freddie never discussed his practice work. He continued to mention this, and up to a few days before his birthday he was still talking concernedly about his client (who was, in fact, an actor friend of the Sons). I played it cool, showing no interest and supposedly wanting to get back to the campaign.

Jennie had arranged the plan with detailed precision, having people in Australia and Birmingham to back up the story, knowing that Freddie would research every detail. The plan was now common knowledge at his office and the matron at the nursing home co-operated fully with the plan.

There was low lighting in the bedroom, a half bottle of sherry by the bedside, I supplied a tape recorder that was to go under the bedsheets to record the dialogue between Freddie and the "client", who, avoiding grasping relations, insisted on leaving Freddie a legacy of £1,000 and the rest of his substantial estate to his favourite charity. Out of the blue Freddie phoned me at the surgery, "You know that really nice gentleman from Australia I have been telling you about - he died this morning," he said dejectedly. "I went to get the will signed but he was taken to Scarborough Hospital last night and died in the early hours, and he never signed the will. I never lost a will before."

My goodness! He had fallen for it, I couldn't believe it. I said: "Sorry to hear about this Freddie, but I am up to my ears in feet, and will talk to you later."

With almost a week to go to his birthday bash, how could

I conceal the jape? I managed to do so by sticking to the Sons campaign and matters of pollution.

On the night of the birthday, a crowd of Freddie's good friends poured into his house with bottles of fine wine, whiskey and presents galore delivered with an air of celebration. At 8.30 Chris Coole announced that at precisely 9pm that there would be a special satellite message, taking us all the way to the poolside in Florida, for Freddie. Everyone crowded round the Tv at 9pm. Chris had convinced everybody that he had arranged expensive satellite time for this special event. He had already timed each question and Jennie's answers to the second. At first a snow-blizzard screen, and someone said "I don't think we are going to get through", then suddenly there was Jennie, Geoff, and daughters in what appeared to be the tropical atmosphere of Florida. Chris asked what the weather was like in Florida. Jennie replied: "It is wonderful, wish you were all here,"

Freddie said in amazement "This is great. I can't believe we are seeing you - we are having a great party - you should be here"

Then the screen snowed up, followed by a clear picture, with Jennie saying: "We will see you next week when we get back. Bye-bye and Happy Birthday!"

Freddie was now in a state of delightful delirium. "That was fantastic!" he exclaimed. "Fancy Jennie, Geoff and kids sending a message by satellite all the way from Florida."

As he swooned with disbelief Martin, the actor who had played the "client" he thought had died, came up behind him, wearing the same pyjamas he had worn in the nursing home, and made up to look like death and tapped him on the shoulder. Freddie froze like a statue, his face aghast, his eyeballs protruding, shocked and disorientated for a few seconds, his mind rewinding as to how sad and devastated he had been that the man had died on him before signing his will. Now here he was in front of him alive! They embraced like two zombies. The silence, only a few seconds long, seemed endless.

"I can't believe this," said Freddie, "Amazing! Wonderful! I need a malt whiskey and so do you Martin. Why did I not recognise you?" Martin's reply was short and to the point: "Make-up Freddie, make-up!"

Teamwork and amazing planning had floored Freddie. He was flabbergasted. The satellite message was, of course, pre-recorded on video, and Jennie and family were still in Florida.

It was not long before we were back to the harsh realities of the campaign. We took our protest to London for better impact.

The day before we were to go we collected dead seabirds such as seagulls, cormorants, kittiwakes, guillemots, and gannets, along with dead porpoises, seals, and various dead fish and loaded them into iceboxes. All of these poor creatures were regularly found on the beach during this period. Early next morning we set off for the Houses of Parliament, having informed the Press Association of our protest. Our huge white hired van was loaded with the boxes of dead creatures. Captain Syd sat in a big chair in the back of the van, Dave Lazenby was the driver, and Freddie, his son, Paul, and I squeezed into the front. For visual purposes we had acquired a set of huge scales so that we could display the creatures on one side of the scales and a handful of Company shares in the other. 'Don't buy a share in Death!" said the poster. The stench of the dead creatures was awful, but that did not dampen our spirits. The journey seemed totally surreal. I was thinking to myself: "How badly did you want to be a conservationist? How badly do you want to live?" was the answer!

It was a hair-raising experience all the way to London. On entering the City matters got a little fractious over which turn to take and which bridge to cross until, exasperated, we eventually arrived outside the Houses of Parliament and pulled up beside a policeman. As we opened the driver's window he was engulfed by the stench of the rotten fish. "God, what have you got in there?" he said.

Freddie said "We have brought these dead sea creatures here to protest about this Government's continuing pollution of the seas around our coast". Bewildered the PC stood back and with his hands clasped around his face peered at the array of dead creatures in the back of the van. "Well by law you can't protest within a mile of the Houses of Parliament," he said, but seeing how disappointed we were he said "However, you can in a private building or on private land." He winked and pointed to a pub across from Parliament.

Freddie shook his hand and we all thanked him. We pulled across the road, drove into the yard at the back of the pub, and unloaded our stuff for the demonstration. The pub was located on the side of Westminster Bridge. The next problem was to get permission from the landlord, as his land was private property. Diplomatically we ordered beer and sandwiches for all of us and after friendly dialogue with the barmaid and other staff we were told we could hold our protest outside. By this time some media people had arrived - we had informed the Press Association of our location. A Danish TV crew was so keen they filmed our every move. We set up the huge scales with the dead creatures on one side and imitation share certificates on the other, and as a backdrop the large banner declaring "Don't Buy a Share in Death."

Local London radio and TV reporters turned up and after several interviews Freddie and myself set off for the Houses of Parliament. Fortunately we had been asked to contribute to a Parliamentary report on sea pollution, so we had easy access.

We had arranged to meet our local Scarborough MP, Sir Michael Shaw, who had strongly condemned our campaign. As I passed the late Robin Cook, who was standing by a window reading a document, I said to him we were contributing to a document on sea pollution. "A noble cause I'm sure," he retorted. We delivered a copy of the Denness report and our copy of the report "Sewage Disposal to the Sea" to be delivered to the Parliamentary Committee on Beach Pollution, We returned to the pub then dropped off the dead marine creatures at the laboratories of St. Mary's Hospital, where a cheerful technician took them in for analysis.

On our return to Scarborough, Freddie declared: "We have to go through Europe. The EEC is our only hope. The democratic system in this country has failed us."

As George Bernard Shaw stated: "Democracy allows us to make fools of ourselves without interference."

We had now gained a reputation as rebels because of our stance seemed to have put us in contact with higher authority. With the help of our Denness Report and the Neptune Project, Louise Ellman, Leader of Lancashire County Council, was able to force the Lancashire County Council to implement a public enquiry. Dr. Wheeler gave his evidence to the County Council. Louise Ellman said: "We are concerned with the views of the residents of the area, tourism which is a major industry and fishermen in this particular instance are concerned over their livelihoods. We have registered our objection to its application with the Department of the Environment and we have registered our concern to the European Commission and we have called for a public enquiry. We don't yet know if the Department of the Environment will accede to that request, but we have a great deal of concern as we feel that this is an issue which has led to a great deal of public disquiet."

Meanwhile groups such as the Fylde Boat Angling group gave this message for the environment committee: "The Morecambe Bay and the North Fylde coast is one of the most important coastal areas in the UK for both boat and shore fishing especially in the immediate vicinity of the proposed outfall. It is one of the most heavily fished grounds in the area, cod, whiting, plaice, dabs and conger eels are some of the species prolific in the area, attracted by the rich variety of food that can be found. In the early summer months large quantities of female tope move in to breed so that their young can take immediate advantage of these pickings. The proposed outfall, daily depositing over 100 tons of sewage sludge onto the seabed would have a catastrophic effect on the food chain, rapidly making this sea area a lifeless wasteland. This has already happened at Weymouth West Bay. I have eaten mullet caught in the vicinity of a sewage outfall and would not recommend it to anybody. Lately a big advertising campaign has been promoting fish with the slogan 'Give 'Em Fish' but with the recent controversy over eggs, chicken and quick-chill salad foods, I wonder who would be liable if effluent-fed fish were ever tested. The vast majority of sea anglers living at the coast and living inland are totally opposed to the NWWA's proposals and feel the overall proposed outfall will be severely detrimental to sea angling."

A further statement by the commodore of the Fylde Coast Wind Surfing Club said: I have sailed at Fleetwood since 1980 and noticed every time I have swallowed water, I have suffered sickness, diarrhea and a sore throat. These clear up if I do not windsurf for a day or two. Members of the Windsurfing Club have missed work with gastroenteritis, ear, nose and throat infections, and skin irritations after swimming in the sea. There are at least 40 sailors windsurfing every weekend, wind permitting on the North Beach at Fleetwood. I have received letters from sailing clubs all over Britain, condemning the practice of dumping untreated sewage into the sea. The sailing club at Barrow has contacted their MP, complaining about the new Fleetwood outfall. We on the Fylde coast have an opportunity to stop dumping in the sea. Let us be one of the first coastal areas not to use the sea as a tip, and with modern methods, dispose of our sewage on land and control its destruction."

However, like all campaigns against the political power of the day it takes enormous tenacity and determination to get to the point of a public enquiry about a major issue. Save Our Bay Campaign leader, Group-Capt Harry King, of Fleetwood, describes in a letter to the Sons (dated 4th September 1989) the frustrations of dealing with bureaucracy and politicians.

'At the beginning of our campaign last summer Keith Mans, a local MP, was somewhat non-committal. I appreciated his problem - he was under pressure from the Save Our Bay campaign and many of his constituents to oppose the scheme, but he did not wish to go against Fylde Borough Council, who, by some political jiggery pokery, had voted in favour of the NWWA scheme.

On 4th September 1988 Save Our Bay issued its first interim report. This was a 6-page report with 9 appendices. It was this report which inspired Lancashire County Council to commission the Robens Institute report. On 10th September I had a long interview with Keith Mans. As a result of this he gave a copy of our report direct to Nicholas Ridley. the then Secretary of State. On 19th October Nicholas Ridley replied to Keith, saying inter alia "The use of long sea outfalls to dispose of sewage is a well-established method which has been endorsed by the Royal Commission on Environmental Pollution. Most schemes for improving bathing water quality are of this type" Ridley did, however, make the point that the question of long sea outfall versus inland treatment must be considered by H.M. Inspector of Pollution and added "I will need to consider in deciding the applications, whether there is a case for a public enquiry." Alan Clark, the Tory MP who published his diaries to the embarrassment of the Tory Government, said: "Margaret Thatcher appointed Nicholas Ridley as Minister for the Environment because he has the utmost contempt for the environment!"

Group-Capt King continues: "On Friday 4th November 1988 Keith Mans spoke in a debate in the House of Commons. His speech is reported at page 1320-1321 of Hansard. In the report Keith referred to a speech by Sir Hugh Rossi saying 'We are becoming increasingly isolated in Europe in using the sea as a way of disposing of sewage. There may come a time when that form of disposal is no longer acceptable'. Turning to the NWWA scheme he asked for a full independent enquiry. He said he used the word "independent" because he was apprehensive that a public enquiry would take too long and there was an urgent need to clean up the beaches. In July this year Keith telephoned me to say that Sir Hugh Rossi, as Chairman of the Select Committee for the Environment had, as a matter of urgency, arranged for the Select Committee to consider the whole question of long sea outfalls.

"To sum up we have had considerable assistance from Keith Mans in ensuring our protests were put into the right hands. He agrees we must ensure that we have the best scheme that technology can offer to clean up our beaches."

Group-Capt King concludes: "We shall always be grateful to the Sons of Neptune for their help in getting our campaign under way."

Later Louise Ellman, leader of Lancashire County Council, wrote to the Sons, saying that the Department of the Environment had rejected North-West Water's Lancashire outfall scheme and had told them to go back to the drawing board because of Professor Denness's scientific report published by the Sons. "Many thanks for all your help. This is a great victory," she wrote. We were very pleased that we had helped in this victory, although the establishment were still reluctant to recognise our role.

Whereas we were delighted to help out other groups around the country, we were disgusted and appalled at Scarborough Council's continuing support for the dumping of raw, untreated sewage into the Town's bays. Even children at local schools from the age of eight upwards were shocked. It was unbelievable that the local council still endorsed a disposal system that would pre-date ancient civilizations. Soon Neptune, the god of the sea, would indicate that he was not at one with man's activities. The Sons were contacted by seafood traders and local people from Sandsend, a beautiful beach resort just to the north of Whitby, which is part of Scarborough Borough, where there was concern about raw sewage on the beach. Local citizen Pat Coakley said: "The local beck flowing onto the beach formed what was known as 'polio pool' because so many kids got ill playing on that part of the beach, which was regularly flooded with raw untreated sewage". A group called Sandsend against Sewage was formed and the Sons advised them on how to proceed.

Sea-front traders at this popular beach were upset by the dysentery reports and sewage scares for holidaymakers reported in the press, which led to the local health authorities closing part of the beach from Sandsend to Whitby at a crucial earning time of the year. Shopkeeper Mrs. Irene Raine, chairman of Sandsend against Sewage said: "It's just not worth opening".

Another local trader, Mrs Christine Hodgkinson who sold beach goods and snacks demanded a reduction in rates from Scarborough Council due to lack of trade. On the 4th September 1991, angry mother Mary Picketts O'Donnel who with her children Joseph, Stephanie and Guy, had visited Sandsend, contacted the media after one of her children contracted dysentery and the rest of the family were struck down with illnesses after their visit to the resort.

The Sons went to the aid of the Sandsend group when a meeting was called to discuss the pollution problem. On arrival we were warned by the Sandsend group that we would be refused entry as Scarborough Council had stated that they would not attend if we were going to be present.

So we diplomatically agreed with the group to stay away so that they could hear what Scarborough Council would do to prevent further pollution happening. Trebble and Bosomworth predictably were still supporting Yorkshire Water's policies without question. The Marquis of Normanby, the local symbol of the establishment, gave us a condescending stare on his way into the meeting and was clearly as alert as a zombie to our group's aims towards sea pollution

It was clear that the Town Hall chiefs had neither read nor understood the crucial contents of the Denness report and how important it would have been to Scarborough's tourist industry. The Yorkshire coast could have led the UK in beach and sea cleanliness had they done so.

There was now increasing evidence from all over the UK that sea bathers, divers, and surfers were feeling the effects of pollution. The most common were eye, ear and stomach disorders, this apart from the common sense factor was strong enough evidence to stop the outfall schemes without treatment, but the more sinister picture of serious virus infections should have been enough to have stopped this insane practice immediately.

A series of newspaper reports confirmed our fears:

'In 1988 two boys contracted an illness with paralytic symptoms similar to polio after swimming in polluted water at Southend. Monitoring of two local beaches revealed salmonella and polio-type viruses, some of which cause meningitis.

'A week after 1989's snorkel race in Bristol docks, 27 per cent of the participants developed gastroenteritis'

'Blackpool GP Dr. Martin Lucking told the recent inquiry into Britain's beaches that onshore winds in 1988 and 1989 coincided with "a tremendous amount" of gastro-intestinal and respiratory infections-including vomiting and violent diarrhoea". The inquiry concluded that sea bathing could lead to stomach upsets, skin problems and ear, nose and throat infections.'

'In September 1989 checks on divers who spent a weekend diving in and around Plymouth Sound revealed a higher incidence of gastroenteritis than among a comparable group of non-divers. The rate was twice as high among divers who were active outside the harbour, and three times as high among those who dived inside the harbour.

In 1988 over 5,000 seals had been found dead in the North Sea in less than three months. This highlighted the deteriorating condition of Europe's dumping ground, the North Sea, reported Harry Mead in the Northern Echo on 19 May 1988.

"The seal were dying from this virus and other pathogens, first located off the coasts of Denmark and Holland. Very worrying for both seal and humans, the virus and other forms of infection are much more persistent in the sea than has previously been supposed. It looks like becoming a major health hazard", he reported.

"The uncertain basis on which sea water has been judged has already been exposed by the Sons of Neptune, who are fighting against the sewage outfall scheme at Scarborough. The death of seals on the Humber and Yorkshire coastline has been described as a holocaust. This is also happening along the East Coast. At the Norfolk Seal Rescue Centre they are treating the common seals which were suffering from septicemia poisoning. Jim Ward, founder of the Scarborough Animal Welfare Service stated: "They have rotting flippers and tails and try to get ashore before they are drowned".

Both Freddie Drabble and Jim Ward blamed the cause of the pollution on Yorkshire Water and other water authorities along the coast. But water chiefs vehemently defended their legal right to dump tons of untreated waste and toxic material into the waters off our coastlines. John Taylor, of Yorkshire Water, said there was no justification in saying that discharges into the North Sea played a contributory part in the ouitbreak of the seal virus. The Sons said that evidence so far had identified a group of bacteria which had caused the seals' deaths as picorna virus. "This is the same group which causes such diseases as meningitis and hepatitis. This is the same group of viruses found in human sewage." said Freddie

Drabble. The Marine Conservation Society said the Yorkshire Water chief should be sacked for his statements.

During our daily dip in the sea over a period of time, we noticed the amount of dead seabirds and fish on the beaches. Life in the rock pools also declined, creatures such as starfish, shrimps, rock salmon and sea urchins disappeared The decimation of thousands of seabirds on our coastline was now very evident.

Jim Ward reported the death of seabirds: "450 kittiwakes had been found dead on a beach off Scarborough. Preliminary post-mortem results indicated that the birds could have died because of the shortage of sand eels. I believe that pollution is the cause of this".

We also noticed the decline of sand eels as well as the increase of dead marine and birdlife of all varieties at Bempton Cliffs, a noted seabird colony for all species especially puffins, gannets, gulls etc. These were all now affected by the state of the North Sea. The best example was in the case of the guillemots. Thousands were dying. Usually they would dive near the coastal cliffs and shores but because of the lack of sand eels they began to fly further out to sea. Soon they had to fly so far that when they flew back to their nests the food was already digested and could not be regurgitated in order to feed their young. There were reports in the media of shellfish farms all over the UK being affected by pollution. For example in The Guardian August 1992 under the headline of 'Shellfishing livelihoods could be sunk by government-approved sewage. It was stated: "The produce of various shellfish farms all over the UK were classed as unfit for human consumption'- these included Morecambe Bay, Hull, Kings Lynn, Whitstable, Plymouth, Barnstaple and Falmouth.

Ancient shellfish beds in Poole Harbour were threatened with extinction mainly because of sewage pollution being piped into the harbour by Wessex Water. Official Ministry of Agriculture figures show the quality of mussels going down as pollution rises. A mussel farmer, David Davies, who runs a business with his son in Poole said that less than twenty years ago the harbour was one of the cleanest in Europe and was designated by the EC as a shellfish fishery in 1979. Wessex Water admits that the development of

Poole without comparable updating of the sewage works has meant increasing discharges. Mr. Davies continued 'We have not caused the problem but it is us that suffer, we do not know who to turn to, to sort this out. We believed that the quality of sea water was being looked at constantly and would not be allowed to drop below that needed for shellfish-designated areas. This has come as quite a shock.'

Andrew Lees, of Friends of the Earth, asked: "Whatever happened to the government's 'polluter-pays-principle', the reality is that the victims of pollution pay. Wessex Water should pay these fishermen compensation out of the millions of profits they make, until such time that the water quality is restored to its previous level."

A spokesman for Wessex Water accepted that most of the pollution came from its outfall.

A native American Indian tribal belief is that whilst polluting might save you money, eventually you find you cannot eat money. Most tribes, when making decisions about conservation and environmental matters would use as their guide the question: How will this affect seven generations from now?

David Bellamy, noted biologist and broadcaster, had stated as far back as 1969: "You name it, it all goes in the sea."

Gerhard Ehrke, Chairman of the Schleswig Holstein Tourist Board, said in 1971: You can sail the North Sea today without a compass. Simply follow the sewage trails to a port."

Ted Clighton-Hinton, marine biologist and secretary of the Durham County Conservative Trust, said in 1971: "Judging by the number of nitrates coming down the Rhine and from other sources, in fifteen years we will see the end of the North Sea."

Gro-Harlem Bruntland, Prime Minister of Norway, fired a salvo at the Thatcher government over the coal-fired power-stations in England causing acid-rain. She told the Queen at a banquet in honour of the King of Norway in 1988: "It is in the interest of both our nations that the health of the sea is maintained."

It is clear that between 1983 and 1992 the build up of pollution in the North Sea was alarming. As all-year-round sea-bathers we the Sons witnessed this deterioration of marine environment on a daily basis. Our knowledge and concern was giving us a clear picture of the crisis that was building up, not only for our species but for the whole of marine life. Even more disturbing was that it was becoming a worldwide problem. 'Our Common Future' the title of the Bruntland report, published by Oxford Press 1987 for the World Commission on the Environmen, indicated in the chapter title 'Oceans' the balance of life and the delicate threshold of life on our planet as follows: "Covering over 70% of the planet's surface, the oceans play a critical role in maintaining its life-support systems. In sustaining life - animals, plants, minute oxygen-producing photo-plankton, in fact all life-forms emerge from the sea.

"In the last few decades the growth of the world economy, the burgeoning demand for food and fuel, and the accumulating discharges of waste has begun to press against the bountiful limits of the oceans. In short, mankind is destroying the source of life itself."

Around this time Freddie and I had met the celebrated astronomer Sir Patrick Moore. I asked him if mankind would destroy this tiny, beautiful and extraordinary planet of ours with greed and pollution. He immediately replied with his demonstrative gesture: "There are many such worlds out there that have already been destroyed by such matters - next question."

This remark hit a major chord with both Freddie and I and added fuel to our already indestructible determination to stop the insane scheme that Yorkshire Water had imposed on Scarborough. Whereas there were problems on a worldwide scale, our attention was mainly focused on our own area and helping similar groups in the UK. The Hon. Tom McMillan, Minister of the Environment, Government of Canada, said on 27th May 1986: "The world's environmental problems are greater than the sum of those in each country, and certainly they can no longer be dealt with on a nation-state basis. The growing trend towards isolationism demonstrates that the current rhythm of history is out of harmony with human aspirations, even with its chance for survival. "

Captain Sydney Smith told us: "The factor that contributes to the decline of the North Sea is that it is a very shallow sea, and it cannot continue to absorb the industrial waste, sewage and other pollutions. Fish catches have declined by a third since 1974. The North Sea is in trouble. But I believe that if they stop the dumping of untreated sewage sludge and industrial waste, they will reverse the process. The sea is very resilient."

UK coal-burning power stations were contributing to acid rain affecting not only the UK, but the lakes and rivers of Northern and Central Europe. So much so that acid rain in Norway, caused by UK pollution, stripped the pine forests of their needles and floating dead fish in Norwegian lakes became a frequent news item on our television screens.

The Norwegian PM condemned the Thatcher government for its pollution of the atmosphere, lakes and forests with acid rain. But the so-called Iron Lady Margaret Thatcher was in no mood to consider environmental matters. After presenting awards at the Better Environment Awards for Industry to ICI, Sainsbury's and other companies for their contribution to overcoming environmental problems she defended the dumping by British companies of toxic chemicals in the North Sea and warned against hasty action against global warming with the greenhouse effect. "I find some people thinking of the environment in an airy-fairy way as if we could go back to a village life. Some might quite like it but it is quite impossible. We have created enough wealth to enable us to consider very carefully how to reduce pollution and how to design things for the better. We are not going to do away with the great car economy for example."

In reply Paul Horseman, a Greenpeace spokesman said "Mrs. Thatcher is completely out of touch, she is trying to defend the cosmetic changes of dirty industries while environmentalists and other European governments look to a future of phasing out pollution and phasing in clean, non-polluting production."

Jonathan Porritt, of Friends of the Earth, said through a spokesman, that he resented her comments. This was no surprise to the Sons. Thatcher's philosophy of the time was that market forces and improved technology could bring sustainable economic growth. She dismissed the global warming theory. "It could be from a completely different pattern of winds across the Atlantic," she insisted.

I approached former Tory MP and businessman Wilf Proudfoot in Scarborough, and asked him about the effects of global warming. He was immediately dismissive, insisting that "market forces will sort it out". A self-made and successful businessman, this had moulded his philosophy.

A Labour spokesman for the environment retorted "Mrs. Thatcher's attempt to smear everyone concerned with the environment as wanting to return to a rural idyll, is a grave insult to the many millions of people in Britain and throughout the world desperately worried about their quality of life and the kind of world we are bequeathing to our children"

On July 9 1989 we became aware of Thatcher's possible motive in supporting toxic waste dumping in the North Sea. The Observer reported, under the headline Exclusive: 'Attwoods buys firm with 'Mafia Link', that Attwoods, whose deputy chairman was Denis Thatcher, had been linked by the FBI to an alleged Mafia associate. "Two months ago Attwoods agreed to pay $20m for a US national waste company, run by the two sons of John Zuccarelli, employed as a consultant by the firm. In August 1981, the then FBI director William Webster, in a letter to the US Congressional Committee investigation of Mafia involvement in the New Jersey garbage business, identified Zuccarelli as a reputed associate of organized crime, allied to Ocean Combustion Services."

Thatcher's firm was connected to Ocean Combustion Services, which was involved with the dumping of highly toxic and poisonous waste via the Vulcanus I and Vulcanus II ships, which burnt more than 100,000 tons of hazardous waste every year off Scarborough. A local builder, Frank Smith, said: "I used to see the ships burning toxic waste off Cayton Bay, but when I informed the coastguards they said it was merely the light from passing ships." Not so. The Sunday Times Magazine pointed out the truth in July 1989.

Thatcher was up to his neck in it.

Professor Pat Gowan showing Freddie the scientific process for testing for safe bathing water.

YORKSHIRE POST

The country's biggest selling regional morning newspaper

Estab. 1754 No. 44,188   WEDNESDAY AUGUST 30 1989   PRICE 27p. Tel. LEEDS 432701

Double blow to Clarke's plans

Poll finds

The anti-pollution group, The Sons of Neptune, stage a protest by the new sewage pipe.

Sewage-pipe launch upstaged by protest

By MIKE WOODCOCK

A MEDIA photo-opportunity, arranged by Yorkshire Water to publicise work on a huge sewage outfall pipe on the Yorkshire coast, was

By RICHARD SADLER
Environment Correspondent

"We will continue to fight this and all similar plans which continue the disgusting practice of dumping raw sewage, for the sake of future generations."
Yorkshire Water's scientists claim the

─ INSIDE TODAY ─

Heroin gang jailed

A SMUGGLING gang from Yorkshire received heavy jail sentences yesterday for trying to bring heroin with a street value of £300,000 into Britain.
Customs officers found the high-purity drug expertly hidden in two suitcases at the Welsh port of Holyhead where the gang had arrived from Ireland. P.3.

Japanese link

THE electronics group, Plessey, which is fighting a hostile takeover bid from GEC and the West German, Siemens, is planning to link with a leading Japanese microchip company. P.4.

'Riots' rally row

ATTEMPTS by the British National Party to hold a rally in Bradford — after riots at a similar event in Dewsbury — have provoked an angry reaction. P.3.

Adverts attack

THE Labour Party has attacked an £8m advertising campaign to tell the public about two private power-generating companies. P.5.

ARTS & ENTERTAINMENT

See Page 8.

Fraud 'letter'

As the result of the Sons scientific evidence media interest on a worldwide scale resulted in several T.V. crews filming them. A crew for Germany's TV Channel ONE 'World Mirror' programme came to Scarborough to do a documentary.

Motor car economy defended at environment awards

PM angers greens with 'airy fairy' tag

Green Peace spokes-
man Paul Horsman,
Charles White and Pro-
fessor Alasdair McIntyre
who backed the Sons
scientific evidence.
Paul Horsman said
Mrs Thatcher '..was
completely out of touch
she is trying to defend
the cosmetic changes
of dirty industries while
environmentalists
and other European
governments look to a
future of phasing out
pollution.'

James Erlichman, Consumer Affairs Correspondent

THE Prime Minister yesterday accused some "airy fairy" environmentalists of demanding the end of the motor car economy and a return to village life to halt pollution.

Mrs Thatcher defended dumping by British companies of toxic chemicals in the North Sea and warned against taking hasty action against global warming from the greenhouse effect.

She was speaking after presenting the Better Environment Awards for Industry to ICI, Sainsbury and other companies for their contribution to overcoming environmental problems.

"I find some people thinking of the environment in an airy-fairy way, as if we could go back to a village life," she said. "Some might quite like it, but it is quite impossible . . . We have created enough wealth to en-

The Prime Minister said she was a great admirer of Jonathon Porritt, the director of the Friends of the Earth, and said true greens were very constructive.

A spokeswoman for Mr Porritt, who was in Holland, said: "This is a mammoth case of appropriation by the Prime Minister and I rather think Jonathon would resent it."

Paul Horsman, a Greenpeace spokesman, said: "Mrs Thatcher is completely out of touch. She is trying to defend the cosmetic changes of dirty industries while environmentalists and other European governments look to a future of phasing out pollution and phasing in clean, non-polluting production."

Mrs Thatcher's remarks were little more than a restatement of the Government's belief that market forces and improved technology can bring sustainable economic growth. It was the "airy-fairy" jibe, repeated twice, which angered environmentalists who believe more

bon dioxide effect which we have to sort out. And then, at the end, there was a conclusion: although this could be from the greenhouse effect . . . it is more likely to have come from a completely different pattern of winds across the Atlantic."

Bryan Gould, Labour's environment spokesman, accused Mrs Thatcher of a U-turn on green issues. "Mrs Thatcher's attempt to smear everyone concerned with the environment as wanting to return to a rural idyll is a grave insult to the many million in Britain and throughout the world desperately worried about their quality of life and the kind of world we are bequeathing to our children," he said.

ICI received a pollution abatement award for its design of a new ammonia-making process. Britain's insistence that ICI be permitted to continue to dump 165,000 tonnes of chemical waste into the North Sea each year led to condemnation at the North Sea Conference in the Hague last week

Charles White promoting clean seas on TV and at conferences seen here (clockwise) with Jonathan Porritt director of Friends of the Earth, Robert Kilroy Silk TV presenter 'Kilroy', Bill Odie and Julian Pettifer who were about to commit to conservation programming.

Newsnight team with Sons of Neptune, filming in Scarborough for a special edition devoted to Professor Dennis report and featuring Professor Jay Grimes from the USA that went out in June 1987

Eammon Gallagher, former EEC fisheries minister with Charles and Ann White, and Ms Pat Hourican in Brussels, as guests of Mr Liam Hourican, European Commissioner.

The Thatcher Loo v. The Thatcher Lie

The Prime Minister, Margaret Thatcher, said in an interview with Michael Buerk on the BBC environmental programme "Nature", on 2nd March 1987, when taken to task on the dumping of untreated sewage in the sea around the UK: "It's treated. It's not untreated. It's treated; you will find it's treated."

Buerk rejoined: "Yes. But we have a lot of long sea outfalls that take raw sewage out to sea and we're still building them."

The PM: "I think you will find it's treated. Well, it should be treated sewage that goes out. I think you will find it is treated. All of it. Treated sewage."

Buerk: "The truth is that all over the country, a number of water authorities are pumping raw sewage, untreated in any way, straight into the sea."

At this time the job of cleaning up Britain's beaches would soon pass to a privatised water industry. Buying a stake in that industry has been likened to buying a house without any drains. Replacing the country's inadequate sewage systems was to cost hundreds of millions of pounds. Water charges would probably have to rise to meet those costs. The Government was not going to pay - the customer would have to.

This was the 1980s, the era that produced financial plunderers known as fat cats and yuppies. The yuppies were a new phenomenon, young professional men and women out to exploit the world of economics for as much financial gain as quickly as they possibly could. Theirs was a laissez-faire attitude, founded purely on self-interest that was eventually to lead to the foundation of a change in the British character. A new level of greed known as the free market.

As the Sons of Neptune, we realized that this was happening – especially as conservationists who were trying to protect the marine environment. Against a Government who were prepared to impose a Viking settlement-style plan for sewage treatment which did not feature treatment in any way shape or form: just dumping raw untreated sewage through long sea outfalls.

Only solids which could not be pumped through a screen, such as condoms and tampons and other bio-nondegradables were removed, but that was all. This was called screening and relied purely on the action of sea and sunlight to kill off any dangerous bugs in the effluent and sewage sludge. Our group had proved, with the aid of the world's leading scientists, that this was a danger to our species and marine life which it would ultimately build up a microbiological time bomb for future generations, creating "super-bugs" with resistance to our immune systems - or anything else medicine could come up with.

We had no doubt that we were one hundred per cent right and we had no doubt that the Government was determined to forge ahead with this outdated, and now proven lethal practice.

Locally, the Yorkshire Water so-called sewage plant at Bridlington was hyped as a success. We knew this was not possible because it could not pass the EEC tests. A Yorkshire Water spokesman had said: "In the end our purpose is to make money. We cannot function without money."

Even though we continued our protest, the atmosphere in Scarborough was one of apprehension. Though we had great support from many local people, there was a feeling amongst some that our campaign was undermining the local tourist trade, so we were placed on a delicate threshold. However, the hard work and research involved had brought support from the U.S. and around the UK – and especially in the E.C. On July 17th 1987, the E.C. Environment Commission accepted the registration of the Sons' formal complaints that the ability of bacteria and viruses to survive in the sea for longer than previously believed. This made the Scarborough scheme not only obsolete before completion, but unable to comply with the existing bathing water directive, and that it would constitute a danger to human health and the marine environment.

At this time we were gaining support from UK politicians such as Helen Jackson, MP for Sheffield; Louise Ellman, leader of Lancashire County Council; and MEPs such as Ken Collins and Edward Macmillan-Scott. The latter on the ninth of June 1989 confirmed that our complaints to the EC, backed by the world's leading scientists, which demanded full treatment of all effluent through long sea outfalls.

In June 1987, we were more determined than ever to battle on for clean seas and beaches.

"We will fight them on the beaches," Freddie would often declare. "Aye," would say Captain Syd, "Confusion to our enemies."

This would be the clarion call to the Sons' meeting on Thursday nights at the Sons of Neptune hall to discuss our latest strategies to achieve clean seas.

The new BBC2 "Nature" programme on environmental matters, presented by Michael Buerk, whose professionalism as a broadcaster gave to complex issues the clarity of clean spring water – got us involved when we sent a press release discussing sewage outfalls.

This was the catalyst for our biggest and most audacious demonstration yet. On seeing Margaret Thatcher's performance of barefaced lies on the programme, we protested so loudly to "Nature" that it was obliged to correct the matter on the next edition of the programme.

Finally we had our legitimate weapon: Thatcher had lied on national TV, and we could prove it.

At this meeting the Sons' idea evolved to build a public toilet with a cistern sitting on the roof with its chain pull flush dangling down the outside. It would naturally be equipped with its own sewage outfall pipe and a large billboard on the side proclaiming "Thatcherloo proves Thatcher Lie"

The plan was to use it on the Thames at the upcoming North Sea Conference. The idea was to site the mock loo on a large inflatable craft. The loo was to be constructed on plywood with walls papered in a red brick style and its roof postered with the words "Britannia Waives the Rules"

The idea was to take the craft to London the following Thursday and sail it up the Thames from Tower Bridge to the Houses of Parliament. We only had six days to build and test it in the sea. Captain Syd's involvement was once again essential since he had experience of many types of sea craft - although nothing quite like this!

"It will have to be steady away on the Thames river, as the currents there are treacherous," he observed.

Freddie and I and Chris Found spent all day Saturday getting materials together for our new project – wood, glue, and nails – and through Captain Syd, we managed to get an inflatable raft, a large dinghy as used by the inshore rescue. Could we get this assembled and tested by Thursday? High pressure on all fronts. Over the weekend, the smell of glue and paint and the hammering of nails dominated the sons meeting Hall (Freddie's old barn). On the Sunday we were at Freddie's office, faxing and phoning the media about our planned protest. The "Nature" programme was our goal, as this would show our protest nationally and expose Mrs Thatcher's misrepresentations of the true facts, and the damage that this would do to our marine environment. We had the ammunition, it was now just a matter of hitting the right target.

We protested our complaint to the Nature programme, and demanded right of reply, armed with our scientific reports.

Early on the Monday morning Captain Syd, El Foundo, Freddie and I gave our craft a test in Scarborough Harbour, before the town stirred. Conditions were perfect for the test, and it went well. Captain Syd once again cautioned us: "This seems fine, but conditions on the Thames will be a lot different. The balance of the loo, and the steadiness of the craft will be all-important."

The tension and excitement mounted as Thursday approached. Freddie's law practice was running at high pressure with four offices and thirty odd staff. Planning the launch on the Thames was only possible with Freddie's office manager, Jennie, taking charge once again! As for the pressures of my chiropody surgery, my wife Ann and I were bursting at the seams – both working full-time at the practice and doing other clinics as well. As for the children Sue and

164

Liam, they were fully occupied with forthcoming exams.

We continued to credit our families for their support, but our main inspiration was Neptune: our daily dip in the sea, which gave us this inexplicable extra energy. After work on the Wednesday, Freddie and I called at a local garage to hire two large white vans to transport the Thatcherloo to London.

Barry the garage owner was quite petulant, and continued to shout like a hyena as we maneuvered the vehicles. One van contained the dinghy on which the loo would float, and the other the Thatcherloo itself.

When we left the garage, I turned to Fred and said: "He could do with a year at the Rank school of charm, but there's no way he could possibly be given entrance to any school of charm. You can't make a silk purse out of a sow's ear."

Thankfully, both constructions were just able to fit into the pair of vans. On my return home, my wife Ann was busily preparing for a trip to Paris with her friend, Jan. Later that evening the Sons made final plans for the expedition to London, including the timing of the launch into the Thames and the arrangements and confirmation to meet reporter Grant Mansfield and crew from the "Nature" programme, as well as confirming our schedule to the other media.

Plans to stay at my sister's house in Beckenham were scuppered as it would take too long to get into London on the morning from her house. Instead we decided to stay at the Thistle Tower Hotel – next to Tower Bridge. It was also right by St Katharine's Dock, for access to the river.

We hesitated over our plans as we had to be very careful. The Scarborough tourist season was at its zenith, and any negative publicity would be damaging to our cause. Already the Council were totally against us, and blamed us for any decline in the town's income.

Although we appeared to have the support of the majority of the town's people, the establishment glowered on our efforts. This in no way hindered our determination to win the battle at all costs.

So we set off for London early Wednesday morning.

I had already contacted Dave Webb, a Londoner through and through, how to get permission to sail a vessel up the Thames past the Houses of Parliament.

"Chas," he said – "Bleedin' 'ell, you have to get a permit from Lambeth Council, Southwark Council, Hammersmith Council – all the councils on the river, mate."

I mentioned this to Freddie – "No!" he exclaimed. "The element of surprise will have far more impact."

We arrived at the Thistle Tower around teatime. We did a reconnaissance tour, which was imperative for a successful mission. We parked the vans in the hotel car-park, and soon discovered that St Katharine's Dock was heavily secured, with big gates, guards, and membership required to even open a gate. How were we to float the Thatcherloo among some of the most expensively moored yachts in the UK, in a Thatcherite stronghold to boot?

We checked into the Thistle and met in the cocktail lounge for a discussion.

Fortunately, we had brought copies of the Professor Denness report on Marine Pollution, which we had published. A plan took shape. Captain Syd, Freddie and I would approach the security of the dock, asking to see the commodore of the yacht club, and present him with a copy of the Denness report.

Fortunately, as we did so, we found there was access to the dock via the hotel. We were unsure as we approached, of the attitude of the security guards.

"Good evening, this is Captain Syd MBE and Master Mariner. We are staying at the Thistle Hotel. Could we please speak to the commodore," I said.

"Sorry gents, he's gone home," came the reply. Very good - the security guard seemed very laid back.

"We will come back tomorrow, I said"

"Are you gents staying at the hotel?" he asked.

"Yes – we have a small craft we would like to sail tomorrow."

"You can have that berth over there," he said with a smile.

"Thank you very much," I said, slipping him a fiver, "have a drink on us."

We were delighted. We returned to the hotel ecstatic that we could put the Thatcherloo in a berth in St Katharine's dock.

"Wow! We've cracked it!"

We had dinner and few pints, and hit our nocturnal barges early.

As I went to sleep, I thought: "Is this really happening? Are we really going to sail up the Thames in our Thatcherloo to the Houses of Parliament?"

As I dozed off to sleep, I thought no dream could be more bizarre.

The next morning under cover of darkness we unloaded and assembled the Thatcherloo and carried it along ill-lit walkways until we found a pontoon from which to lower it into the Dock. We crept away as dawn broke but even in half light the Thatcherloo seemed to shout its arrival as if through a megaphone - or perhaps it was the million pound yachts shouting their resentment at this insulting intrusion in their hallowed waters!

It was now broad daylight. How would we get onto the Thames? We walked to see the lock-keeper, who was officious, although at this stage, fortunately, he had not seen the Thatcherloo.

"We have a craft and seek clearance to sail," we said.

"You have to have a permit with the clearance of the Commodore," he replied.

"We have an appointment with the Commodore," I declared.

He seemed to become more human. We went to the yacht house and found that the Commodore's penthouse office was five floors up in what seemed like a huge tower.

His secretary was nervously friendly and flirtatious.

"This is Captain Sydney Smith, MBE and Master Mariner," I said. "And this is Freddie Drabble," lawyer and leader of our group, the Sons of Neptune. And we have come to give the Commodore a copy of our report about protecting the marine environment (I decided against mentioning sewage in a yacht club).

"I am sure the Commodore will be delighted to receive it," she said, "I will see if he can spare time to see you now."

The receptionist reappeared and said, "The Commodore would be delighted to see you. Come through."

He seemed a jolly chap, content and proud of his position in life. We introduced the Captain and told him of his adventures, D-day landings etc. He was instantly impressed, and cast aside his copy of the Times, bidding his secretary to organise coffee and biscuits for us all.

He was enthralled by the Captain's seafaring stories as the tea and biscuits circulated.

Out of the corner of my eye, through the penthouse window, I spotted the Thatcherloo bobbing in the dock, relishing its hours of glory nestling up to millionaires' yachts! I immediately thought, "If the Commodore sees this, he'll have a heart attack."

Freddie proceeded to tell him about the work of the Sons and said he was not happy with the Government's policies on marine matters. A quizzical look emerged on the face of the Commodore.

"What are you going to do?" he asked.

Freddie explained we had a craft, and that we planned to demonstrate against government policy from the Thames.

Freddie, with his straightforward Yorkshire style explained it was here in the dock, led him to the window and pointed out the Thatcherloo.

"My God!" shouted the Commodore. His reaction was as

though the place had been silently bombed to smithereens since he last looked.

"Get that out of my lock immediately," he howled. "Now now now! Now!"

We were ushered out, and hurried across to the Thatcherloo, leaving the Commodore awash in a tidal wave of neurosis.

When we got back to the lock-keeper, we said we had to leave immediately. By now the lock-keeper, was joined by his attractive daughter. I jested with her, saying, "Who takes care of the lock-keeper's daughter, while the lock-keeper tends the lock?"

"You'd be lucky, mate," she says.

"So the commodore says we have to leave immediately," says Freddie.

"The tide's not here," said the lock-keeper. "Two hours."

"Aye" said the captain, "Tide waits for no man, but all men must wait for the tide."

Another layer of tension – would the Commodore allow us to wait that long or would he have us thrown out of the berth. At that moment, a message came from Grant Mansfield, of the "Nature" programme. He would like to an interview with us in an hour. This became a temporary distraction that eased the situation. Fred had prepared a statement for the media.

We went over the statement together, highlighting and emphasising the key points. By now, Freddie was used to TV and was ready for action.

Mansfield opened up his package with a piece to camera. "They call themselves the Sons of Neptune. Others call them eccentric. They are dedicated to cleaning up Britain's seas and beaches, and they say the Prime Minister is not."

Freddie rose to the occasion: "We are fighting for the right of every man, woman and child to swim in the sea without fear of disease or pollution. Our government must be prepared to put this

169

right."

I could tell that the interview was just superb, with Freddie oozing passion and sincerity. The crew agreed that they would film us sailing out of the dock in an hour. We had managed to get the Thatcherloo in the exit lock and were anxiously awaiting the level of the Thames to meet that of the water inside.

The lock-keeper's daughter was now left in charge. We persuaded her to let us out early so we could meet the requirements of the film crew.

"Here's ten quid for the lock fee," offered Freddie.

"You must be mad, going out there in that," she replied.

We descended into the good ship Thatcherloo, now floating out of sight of the Commodore in the lock, which was about a quarter of a mile square, and able to take much bigger craft..

Soon the sound of water flooding into the lock filled our ears and terrified us. We positioned ourselves at the back of Thatcherloo, quickly realised it was taking in water, and began to bail it out. Our outboard motor had not even started yet, and we had to rise another twelve feet yet to meet the Thames. El Foundo was in charge of the vans. Fred said, "El Foundo, you better nip up and get the vans sorted. We'll contact you at the hotel."

El Foundo needed no encouragement to leave the Thatcherloo, although a Son of Neptune and superb athlete, he could see that the frail craft would not take the weight of another man. So here we were in the Thatcherloo, taking on water as fast as we could pitch it out, ears full of noise, and not even on the river yet. Scary.

Suddenly there was silence. We were level with the River Thames and ready to go. The Captain started the outboard motor. The huge lock gates opened slowly. We and the Thatcherloo were swept out into the tidal paths of the River Thames. It was like doing a Strauss waltz as we span around under the Tower Bridge. Astounded by the speed of our travel in the currents, we were awestruck, bailing out the water, while the Captain coolly manned the outboard, which rapidly proved pretty ineffective. But the vessel was caught by the wind – the loo acting as a sail to push us upstream.

Unknown to us, the Security Services were expecting a terrorist attack from the river by mortar or bomb, from either Arabs or the IRA among others.

As we sailed under the Tower Bridge, past the Royal Yacht, two police launches set off towards us. By now, the Thatcherloo had begun to sail quite smoothly. The police launches surrounded us with megaphones blaring, "Stop this vessel at once," they demanded.

Freddie shouted back: "This is a free country, we are making a legitimate democratic protest against the pollution of this country's beaches by the Government. We have the right to protest to Parliament."

But the police seemed determined to stop us. "You must stop at once," they demanded.

I could see an armed unit on a smaller vessel on the other side of their launch, and for once in my life, fell speechless. The Captain remained coolly quiet, as though on a Sunday afternoon boating trip. The police launches threw ropes and began to tow us.

We had no alternative but to accept the situation as they towed us to Wapping jail. As we were pulled to the bank, a group of security men rushed to the Thatcherloo, and began a frantic search for weapons and explosives.

We were half way up the steps when some kind of alarm went off.

"There's something in there," said one of the security men. Suddenly, the Captain turned around and headed back towards the Thatcherloo, in a state of sudden urgency. "My medals are in there," he cried. The security men stepped back, and the captain fetched his array of medals. On entering the police station we were faced by three senior police officers.

"You first," said the front one to Freddie. "Empty all your pockets."

Keys and a wad of notes were emptied out and Freddie put them on the desk.

"Name and address please," said the policeman.

It was supplied.

"Take him to the cells."

"Next. You."

He pointed to the Captain, a man well into his eighties. I was really worried.

He walked slowly to the desk.

"Name?"

Captain Sydney Smith, Master Mariner.

I interrupted: "You can't arrest Captain Syd, he's an MBE, did twelve D-Day landings under fire and received the King's commendation for it by recommendation of Winston Churchill himself."

"Hold it", said the Super, "are you Irish?"

"Yes I am", I said.

"Well we are on high alert here, expecting attacks from Irish or Arab terrorists. It's a good job you didn't speak on the River, you'd have been shot."

"I'd have been the first Irishman shot defending England against its own disease-ridden pollution."

"Shut up. What's your name?"

His colleague was ringing Scarborough police station to check our identities.

"Charles White, I'm also known as Dr Rock. You can ask Superintendent Scutt at Scarborough police station about me, I'm playing squash with him next weekend."

"Have you got a lawyer?"

"Yes," I replied, "but you just locked him up."

"Take him to his cell."

It sounds funny, but what a terrible experience this was to be. A long corridor of prison cells, only silence. A green metal door with a peep hole in it was opened. I walked into this Victorian structure, high ceiling and a small metal sink. I felt really scared. The door slammed shut, then the rattling of keys, a loud click, and total silence.

I was only there for an hour and it seemed like forty years in the Bastille. My mind wandered through the tapestries of fear. But it was the loss of freedom that was the most terrifying of all.

Then, after an hour, the door opened – freedom, freedom, precious freedom – a state we take too much for granted. It was exhilarating to be out of captivity. I walked back up the corridor and worried more than ever about Captain Syd – how would he cope? There he was, standing by the desk, lighting a cigarillo and laughing with Freddie.

"I was worried about you Captain," I said.

He replied, "There was no need to Charles, I've not had so much fun in years. To think I've been through two world wars and never been in jail before,' he chuckled.

El Foundo the magnificent arrived to collect us and we walked two hundred yards to the nearest pub, the Hope & Anchor, raised our glasses with finest ale, and toasted:

"To the success of the Thatcherloo – cheers!"

Then Captain Syd added, "And more confusion to our enemies!"

Freddie said, "We better not let this story get to the Evening Nuisance (meaning the Scarborough Evening News)". They might have given us great support, but this would be used against us in Scarborough."

We all agreed. However, while we were in London Bryan and

Pam Dew and David Lazenby had been protesting in favour of the Sons on Scarborough beach, which took the spotlight off our activities, although in a phone call home to the family I revealed that we had been in jail. My wife Annie, who had called up from Paris just afterwards, had asked after me, and my son replied impishly, "He's in jail in London."

My wife laughed hysterically, thinking it was one of his jokes. It was nearly three months later that she found out.

A week later, the Thatcherloo and our protest was the lead story on "Nature". We had achieved our aims of attracting national publicity and exposing the false claims of our government. This was a powerful blow in the fight to outdate the dumping of sewage to the sea and boosted our resolve for the fight tremendously.

The Thatcherloo being sailed on the Thames to the Houses of Parliament as a protest against the continual dumping of raw untreated sewage off UK beaches. During the 'International Protection of the North Sea' conference, 1987. With security services on high alert we risked being 'mistaken' for terrorists. Arrests by the River Police followed.

Minister of Health and former Environmental Minister Virginia Bottomley, Listens as the Sons as they explain that their scientific report warns that the continues sea dumping of untreated toxic waste will increase the disease levels for future generations. 1990

Sons V. Environment Minister

When the Minister of the Environment, David Trippier came to Scarborough to open the Scalby Mills plant on the 12th of September 1991 we had our greatest impact. We had planned to set up a display stand with buckets of the recently collected sewage-sludge-contaminated sand - which was putrid – next to the sand we had collected before the Scalby Mills plant opened, and deposited in a bank safe.

Trippier, who was recently appointed by Margaret Thatcher, had proved himself as a decent political street fighter with a nice line in bons mots. He had previously been Minister for Inner Cities, where he had experienced some intense protests, especially with the activists against the Housing Action Trust, which was a scheme to turn around sink estates in UK inner cities. In his autobiography Trippier explains it was doomed because whichever estate was named as a target for action was automatically tainted. On one trip to Gipton House estate in Leeds, a mob was baying for his blood. Trippier recalls an enormous lady producing an equally large-size pair of knickers bearing the legend, "Knickers to you."

The Minister replied, "Yes Madam, as I've said throughout, I've come to take everything down."

A much more riotous experience came from a similar meeting in London's Tower Hamlets, where it required twelve policemen to protect him on the way in and twenty on the way out. BBC's Panorama filmed the event, and although visibly shaken, his wit proved more popular than his policies:

Panorama reporter: " What do you hope to get out of a meeting like this Minister?"

Trippier (shrugs): "What about the Victoria Cross?"

We were totally unaware of Trippier's experiences, but had heard of his reputation as a sharp cookie, so when setting up our protest we were quite amazed at the high level of security employed for the official opening of the Scarborough scheme. This included high riot barriers around the reception marquee and a flock of

177

security staff.

We had been let down by everyone who was supposed to be concerned about this, and major offenders were the local Labour politicians, who had a wonderful opportunity to oppose the Tories on this matter, but instead rolled over. The Fabian Society, the intellectual socialist group, came to Scarborough to debate the issue, then fell into line behind Thatcher's policies. When Barry Hampshire, a lifelong member of the Labour Party, former member of the local executive committee and supporter of the Sons, explained his position to Mavis Don, the local Labour Leader, he was given a public dressing-down in a petulant display. Mrs Don, who had been an excellent junior-school teacher, later seemed to develop a form of megalomania, and was eventually kicked out of local politics in what should have been an easy ward to win. Her attitude summed up that of the Council: "If we dilly-dally, the YWA will spend the money elsewhere, and then we will lose our clean beach status." Hampshire later observed: "I honestly don't think that these were inherently bad people – just that they had swallowed hook, line, and sinker the water authorities' line about going elsewhere, and that story had been confirmed by the paid officials of the Council."

Scarborough Council's Environmental Committee voted for the Scalby Mills Scheme to go ahead,

Councillor George McIntyre, a medical doctor, said: "Sewage disposal to the sea - ecologically, these proposals would cause no problems and could prove a positive benefit."

Environmental Health officer Roy Ayrton: "The sea is an extremely hostile environment for sewage bacteria. Sewage released well out to sea...a clean and simple operation."

The local councillors, who had vigorously supported the scheme, arrived at the event in two large coaches, as many people booed them. They were whisked into the marquee to be introduced to the Minister of the Environment. We realized that due to the intense security we would be unable to confront the Minister with our display and our usual appeal to the TV cameras. We would have to go for something more direct to get our message across.

Over a year before the outfall was opened we had, on Captain Syd's advice, taken samples of sand along the shore at the point where the planned outfall would go out to sea. When it started to function the sands were soon coated with horrible sludge, which had the colour and consistency of Marmite. Local marine scientists described it as "estuarial decay." The accepted theory was that the sea was a huge disinfectant tank. On analysis the sludge contained high numbers of dangerous bacteria and viruses, nail clippings, hair and more repulsive matter that came from toilets, abattoirs, hospitals, and factories.

The Sons were well prepared for this new major battle - in fact we had been preparing for years for the possibility that this dreadful event would take place. Captain Syd, and Freddie had anticipated that a huge that a grey coating of sewage sludge would cover the beach directly behind where the outfall projected out to sea from Scalby Mills. The sands were clean previously, like a mixture of sand and gold dust that tested free of pathogens. Freddie insisted we dig buckets of this and deposit it in his barn. Some were also lodged in his office vaults, as well as some in the local bank. The Captain knew because of his experience in dredging the shoreline that there would be no doubt that this natural sandy beach would be covered in sewage-contaminated black sludge. The Sons once again borrowed coffins from Bert Bernard, the local undertaker, and Freddie was anxious as he drove his Volvo estate around with two or three coffins protruding under the tailgate. "It doesn't look good for a solicitor to be seen moving coffins about," he quipped. We decorated the coffins with black plastic and white stickers indicating the diseases caused by sewage, then three days before the opening we dressed up as Victorian funeral directors and marched across the beach carrying the coffins, led by Captain Syd carrying a trident. The previous week-end we had bombarded the media with faxes and phone calls telling them that we were going to enact a spoof opening of the outfalll three days before the official opening.

The imagery made a great impact – we even got the front page of the Yorkshire Post, and the photo was used in a GCSE paper asking the question: What is this group protesting against? We had upstaged the YWA's plans by firing a media guided missile into their proposed launch, indicating what a disaster this would be. On the day of the official opening we all wore suits like professional businessmen. On the promenade we had two tables – one with the "gold dust" type sand and the other with buckets of the sewage-contaminated sludge which the sand had now become.

The YWA had blocked off the area with huge wire fences and had employed security men to march menacingly about with alsatian dogs. Later the security men remained in the background without the dogs and dressed in suits under instructions to keep the Sons at bay.

We knew that their plan was to keep the Minister away from us, so our idea was that Freddie, as leader of the Sons, would invade the marquee reception and persuade Mr Trippier to come out and have a look at our display and outfall protest, then I would pulverise him with my anti-outfall diatribe. I was hesitant, but our determination was at a peak. At the time it seemed most unlikely that the minister could be persuaded to come out, but amazingly, by the coolest of charm and his legal expertise in communication, Freddie brought him out, surrounded by the media, who followed them in procession.

Freddie described his entrance like this: "I walked in and the security guards looked surprised – I was number one unwelcome guest. Certainly the water authority regarded us as undesirable company. Our campaign had already traumatised both the local incompetent council and attendant sycophants, who were all here busy cooing round the Minister and generally sliming up.

"The security guards asked me what I was doing here, and I said I was here to see the Minister, which was completely true. They were surprised to say the least, and I walked straight in.

"This party for the sewage scheme was in a marquee tent – right next to the outfall pumping station. He was surrounded by the local sycophants and all the backers of the scheme from the council. When they saw me their coffees slopped into their saucers. I thought a couple of them were going to drop dead on the spot. I introduced myself to the Minister, who I knew was a QC

"You are a lawyer, aren't you? You would agree that there are two sides to every story? Why don't you come and see our side of the story of this scheme?"

Trippier was a strong and confident chap, and was unaware – it appeared to us – of all our work and research."

Sure enough, when Mr Trippier wandered out after Freddie, relaxed and casual, with tea and biscuit in hand, I leapt on him like a starving panther on a newborn lamb, much to the delight of the gathered media crews. I must explain that the National Rivers Authority was the shield to protect the population should the Water Companies overstep the mark, i.e. pollute the rivers or the sea, our experience was to see them as an impotent body, who were toothless against the water authorities and the government bodies. To mention them to us was really a red rag to a bull.

What follows is a transcript of an audio tape of the encounter. *(DT is David Trippier, FD is Freddie, and CW is Charles White.)*

DT: This is the job of the National Rivers Authority. Do they confirm what you say? Because they will prosecute the water company if they are not satisfied.

FD: Then I think they should do that immediately.

DT: But why is it that they are not doing it when they are employed by us to prosecute the water company if they are not satisifed. Just a minute. Why is that they are not agreeing with you – and they are scientists and you are not.

FD: I am asking you to prosecute them.

DT: You're asking the NRA to prosecute them. And when you talk to them why is it that they are not agreeing with what you are saying?

FD: You have powers under the Water Act to . . .

DT: Answer the question. You're not answering the question.

FD: I'll answer the question. I do not know why they are not prosecuting them.

DT: But you must know, because when you have gone to them and talked to them, and they have said we don't agree with your scientific analysis. They have prosecuted many water companies. They have prosecuted this one.

FD: I'll answer your question. They are not in a position to disagree because they have made the official statement that they have a count of 3,500 of the bacteria e coli – which can only exist in excreta – and they admitted a delay of 60 hours between taking the sample and counting. So you can take the 3,500 and multiply it by eight to get a count of twenty thousand.

DT: Well, I think this is all absolutely wonderful stuff, but I have to tell you that whether it is the National Rivers Authority or the drinking water inspectorate – who are not slow to prosecute in any event – if they are not satisfied that what you are saying is right, then nor am I. We set them up. And I am proud of the fact that we set them up. They are the police force. You are not. If they say that you are wrong, and they must be, because otherwise they would be prosecuting . . .

FD: They haven't said we are wrong. They haven't said we are wrong.

CW: The problem, minister, with respect, is that they expected our children to swim in raw untreated human sewage. The beach report by the Which? magazine independent scientists, proves that the bacteriological threshold and the virological thresholds have gone up since this obnoxious scheme which intensifies raw untreated human waste into our beautiful bay here. And as a Tory minister, you should be absolutely ashamed. This is a Tory town. This is historically the most tragic day for Scarborough because you are imposing an outdated disease-ridden scheme on our beautiful town. And that's scientific proof. And I as a swimmer, I have gone in there and got violently ill.

(Applause)

DT: As a swimmer, er, I would be entirely satisfied and convinced of what you say if I got confirmation from the NRA.

CW: But we have been to the world's leading scientists. We

had Professor Jay Grimes, who wrote the Congressional report, we have had Professor Bruce Denness who is a former Professor of Marine Science at Imperial College, London, and former Professor of Ocean Engineering at University of Newcastle upon Tyne: both totally condemning this scheme. We sent copies to the department, you and the government have completely ignored them.

DT: Just a minute . . .

CW: No "Just a minute", this is the reality minister. Don't be trying to give me a load of baloney, I'm used to that.

DT: I'm listening to a load of baloney from you, actually.

CW: You're not, you're listening to scientific fact backed up by the world's leading scientists.

DT: Well why is it that the scientists in the National Rivers Authority don't agree with you.

CW: Because minister, you in the department are putting the finger on them.

FD: No, I have just said they do agree, they have their own bacterial count which is conclusive.

DT: Well if I see a report to that effect...

FD: I will let you have that report.

DT . . . and that is the honest truth, this not baloney.

CW: Your department is very inefficient, minister, they should point out to you the dangers of bathing in raw untreated human sewage. This is 1991, this is no longer a Viking settlement. You are asking us to accept a Viking settlement solution to a twentieth century problem.

DT: I am not asking you to accept anything except a proper scientific . . .

CW: You are!

DT: Do you mind if I speak? I mean even in a democracy ministers are allowed to speak?

If I could make it clear that I am only going to be satisfied with the scientific findings of the National Rivers Authority. Not a group of people who are not qualified to actually judge as to whether the scientific basis of what they are saying is right or wrong.

CW: The scientific basis . . .

FD: We are non-political, I do my own lab work with my own hands. This is sewage sludge in front of you. Are you satisfied with a beach that was that [points to the golden sand] – and is now black sludge? You've asked me to answer your questions, will you now answer my question: are you satisfied with this? I've answered your questions will you answer mine?

DT: If the National Rivers Authority say that it is not satisfactory, then I am not satisfied.

FD: But you haven't answered my question: are you satisified with it?

DT: I don't know what it is. For goodness sake, it looks like a bucket to me with a lot of rubbish in it, How am I supposed to know what it is?

FD: Are you satisfied with it?

DT: What am I satisfied with? A bucket or what's in it?

[Trippier starts to walk off]

FD: Are you satisfied with black sludge? Are you satisfied with that?

DT: I don't know exactly where it's come from.

CW: Would you let your children swim in that minister?

[DT walks away faster]

DT: I don't think anyone could actually walk on that, let alone swim in it. It's a silly question.

CW: Well that's what you expect of us.

FD: You're saying you're satisfied with that.

DT: I have actually given you the courtesy of meeting with you, which you asked me to do.

CW: Very kind of you to come down.

DT: And I've given you a fair crack. If the National Rivers Authority confirm any part of what you are saying, I promise you I will take action.

FD: Right

DT: But I need that confirmation from them, otherwise it would be stupid. And it would have been silly to set up the organisation in the first place. And you should have the decency to recognise that we set up the NRA in the first place, to carry out that kind of work.

CW: But we have no evidence that they are protecting the environment, minister. There's no evidence that the NRA has any serious . . .

Trippier walks off.

The NRA , were supposed to protect the rivers and sea, but were of little use. They were rendered toothless by Government policy.

To get further inspiration for, and a break from, our battle for the environment we began to hike abroad, and on one of these adventures we flew to Girona, in Cataluna, Spain, with the intention of hiking from Nuria, in the Pyrenees, across to Mont Louis. It was a warm autumn afternoon in late October as we checked out the funicular railway which would take us to the starting point of our hike in the majesty of the mountains, the awesome spectacle of the valleys raising our spirits. We went back to the village and prepared for an early night – after we discovered a tapas bar and ordered large quantities of sangria tipico to help us caress the shores of inebriation. Planning an early start in the morning we hit the nocturnal barges, leaving the room shutters open as it was still warm. About 1 am I woke up freezing, and going across to close the wooden shutters I was astounded to see everything covered with snow. At breakfast we realised that the hike across the mountains was off, so we drove in the icy conditions to Mont Louis, intending to walk in the Spanish national park. We intended to drive south to escape the weather, and with my vestigial Spanish language ability I chose the town of St George de Flores, which sounded to me like a beautiful place. Wrong! The town was an industrial nightmare, with concrete factories and a smelting plant, and the hotel we chose for the night was Cockroach City. Next day we hiked across a couple of valleys and came to a vineyard, where we were entertained with wine and cheese in the warm Spanish sunshine. We went as far as Peniscola, the town where El Cid was filmed, which was in tourist garb, with dozens of souvenir shops decorated with dildos, marking the town's name. We walked on the beach where the final battle sequence of El Cid was shot, then turned back to look at the majestic castle, the sight of which was completely ruined by block of flats erected in front of it, like concrete blockhouses.

Freddie was horrified. He could not believe that they had built cheapo-cheapo flats in front of the superb castle. He spotted a tourist office at the end of the beach and marched in with an air of fury. Two pleasant young Spanish ladies greeted us with a charming "Buenos Dias", but were taken aback when Freddie burst into a diatribe against the buildings in front of the castle, completely oblivious to the fact that they couldn't understand more than a couple of words. With my feeble Spanish I pointed to the large poster of the castle and the concrete montrosity "Edifico malo" I said forcefully. The ladies gestured that it was not their fault, and Freddie wrote a note to the town's mayor. "Careful," said El Foundo, "You could wind up on the Judas Cradle or get the Heretic Fork treatment – both torture implements we had seen earlier in an exhibition about the Spanish Inquisition. El Foundo wandered on while Freddie and I spotted a replica of El Cid's sword in a jeweller's shop, and we decided to buy it for El Foundo and surprise him with it later.

Later that day we set out to drive to the seaside resort town of Sitges, on the way finding wonderful old Spanish inn, run by a lady speaking classical Castilian Spanish. She was a wonderful cook, so we stayed for lunch, absorbing more sangria, then set off in a totally inebriated state to head for Sitges. As we approached the town we gasped with amazement to see, apparently on top of the superb medieval church, the gigantic gorilla King Kong! As we went further into the town we were amazed to be confronted by further images of horror – vampires suspended over the street, Frankenstein standing at a corner. El Foundo gasped: "That blooming sangria was stronger than we thought!" Turning onto the seafront we saw the beach teeming with more horrific monsters – Godzillas,Tyrranosaurus Rex, mummies, and bats appearing to fly out of the trees. Eventually a large banner across the street explained it all. It wasn't the sangria which made it like driving into the supernatural, it was the Festival Internacional de Cinema Fantastique de Sitges – a horror-film festival!

Amused and disorientated, we decided to make the best of the situation, booking three rooms at an old-fashioned hotel facing the beach, and went straight into the sea for a refreshing swim. We returned to the hotel and realised from our fellow guests that the Spanish campasinos had been replaced by the greatest collection of pretentious posers ever gathered in one place. They were here to enter their mainly sub-moronic brain-damaged movies in the festival. The whole thing had converted the elegant resort into a plastic nightmare, a cross between Woolworths and Hammer Horror studios. However, the representatives of the horror-film industry were in their element.

We had a hike round the local hills, during which El Foundo left us to make a detour through a wild area of bush land, the kind of thing he loved to do, and this gave us chance to plan a surprise birthday presentation to him of the replica El Cid sword we had bought earlier. On his return I was deputed to take him around the town while the lads arranged a meal at a local restaurant at which the presentation would be made. El Foundo had quite an array of cuts and bruises suffered while battling through the thorns and cacti of the scrub land, and after he had a quick shower I persuaded him to go for a walk around the town – something he would never refuse to do. As we were exiting the hotel we were stopped by someone we had met earlier – a very attractive young lady whom we had privately nicknamed Heidi, but who was a Polish movie director. She stopped us and began to expound the plot of the film she was exhibiting at the festival —a horrific story, which I had to cut short as I needed to get El Foundo out of the way while a grateful local trader relieved himself of the magnificent (reproduction) sword of El Cid. So we set out to walk round the charming streets of Sitges, noticing at the end of one street the local town hall, with red carpet laid in front, with an armed police guard and quite a lot of activity. "Let's go over and see what's going on," I said. We approached confidently, and though I was dressed like someone who had had a traumatic experience with a kaleidoscope in my gaudy Hawaiian shirt, shorts, plimsolls and a loud baseball cap, we were saluted and ushered up the stairs and through the entrance just before a fleet of limos arrived behind us. A smartly dressed woman pronounced: "You are welcome", and noticing an array of media folk behind her, I said: "Thank you. I'm from the BBC" (I was doing a weekly programme for the Beeb at the time) and introduced El Foundo with his title of "The Magnificent". She was strangely impressed, and said how nice it was to have the BBC present for the festival. A tray full of glasses of champagne made its appearance, and we were introduced to the Spanish Minister of Tourism and other VIPs. Then a familiar figure was presented to us as being there to open the festival later, and I shook his hand trying to place him. My anxiety was to get El Foundo back to the hotel, so we thanked the charming lady for her hospitality and said we had to get off to be properly dressed for the evening. "So glad that you met Gerard Depardieu," she said as we left the building. "Gerard Depardieu . . . GERARD DEPARDIEU! The star of my favourite films "Jean de Florette" and "Manon des Sources"! The delirium set in as we rushed back to the hotel for the big surprise. The restaurant was booked for 7pm, and the waiter, who had been previously primed by Freddie, made a huge deal out of the presentation, fitting El Foundo with a bullfighter's cape as he raised the sword in triumph, a huge smile beamed on his face.

The Sons led a protest as Minister of the Environment David Trippier (Stock Broker), visited
Scarborough to open the long sea outfall, which was outdated and a blatant waste of public money, as
it continued to spew untreated sewage into the family bathing bays.

Poster from the Sons wander into the Horror Movie festival in Sitges after a long hike, expecting a refreshing dip in the sea only to find the beach covered in the most horrific horror movie monsters ever assembled.

The Sewage Sniffers

It was a surreal experience, giving rise to a bizarre situation.

After Yorkshire Water announced the cancellation of the Marine Drive/Castle Headland scheme in September 1984 little was heard from the company for most of the year. Because they had, under pressure from the Sons, costed two alternative schemes for Scalby Mills and Cowlam Hole we had assumed that they would be putting together an application for Cowlam. Instead it was announced, late in the year that Yorkshire Water were planning a sewage works at Scalby Mills!

The preposterous decision to build a sewage plant at Scalby Mills, smack dab in the middle of a residential area, adjoining a superb golf course, next to a delightful bay and excellent beach which was such an important asset to the town's tourist industry, was proof to us that those in charge of the town's welfare were guilty of dereliction of duty and a lack of plain common sense. We felt that generally they had neither conception nor realisation of the importance of the environment. To be a conservationist in the 1980s was like being a leper in ancient biblical times, and Freddie would often say at election times we would be better off with a bunch of baboons running the town. This may seem funny but to us it seemed like reality.

When the scheme got the green light David Lazenby, who vigorously supported the Sons and had worked with Professor Sydney Cross-Harland FRCS, a professor of botany and genetics, and also with scientists on the Farne Islands with marine and birdlife, made an urgent statement in a letter to the Scarborough Evening News

"It will be a mistake to proceed with the plant. The site which Yorkshire Water Services envisage as suitable for their purpose is, from this point of view, totally unacceptable. There will be the problem of smell, which will not be rectified by the addition of toxic chemicals. The inhalation of chlorine or ozone in the concentrations which would be required would be detrimental to the health of those living in the area and this would be unpreventable under certain weather conditions."

The water Authority and Scarborough's Environmental Health department, run by Chief Health Officer Roy Ayrton, assured us that this could not happen and implied once again that the Sons and their supporters were giving the town a bad name.

Freddie and I continued to run round the Marine Drive every morning before work, and go for our morning swim in the North Bay with Freddie's dog, Bo. Here we would discuss the latest events in the campaign. We had for some time been noticing a decline in the level of sea life in the rock pools, such as starfish, shrimps, mussels, cockles, crabs and seaweed. Fred had contacted Dr Pat Gowen, an environmental scientist for the EC and Friends of the Earth, who fully supported our campaign. He said: "I primarily got interested in pollution of our marine environment when I was at the University of East Anglia. I have been in various scientific jobs and I became aware that people were getting diseases when I studied marine biology. When I retired I decided to put my scientific knowledge to use in stopping this type of pollution which is a danger to human and marine life. The dumping of raw untreated sewage and other materials into the sea is very primitive and outdated and there are adequate methods of treatment which would destroy this dangerous material - you could utilize the sewage sludge from a proper sewage works to create valuable fertiliser to put on the land. There is no excuse now whatsoever for putting it into the sea or rivers and polluting the beaches which is endangering people's health and the whole of the marine environment."

Dr Gowen had taught us how to monitor sewage pollution by carrying out our own bacterial tests on the bathing waters, as we could no longer rely on the Water Authority or the Council for credible results.

We had noticed large vats of chemicals at the proposed new pumping station on the Marine Drive, but no-one would tell us what they were, and when we tried to get independent tests to find out what chemicals were being used laboratories turned us down, we guessed, because working with us could jeopardise their contracts with the local council.

Dr Gowen had taken some sewage samples back to his laboratory in Norfolk and, under microscopic examination found that the plates were completely blank, indicating that the YWA were desperately trying to treat the sewage with a variety of toxic chemicals in order to pass the EEC tests. "You would at least have expected to find small levels of bacteria in the samples," he said. We had noticed that Yorkshire Water's testing personnel had worn full-body protective suits as they took seawater samples – whereas we went in in our bathing trunks. Something funny was up – or not so funny in our case.

On a beautiful sunny day, with Scarborough's beaches packed, kids paddling and splashing in the sea or having donkey rides, eating ice cream or candyfloss, adults walking on the seashore, suddenly down the steps of the sea wall steps a huge monster-like creature, a cross between a Michelin Man and a Dalek, with a sampling jar grasped in a large rubber-clad hand. The apparition walks into the sea to take a scientific sample of the bathing water. Local photographer Bob Rewcroft on first seeing this scenario, said "I was furious as I had paid the Council to have Kermit the Frog and Mickey Mouse suits organised for people to have their photo taken, and at first I thought that this was competition moving into my patch." But if the Water Authority felt it essential to have people in full-body suits to take samples among little kiddies bathing in the sea - no wonder the independent samples that our group took yielded blank plates in the lab.

Our first perceptions were that, on the completion of the Scalby Mills pumping station, there was a lot of activity with large containers of chemicals being delivered to the station. Then a huge chimney stack was put up in the middle of the most important part of the North Bay, overlooking the stunning backdrop of the Castle headland. The worthy (and unworthy) citizens were in a dilemma about the effect a huge sewage plant, with matching chimney stack would have on their existence. The Sons were not too popular as they pointed out it would create emission problems – foul odours and chemical vapours, as well as thousands of gallons of various chemicals and raw untreated sewage going into the sea. Eventually we were informed that the Water Authority would be using peracetic acid to neutralise the odours and after taking scientific advice we objected vigorously to this. Later the YWA were forced to withdraw the use of the chemical.

Yorkshire Water, undeterred by scientific and media reports that the scheme was out-dated and would be a huge waste of public money, continued their plan. The Sons' major weapon was the use of the media in condemning the scheme, and we spent our weekends composing and sending out press releases to the media and contacting leading politicians, including MEPs representing the marine environment in Brussels. We decided to use demonstrations designed to ridicule the policies of the day on marine matters. Writing letters to the media was crucial, although we were aware that in some quarters we were a political taboo. The Yorkshire Post, however, did publish a supportive piece on our campaign, headlined "Dirty Work", on July15 1988 – even though Sir Giles Shaw, chairman of the Yorkshire Post board, was also on the board of Yorkshire Water.

While appreciating the political subtleties woven around our activities we tried to be apolitical but found it impossible. However our fight was on our own territory, and as we went in the sea daily we were aware of what was happening to the marine environment. BBC Radio York, our local radio station and their star reporter Nick Wood were 100% behind our campaign and did a professional job of reporting our exploits and scientific arguments.

Eventually our tenacity in bombarding the media was to yield results - our research was used by the Yorkshire Post in their campaign for clean Yorkshire beaches whilst on our own terra firma we were still being regarded as a nuisance.

Harry Meade of The Northern Echo who fully supported our efforts wrote in an article on Friday October 20th 1989 headlined "Turning the Tide of Seaside Pollution".

"One of Britain's most remarkable environmental campaigns - I would say the most remarkable - owes nothing to Friends of The Earth, Greenpeace, or any of the other big guns in the Environment Game. It is run by six people at Scarborough. Headed by a solicitor and a chiropodist the Sons of Neptune have highlighted what I am sure will become Britain's Public Health Issue No. 1. The issue is the state of the sea - and what it may be doing to us.

"A major step is a new directive by the European Commission

banning the discharge of raw sewage into the sea. Rendering virtually all Britain's coastal sewage plants obsolete overnight, this is a triumphant vindication of the Sons' call for full treatment of coastal sewage. Until very recently no other group took this stand. Meanwhile information fed by the Sons to the EC met an appreciative response."

"Since I first examined the Sons' campaign I have looked at the sea with different eyes. I share their view, gleaned from an eminent USA microbiologist, that the sea is not the disinfecting tank long claimed by the water industry, but a fertile breeding ground for all kind of nasties. If you're glad that cleaner seas are on the way don't thank the Brussels bureaucrats. Send a postcard to Scarborough's valiant Sons of Neptune."

By 1987 our media exposure continued to pay off when Tyne Tees Television produced a documentary called "A Suitable Case for Treatment". This was to be followed the next year by "The North Sea" series for BBC2, which was shown in Denmark, Norway, Germany and Holland. A six-part documentary presented by Susanna York was produced by BBC North-East. This series reinforced our threshold of credibility in Europe, especially in Brussels, resulting in German TV sending a crew to Scarborough to interview the Sons.

Meanwhile a BBC Radio 4 programme entitled "Costing the Earth" featured three members of The Sons who had campaigned regularly against the Scalby Mills plant. The programme was attacked by the local Chamber of Commerce as well as the Council, but it was not long before matters at the Scalby Mills plant became a sewage stench nightmare.

Sir Gordon Jones, Yorkshire Water's chairman, was hostile to our group. He was also chairman of the Water Companies Association, and his job was to guide the water industry through its privatisation. The Water Authority and the local Council assured the local population that there would be no problems, as new technology would remove any foul smells. However, their primary concern of the public at first was the effect on property values, the more serious concerns, such as those on their health, had not yet impacted upon them.

Barry Milner and wife, Pauline, of Scalby Mills Avenue (about 300 yards from the new vent stack), had recently retired and were just beginning to enjoy their new life. It was suddenly turned into a living nightmare, which continued endlessly. The once-fresh air became foul smelling and their neighbours' homes were also invaded by this horrible smell. More locals soon began to complain of illness and breathing problems. Housewives declared they could no longer put out washing as the stench tainted all clothing exposed to the air.

Don and Rebecca Green – who had moved from Leeds to their new bungalow, with magnificent views across the North Bay – had just retired to their heavenly new home when years of hellish tribulations started. They enjoyed looking forward to visits from their grandchildren, walks down to the beach, and playing in the sand. Now they could do neither, as the foul air affected the grandchildren's breathing and black sewage sludge turned a day trip to the beach into a health hazard.

Local businessman Don Robinson and his wife, Jean, have a superb home overlooking the bay. Mr. Robinson had, as a local councillor, vigorously supported the council and water authority and Government policy of raw sewage dumping into the sea. He had been previously persuaded by the Council Health Department to write a robust letter of support for the Castle Headland scheme. However as the Scalby Mills scheme progressed and the odours affected him and his family he was shocked and traumatised. His wife had absorbed the effects of the foul smells and chemicals and became ill, and over the course of our investigations I often met her and concerned myself about the state of her health.

Yorkshire Water and the local Council continued for a long time to imply that the source of the smells was mysterious – and the Council's supportive attitude continued. So Mr Robinson complained to Ofwat about the smells, and they agreed to investigate. There was quite a lot to look into. Not long after the opening, one resident had called the gas board thinking there was a gas leak. Other residents suffered breathing problems which saw them needing to take medicines such as Ventolin to breathe properly, and many suffered from nausea, sore throats and eyes, and general disorientation.

Don Robinson was later to say of Gordon Jones, Yorkshire Water "As a Hitler-type character, he did not give a damn about our suffering, he was just interested in his own huge salary and the YW shares on the Stock Exchange. If they tried to impose this system nowadays they would be sued for millions. The suffering of some of the people at Scalby Mills was terrible. The North Bay has been ruined by this plant."

The residents of the Scalby Mills area felt abandoned by the Council and were denigrated by the Water Authority, so the Sons were drawn more and more into their dreadful situation. Freddie Drabble realised that the residents would themselves have to take on the publicity side of the fight, as the Sons were being derided as troublemakers by the Council. So Scalby Mills and Scholes Park residents got organised, and formed a residents' association, electing Barry Milner their chairman. A man of quiet dignity, he was so infuriated by Yorkshire Water's negligence and lack of consideration for the residents suffering from the emissions from the plant that he hit out verbally at Yorkshire Water area manager Barry Truman, who had implied to the press that the residents were making false complaints.

Barry Milner said: "What Mr. Truman said is absolutely disgraceful, after all the promises from Yorkshire Water that there would be no problems with the plant, he should be ashamed of himself. He should come and live in the area and then he might realise the extent of the suffering his company has inflicted on the residents. Many people, some of whom do not live in the area, including golfers teeing off on the second hole of the North Cliff golf course will testify to foul smells coming from the vicinity of the plant since the new odour system has been installed."

Freddie and I would often visit Alan Robinson, a college lecturer and great supporter of the Sons, who lived on North Cliff Avenue overlooking the golf course, and suffered the toxic fumes and vapour emitted from the so-called treatment plant. He said: "You know there are some people in the area who think we are complaining to get compensation. They are the lucky ones. However, Yorkshire Water and Scarborough Council are using them as an excuse to put us down. It is true that because of climate conditions, some are not affected. However, this is the reality – toxic fumes are seriously affecting people. I frequently talk to the golfers who walk by my house every day, and only yesterday two golfers said to me "The smell is unbearable!" and I asked them if it was the first time they had experienced it, as the stink had being going on for a month. "Well they'll have to stop it, as it will ruin our golf club," he said. "No-one can continue to play golf in this atmosphere – what are Scarborough Council going to do about it?" Alan said: "I told them that the Council say there is no stink, no smells!" The golfer replied: "What madness to build a sewage plant next to a beautiful golf course and a magnificent beach." His golfing companion said: "We can't say much because the club leases the land from Scarborough Council, and they make the decisions. Why doesn't the club captain do something? He's afraid that some of the golf course will be sold off. He's resigned to ignoring the problem and having a few drinks in the club."

It was well known that Scarborough's population at this time was more apathetic than the average town, and an air of resigned apathy cocooned the majority of the townsfolk, together with a fearful reluctance to criticise any decision, no matter how ludicrous or disastrous it was for the well-being of the community. "The council can do what they like" was the general feeling.

Colonel George Talkington is putting up a great fight against this dangerous chemical and poisonous intrusion, even though his wife is seriously ill with cancer - the two daughters of his next-door neighbours have to sleep in friends' houses to get away from this terrible nightmare. Colonel Talkington's reward for his legitimate concern for his family and neighbours came in a threat of libel proceedings from the Council and their officers for daring to criticise them for their lack of concern for the people who were suffering. The letter was delivered, heartlessly, on Christmas Eve. The irony in all this is that we Council-tax payers will have to pay for them to prosecute us."

But the golfers kept quiet. When rumours were circulated that Scarborough Borough Council, who owned the course, intended to sell some of the land leased by the golf club they decided to go low-key over their complaints about the smell.

Scarborough Council continued to deny that there were any problems and the residents found little support from their local councillors Sulman and Willis, who were as in denial as Yorkshire Water over the source or even the existence of the smells.

Continuous headlines condemning the Scalby Mills plant were ignored by Scarborough Council and the YWA, and Don Robinson told the local press: "I think that Yorkshire Water don't give a damn for the residents, and I think they are making fools of the council." There was, however, to be a mysterious turnaround from Mr Robinson. Appointed president of Scalby Mills Residents Association, he came into conflict with association members who had wanted an independent body – Surrey University's Robens Institute - to investigate the terrible smells problem, and had offered to pay for this. Scarborough Council Chief Executive John Trebble would not agree, still denying that there had been a problem. He said: "Council environmental health officers have carried out more than 800 investigations at the site and have not detected any problems." He wanted a different company to make the investigations – Exeter-based W. S. Atkins Ltd. Robinson agreed with Trebble, with whom he had had a close relationship as a Borough councillor, and Trebble announced that the local authority and the association had jointly agreed to offer the contract to Atkins. This caused a row within the residents association, which denied that any agreement had been reached, culminating in Robinson offering to resign as president.

Barry Milner said: "Scarborough Borough Council has instructed its own enquiry and YWA have done the same. Neither of these enquiries has solved the problem. A fresh enquiry should be instigated for the residents so that it is a report to them as well as to the Council."

The residents association also expressed disappointment with Councillor Sulman. "The facts of the matter are that he has done very little to help the many residents who have suffered so much for so long. For nearly a year from when the chemical emissions started he was to continually deny that there were any noxious emissions at all until the truth of this was exposed by the Atkins report," said

Mr Milner, who had reports of local residents who had literally being chased out of their own gardens by foul gaseous smells. At one stage the plant itself was shut down as engineers fled from the building. It was now getting such bad publicity that Gordon Jones announced that he was to visit the plant. Don Robinson eagerly awaited him, but the chief discreetly ducked the meeting.

Mr Robinson, in his disappointment with Councillor Sulman, said in one memorable public confrontation: "Get off the fence Sulman". (Councillor Sulman belatedly tried to ingratiate himself with the residents by writing to the Evening News and offering sympathy, but it was too little too late, and at the next local election the residents exercised their democratic right by kicking him out of office. Later Councillor Sulman explained "We were only doing what our officers told us to do").

Barry Truman continued to downplay the serious situation by devious dialogue. He said: "We carried out odour sampling at the Government independent Warren Springs Laboratory. The results show no detectable smells, but we apologized to the residents for the smells they had reported." In fact no tests had been carried out at the site of the complaints.

So at this stage of events to smell or not to smell was the question! A ridiculous spectacle had emerged. Was it a rejected Laurel and Hardy script or a satire on an Ealing farce? An elegant tourist resort with God-given magnificent scenery locked in perplexing apathy due to unthinkable betrayal and bungling by those in charge. The Council and the YWA had spent £31 million on an outdated outfall which was condemned as a danger to human health and all forms of life before it was even built. And for this criminal waste of public money the public now had a so-called treatment plant, which was producing highly toxic and possibly carcinogenic vapours and billowing them out amongst the local populace.

This was an exercise in self-destruction of our own species and proof that democracy can allow us to make fools of ourselves without interference. At this stage Freddie Drabble, leader of the Sons, was consulted by the residents and was able to come to the rescue in this horrendous bureaucratic problem.

It was early on a May morning - 6.30am, unusually cold with unexpected snow showers. A small group of worthy local citizens had gathered together to perform a major coup. For over a year the residents of Scholes Park had endured a major assault on their existence. Now the tenacity and determination of Freddie Drabble came to the fore. He had contacted the leading firm in the detection of toxic gases, Chemex, and arranged for an expert to come to Scarborough and secretly take samples of the emissions from the stack. The expert was, luckily, a very tall man and because our ladders were about 4 ft shorter than the stack he had to precariously cling to the edge of the stack with one hand and lower the test tubes into it with the other. Other members of the group crept around the manicured gardens of neighbours, placing bamboo canes with further test-tubes and markers attached. The tests proved that emissions were highly toxic and well over the legal limits. It was a morale booster to the campaign, and backed up our convictions.

The YWA were still experimenting with potentially lethal forms of sterilisation, using a cocktail of toxic chemicals in a desperate effort to quell the foul and dangerous gases that pervaded the area. The purpose of having an up-to-date clean beach and sea act as imposed by EEC laws, was to do just that, to have clean seas and clean beaches - but now seemed to be at the cost of poisoned air. However this point was totally missed by the YWA and was not even acknowledged by local bodies due to the distractions of local government policies and the pressure of Stock Exchange privatization of the water industry. The Sons of Neptune were adamant that the plant, built underneath the North Bay miniature railway and the homes of the residents of Scholes Park was a) in the wrong place and b) unfit for its purpose, as the dumping of raw untreated sewage was not a treatment, and was against EC directives. Screening out solids left the pathogenic bacteria and viruses which could survive in sea-bathing waters..

The foul stench continued to give a great deal of serious concern to householders in the area. Not all homes were affected, due to either wind conditions or geographical alignment to the stack and vents from the plant, and those who were not affected were encouraged by those who supported the system to accuse others of hysteria, devaluing property in the area, and trying to seek compensation, in addition to "giving the area a bad name".

However, the general manager of Yorkshire Water, John Taylor, claimed, in an article in the Yorkshire Post, that the proposed outfall was really conservation.

Our campaign and demonstrations were stepped up. When Sir Gordon announced that the scheme would go ahead willy nilly, we placed a bath containing a skeleton on Scarborough's South Bay beach, a lampoon of the YWA chief, labelling it "Sir Gordon Bones". Such was the pressure and adverse media coverage that Sir Gordon then took the step of banning the media from all Yorkshire Water meetings, including shareholders meetings.

Accordingly, when Freddie arrived at the Sheffield for the Company's AGM, Sir Gordon tried to evade him but Freddie cornered him on the front steps of the Town Hall and, pointing to the statue of fallen heroes of the First World War in the Square below, asked him if he had noticed it.

"What has that got to do with me?" replied Jones.

Freddie pointed to the memorial. "Those men died so that we could have freedom of speech and yet you will not allow the press to come into your meetings to hear the disastrous consequences of your policies to our marine environment." We had ensured that the media were there to cover the event, and Jones was eventually forced to observe the democratic process.

The Sons of Neptune had prepared their own independent report, approaching the Robens Institute who were highly respected in this field. The conclusions of the Robens Institute included:

'The microbial analysis carried out for the reports published by WS Atkins and Yorkshire Water is far from comprehensive and, as has been pointed out by WS Atkins, cannot be compared because each group used different sampling methods and sample times.

"The WS Atkins and Yorkshire Water reports do not consider the potential for the transmission of pathogens by aerosols impacting on surfaces.Yorkshire Water measured coliform levels ranging from 0-150cfu/1001 (equivalent to 0-1500cfu/m^3) at the exhaust stack; no other samples were taken. WS Atkins sampled a few points downwind of the site and isolated low levels of coliform organisms. Neither study recorded the species of the bacteria."

Scores of people were flocking to Freddie's legal offices. He was already writing to MPs such as Helen Jackson, of Sheffield, Conservative MP John Gummer and European Commissioners such as Mr K. Kraemer and Carlo Ripa di Meana. The Sons also received another letter of support from Prince Charles.

Not surprisingly the Yorkshire Water staff had not a clue what they were doing with the various chemicals, and we learned that Sir Gordon Jones had another job - as chairman of the chemical company Hickson, the firm experimenting with the plant at Scarborough. (It would not be long before Gordon Jones's chemical firm would be responsible for the infamous explosion at the Hickson plant at Castleford in 1992. The enormous blast killed five and injured more than 200).

Yorkshire Water announced that they would prove that the foul stench and toxic vapours did not emanate from the stack. The Blame was laid on a pig farm a few miles up the coast, and the spreading of pig slurry. Billboards were erected declaring "Sewage Sniffers Paid £5 an hour". A portable testing facility was erected, in which was placed two contraptions that looked like rejects from a Dr. Who set - bulbous tanks with protruding face-masks. Residents were invited to come and sniff the liquid which was contained in these vessels. This was raw, untreated sewage said to have been treated at the plant, and by sniffing this at £5 per head per hour; the YWA hoped that public would be convinced that the sewage did not smell. They became known as the 'Sewage Sniffers'.

Freddie Drabble commented: "If Yorkshire Water do not know themselves what sewage smells like the Chairman of the Board should be sacked."

Unfortunately for Yorkshire Water the public interest in sniffing sewage was not as they had hoped and most residents boycotted the tests. Yorkshire Water was forced to enlist help with their testing from Scarborough Council staff and from Babcock Water Engineering, in Malton.

Eventually some of the Residents Association decided to lend a hand, desperate for a solution to the foul odours. Barry Milner, of the Residen's Association felt that it was his duty, along with his wife, Pat, to try this out. This caused a split in the association, as it looked to many as though they had betrayed the campaign, and there was a shake-up in the hierarchy.

The new Residents Association chairman, George Mark, condemned his four colleagues for getting themselves involved. "When I discovered what was going on I was horrified, absolutely gobsmacked, but the four committee members declared that they had done nothing wrong." They said: "Scalby Mills residents want the smell problem clearing up and we want to help any way we can. We have been paid for doing a job of work, if we had not taken the money we would have been doing Yorkshire Water a favour and they needed residents to join the sniffing panel." This was, of course, a huge con by the YWA designed to demean the dignity of the residents who had complained and to distract them from the main problem. In the words of Evening News correspondent Dave Lazenby: "The emissions constitute a hazard to human health . . . carcinogenic chemicals are polluting the atmosphere over the residential area of Scalby".

Barry Milner later declared "Yes it was a huge con. But what could we do – we were desperate for a solution, and the YWA were the only ones responsible."

Freddie and myself arrived at Rocks Lane to update our information about the Scalby Mills Plant. As we walked to the cliff edge the scenic backdrop was simply magnificent. It was a clear view right over to Flamborough Head, with the glistening white cliffs at Bempton, changing with the light to a silver streak across the coastline. The Castle headland veered up like a huge wedding cake between the two bays topped by the majestic castle. The landscape undulated like a huge carpet of green, whilst clouds like huge cathedrals glided above and beyond us. This was indeed a beautiful evening and such an atmosphere encouraged what we felt was an indestructible determination to stop the madness that was being imposed on the town..

But the groundswell of discontent was huge. The letters page of the local paper was constantly full of the issue. Tourists wrote in to complain about the pollution, and how they had been horrified to see their paddling children suddenly surrounded by sewage. There were even reports of dogs falling seriously ill after going in the sea – and there were we, going in in our trunks! Well, not any more! Black sewage sludge began to build up on the beach, causing patches which looked like small oil slicks, but smelled much worse. The authorities of course claimed this was perfectly normal, and had been there all along.

For years the problem at Scalby Mills continued to make headlines in the local and national media, and between 1991 and 1994 Yorkshire Water insisted that there were no problems at the plant. The Sons were under more pressure than ever since David Trippier, Minister of State for the Environment, officially opened the Scalby Mills sewerage scheme in 1991. We were now fighting on three fronts; 1) to stop pollution going into our bays; 2) to stop the build-up of contaminated sludge on our beaches; and 3) most urgently to stop toxic fumes which were affecting the health of at least 110 families in the Scalby Mills area.

We had one minor victory, however. Our continuous objections to the EEC, the National Rivers Authority, and Ofwat about the use of peracetic acid forced the YWA to discontinue the use of this toxic chemical – although they continued to insist that it was safe to use in the sea.

We had long since lost faith in local government as we found them totally useless on issues concerning clean air and the environment. Now we observed ordinary people go through a living hell, betrayed by elected members who lacked the moral strength to demand the best for their community.

The Sons of Neptune campaign received confirmation in February 1992 from EEC environmental chief Carlo Ripa di Meana confirming that the Sons' complaints about the Scarborough raw sewage scheme had been registered within the scope of the directive on bathing water and that the Commission had given formal notice to the UK government that these observations on the pollution associated with Scarborough's long sea outfall would be submitted. A letter from MEP Edward McMillan-Scott to us confirmed this. We were also invited by the House of Commons Environment committee to contribute to the memorandum of evidence on beach pollution.

The fact that several workmen employed at the plant had resigned claiming ill health, contributed to a rapidly-growing paranoid atmosphere. Freddie Drabble said:

"At that particular point not only did we have our own concerns about these foul stenches which emitted from the stack but the effects of the powerful chemicals they had to use to try and kill this problem all created a carcinogenic and toxic atmosphere. By this time my concerns as a solicitor were so great that the number of families who instructed me to take action was well over one hundred. I had a terrible weight of work, I had to take statements from all these families, I had to take instructions in each case I had to ask how it affected them and their breathing, their lungs, how they could not sleep at night, how they had to keep their windows shut, how their kids were so asthmatic they had to go elsewhere to friend's houses who were not near the stack. How the gaseous fumes were rolling around like balls of toxic gas as they were heavier than air. How people on the golf course were hit by one of these things rolling around from place to place, as a ball of toxic gas would hit them halfway up the golf course and they were almost knocked flying. How people had to shut their doors when these balls of gas were floating about.

"It terrified people in the area like the Jaws film. Still, after all this, Scarborough council denied the existence of any problems in spite of the complaints and the publicity. They sent their officers, who said they could not smell anything, and denied its very existence. They blamed it on the Sons of Neptune's scaremongering, pigswill from nearby farms, muck spread on the land, even though it was harvest time (when you would hardly spread muck) They blamed it on smells from Jackson's Bay even though there had never been complaints of smells from Jacksons Bay previous to the building of the outfall.

"Eventually intense public pressure forced the Council to at last take action against YW and issue a summons to stop this stench. It did lead to a court case and in November 1992 the YW were fined

£12,000, but of course they had to compensate the people, and it only came through my firm. My firm recovered the compensation for the people, it never came from anyone else. We had to fight YW to get the compensation and in the end we got it because we were not prepared to let them get away with it. That was not all, I sought leading Counsel's opinion in London to get an injunction against the YW, to seal the stack and stop the emissions."

"It was one thing getting the compensation, but another matter altogether stopping their poisonous gases from going out of the stack. Whilst Counsel admitted that we had a good case to get an injunction, the difficulty was that YW could appeal. They had the money to keep going in court, we simply could not afford to launch injunction proceedings in the high court because of the high costs. The YW had our money and they could use it against us.

However the increasing media pressure, and because there were now so many cases running against the YW, it forced them to look at their position again and they had to move the plant to another location. We had told them not to build it there, and they should never have built it there in the first place – it was too close to people's homes and property - and to actually site the vent stack just at road level below people's houses within about 100 yards of someone's front door was lunacy. That, together with the fact that we have a sea breeze that is generally southeasterly, and usually just after lunch it blows directly into the front doors of these homes, taking that stench through all the front doors of the people in the wind direction. What does this say about the engineers who can put a vent stack from the biggest raw untreated sewage plant on the east coast and let these chemicals out 100 yards from people's homes? It is unbelievable and we were the only ones that fought to stop it, to actually save people's lives.

"We were prepared to fight against those who supported a scheme which imposed toxic fumes and carcinogenic chemicals on the citizens and their children in order to retain their own selfish interests, even though it betrayed the people and their environment."

The North Cliff Golf Course remains one of the most magnificent courses in the North of England.

Our next jape took place at the other side of town, at the South Cliff Golf Club, with its majestic panoramic views across Scarborough's scenic South Bay. Paul Ridley, Freddie and Chris Found were all school pals, with an air of rivalry still existing between them. As Paul's 50th birthday approached all energy was diverted to another practical joke.

Plan A was to get him onto the golf course early in the morning, entice him into the woods to have breakfast with a bunch of tramps.

Plan B was to make him believe he had got a hole in one at South Cliff Golf Club.

Our main objective - the success of plan B - was thought unlikely without the distraction of plan A.

Paul was a very successful accountant and businessman. He had had great success in the US and was now running a very prosperous business in Scarborough and York.

I thought to myself this is an impossible task, Paul is too sharp to fall for this. The morning of Paul's birthday arrived which started with a game of golf at 7am. Chris Coole had bought a new set of golf balls as part of his birthday treat and had given a similar set of balls to Chris Found. The trap was to be staged on the third hole facing seawards near Filey Road, where Paul would hit the ball uphill to an area surrounded by trees and which was not visible from the tee. Chris Found was hiding in the trees hoping and praying that Paul would get near the green. Chris Coole would distract Paul for a few seconds after he had hit the shot, and El Foundo would rush out and put a similar ball into the hole, removing Paul's ball from the green. I thought that this would fail, Paul was a sharp cat.

However, much to our amazement we pulled it off. As Paul approached the edge of the green he looked puzzled.

"Where is your ball?" enquired Chris.

"I thought it might have been on the green."

"No chance," said Chris

Then another member of the group approached the flag and shouted: "There's a ball in the hole!" Paul rushed over and exclaimed "Its in the hole - bloody marvellous! I can't believe it!"

Chris said "You are kidding! A hole in one and on your birthday -unbelievable!" Paul was just smiling and punching the air. He had fallen for it completely.

Meanwhile the Sons with our back-up plan were dressed and heavily made up as tramps, Having a fry-up breakfast in the woods empty bottles of booze left around the campfire, dead pheasants left around the trees. As they approached the 14th hole, the tramps rushed forward much to the dismay of the other golfers. Paul sighed with disappointment as he was approached by these rag-bag vagrants. He seemed to implode with frustration. When he realized it was actually the Sons pulling a jape on him he said: "You b----- -s!" then came and had a breakfast of a fry-up and champagne with various toasts.

If Paul had suspected a prank then he would belive it was the Sons dressed up as tramps lurking in the woods and was in any case preoccupied with pride at his amazing hole in one! The following Saturday Paul had organised his birthday banquet at the Royal Hotel and introduced his mum to the guests. She had been a single figure handicapper and had proudly showed off her own hole in one medal. That her son should have achieved the same in the week before his birthday was an added bonus of delight. Paul had received the hero's welcome in the Clubhouse and bought drinks all round as is the custom on such happy occasions! Imagine the shock when Chris Found wound up a congratulatory speech with words :- "but sorry about the hole in one Paul. Here's your ball. It landed ten yards short!"

But only months later came sweet revenge! The Sons were led into a trap big time! Paul and Chris Coole were well respected chartered accountants and company business took them abroad from time to time. After returning from France on such a trip it seemed to the rest of us no more than typical act of generosity that they would wish to share with us some quality wines they had been given by grateful clients. El Foundo was proud of his knowledge of wine and had become a member of the Sunday Times Wine

Club and was apt to burst into diatribes about various vineyards. He once held out a bunch of grapes declaring they were sacred as he'd just brought them back from Montrachet!

The setting for this generous invitation was to be Paul's splendid house overlooking the South Cliff Golf Course. On arrival we were not only greeted by our hosts Paul and Chris but as welcoming were the sight of about a dozen bottles expensive - looking bottles of wine. All were wrapped in white linen serviettes which we first assumed were to assure pristine service. We were perhaps partly right but we were soon to be informed that the labels were actually concealed as our hosts felt it would add much to the occasion if their guests were to taste each wine and then write down the region of France it had come from. Naturally the shape of the bottles gave clues to some. There was much frantic scribbling on the test sheets provided and much swirling of each wine backwards and forwards on the tastebuds. When most of the sheets had been completed one of the guests - Pete Emms, a beer-loving rugby player, came up with a guess which on the face of it might have been seen as an insult to our hosts. That guess emanating from the top of about the last sample was that it tasted 'like out of a Boots Kit' (also known as Boots Plonk) - which he promptly wrote down on his test sheet. When all the tastings were completed our hosts collected all the test sheets and we were told that the results would be announced after supper. The look of triumphal glee which greeted us - suggested there were some surprises to come! We were wrong - there was only one surprise - It was **all** from a Boots Kit! Pete Emms was the unlikely winner. The Sons had all been duped! They had got away with it by serving it at different temperatures it seems. Suggestion had also played a big part!

Paul had avenged the hole in one scam. Or so we thought! A few months later Freddie was shocked to hear that Paul was in a very serious condition and had been admitted to the local private hospital suffering from concussion which had led to amnesia. His wife was away at the time and he had been playing snooker with his son and somehow had been struck on the forehead by the ball. Whilst shocked at the time - the concussion was delayed and had come on later in the day during a round of golf with Chris Coole when the state of amnesia was such that he could not remember who he was playing golf with! Chris got him into hospital and later informed his son and that was when the accident with the snooker ball came to light. After several hospital visits by concerned friends over at least a week, including a third visit from Freddie in his solicitor capacity to see whether he would be able to execute a Power of Attorney, he had sat up in bed but dealt with all conversations as if he was talking to complete strangers! We were all left in no doubt that he was suffering from chronic amnesia. The reality was very different! Eventually a call came from Chris that we all had been taken in again! Paul was merely in hospital for a minor operation!

SCARBOROUGH
Evening News

Over 50,000 readers every night **THURSDAY 20 FEBRUARY 1992** 25p Tel: Scarborough (0723)

In YOUR 32-page News

Royal Hotel's glory days – page 7

Classy way to keep fit – page 1

THE SNIFFERS!

People paid in sewage smell tests

A PROTEST group chairman has resigned in disgust after members of his committee were paid £5 an hour to sniff sewage smells in controversial Yorkshire Water tests.

George Mark has condemned his four colleagues for taking money from the water company.

But they insist they are working for the good of their community in a bid to banish the unpleasant smells which plagued the Scalby Mills area of town last summer.

The Scalby Mills Area Residents' Association has criticised Yorkshire Water over smell problems caused by the new long-sea sewage outfall.

But Mr Mark says that — having taken the water company's

EXCLUSIVE by ANDREW NORFOLK

cash — the group will no longer be able to hold an independent position.

"When I discovered what was going on I was horrified, absolutely gobsmacked," he said.

Mr Mark described walking into the sewage plant and finding four of his committee members, sitting in

a semi-circle sniffing into funnels with pipes leading to a central machine.

"This is a paid operation. We should not be in the business of directly assisting Yorkshire Water. If they have a problem it's up to them to sort it out.

"I had told the committee I was planning to resign anyway, but this

LEFT: A Yorkshire Water employee brings in the samples to be sniffed. CENTRE: Residents' Association secretary Pat Milner and husband Barry, and RIGHT, members Christine Rush and Trevor Adams arrive for the smell tests.

is the final straw."

But the four committee members — association secretary Pat Milner, her husband Barry, treasurer Christine Rush and Trevor Adams — say they have done nothing wrong.

Mrs Milner said: "Scalby Mills residents want the smell problem clearing up and we want to help in any way we can.

"We have been paid for doing a job of work. If we had not taken

money we would have been doing Yorkshire Water a favour. As it is, we remain independent from them and they understand that."

Mrs Milner said Yorkshire Water contacted her, looking for residents in the area to join the sniffing panel. The four committee members only joined in because they could not find enough volunteers.

Yorkshire Water say the tests —

Turn to page 2

THE director of Scarborough's St Catherine's Hospice is to meet Prime Minister John Major at Downing Street.

Geoff Bishop will meet Mr Major at a reception to launch a new national Hospice Council next Thursday.

Mr Bishop has been selected to represent the Yorkshire Health Region on behalf of hospices and similar care centres in the region.

The new council will represent hospices and care units.

It will deal with all matters affecting hospices, including Government funding, NHS referrals and standards of care.

Mr Bishop said he felt very privileged and excited about the invitation.

Post Office's public pledge

THE Post Office today unveiled a customer charter to improve its service to the public.

Staff will wear name badges, complaints will be dealt with in 10 working days and waiting times at post offices will be published to show how they compare with target times.

Yorkshire Water had built a sewerage plant at the edge of Scarborough's magnificent North Bay, beside a superb golf course, which produced foul smells, chemical odours, and poisonous gases – to the anger of residents. YW continued to deny that there were any smells and set up a ludicrous system to prove this.

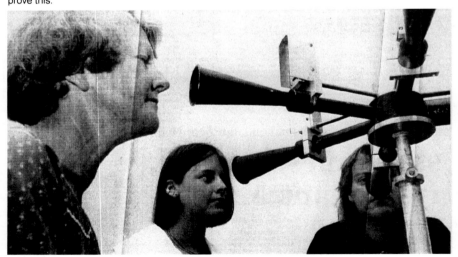

The Sons v. Dracula

The very survival of the human species depends upon the maintenance of an ocean clean and alive, spreading all around the world. The ocean is our planet's life belt

– Jacques Cousteau

It was Christmas morning and the Sons of Neptune were on their way to the south bay for their usual dip. A cold frosty morning was not only boosted by the Christmas spirit but also by a glimmer of sunshine through the grey clouds. As usual we parked at the Spa slipway and were not very pleased when we discovered that the tide was nearly half a mile out. That meant a run across the beach with a cold wind peppered with insalubrious icy particles.

Freddy's brother in law, Cameron, had just arrived from Bondi beach which was literally 100 degrees warmer than here. The night before, having consumed a degree of alcohol with us, he had volunteered to join us at the appointed time of 10a.m. We waited for ten minutes, then, prompted by the chill factor, started to dash across the beach toward the freezing sea. Just then Freddy shouted "Cameron has arrived we will have to wait for him!". By the time he had got to the waves my legs seemed to be made of painful steel, the initial invigorating levels of cheer had dropped as the waves crashed on our bodies. The run back to Freddy's Land-Rover seemed endless, but the thought of whiskey and warm clothes kept us going. Suddenly we saw the BBC Radio York's outside-broadcast jeep driving towards us, reporter Nick Wood waving us down for an interview. I shouted at him from my numb body "Not a bloody interview now, wait till we change, we are all in a frigid state thanks to Cameron here who has just flown in from Bondi Beach"

Radio York had given our campaign fantastic coverage. Our policy was to make Scarborough as attractive as possible even in the depths of winter. "Ok," he said, "I will wait here, this will make a good story for the audience in their warm comfortable homes." We grabbed our towels and began to feel the first signs of life returning as we quickly dressed. Freddy as usual had brought a bottle of the finest malt whiskey "A toast to the Sons and confusion to our enemies and especially to Cameron who has braved the glacial sea", he declared. By now several people had gathered along the walls of the spa, either giggling hysterically or bewildered by the whole event. "Look, Nick is shouting frantically, I think he is stuck. If he doesn't move the tide will get him" Freddy says "Let's go - we had better help him out". When we got there we pushed frantically and eventually the Jeep dragged itself out of the shifting sand, in which, in another half hour, it would have been submerged. We did the interview, then drove seven miles to Staintondale to our favourite pub, the Shepherds Arms.

The Shepherd's Arms was a delightful pub near Ravenscar overlooking the stunning Staintondale and North Sea. The Sons would often walk or cycle there on our Thursday evening outings to enjoy its amazing setting. We would meet every Thursday either in the late afternoon or later depending on the route or length of the hike. Various routes between Scarborough and Robin Hood's Bay, if not along the old disused Whitby railway line then often along the cliffs, depending on which of our favourite pubs - the Shepherd's Arms, the Hayburn Wyke, or the Dolphin or the Bay at Robin Hood's Bay –was to be our destination. These events, in such a marvellous environment, always elated us, along with our swimming, with a sense of being fully alive.

The dramatic backdrop overlooking Beast Cliff gives the impression that it was still a Jurassic park. For decades we enjoyed the splendour of this coast which became part of our psyche. The views from Ravenscar to Robin Hood's Bay are stunning, together with the constant ever-changing cloud structure, and sea-states are constantly fascinating. The dramas of life, existence, and evolution, have been played out on this land since time began. It is known as the Dinosaur Coast, footprints of dinosaurs are still visible and the remains of prehistoric creatures have been found on a regular basis. Along the beaches, ammonites are easily found embedded in the rocks and towards Whitby jet abounds, a much-prized precious stone. The cliffs themselves continue to reveal fossils of marine lizards and a variety of prehistoric reptiles. The atmosphere here and the huge fissures in the massive rock-face could mislead you into the belief that you are the only person to have walked there since prehistoric times.

That is not so of course, and you will be amazed to find out that on the cliffs overlooking Ravenscar and Robin Hood's Bay stood the first and largest chemical factory in the country. In the 18th century a valuable mineral was hacked out from a stratum of the cliffs in this area. This mineral was converted by various processes into a very valuable chemical, called alum. One of these processes involved ammonia, which led to hundreds of ships carrying human urine from the city of London, landing their cargo in Robin Hoods Bay. The ships were built with flat bottoms so they could rest on the rocky plateau of the beach until the urine was unloaded. The ammonia contained in the urine helped to convert the mined mineral into alum, which was used to enhance the colours in clothing used by the fashionable rich. The heightening of these colours in the dyeing process indicated to society that the wearers of these apparels were upper-class. This gave rise to the phrase 'taking the piss'.

On many occasions we would hike down the cliffs from Ravenscar to Hayburn Wyke. Often when a sea fret occurred, it would reach the same height as the cliffs, with the land on one side and a huge white vastness on the seaward side, you could easily get the impression that you were walking on clouds.

During the days when steam trains were a regular sight on the route between Whitby and Scarborough, the hotel at Hayburn Wyke was an important stop for both locals and visitors. However in earlier times these cliffs had been a haunt of pirates smuggling their contraband. This gave rise to another phrase that entered the English language. Farmers along the coast were aware of the smuggling and would often lend out their mares (fine strong horses) to haul barrels of brandy or whatever up the steep cliffs. This is the origin of the word 'nightmares'.

It was at the Shepherd's Arms that the Sons planned some of their best pollution stunts. It was a fairly basic pub with wooden tables, a few hunting prints on the wall, brass and copper ornaments, darts and domino boards and always an inviting cosy fire.

The regular clients always included some marvellous characters. Fred Ulliott also known as The Sage was a farmer on Duchy land and had met HM The Queen when members of the local Duchy land had been invited to a garden party at Buckingham Palace. On being introduced to Her Majesty who asked him if he was enjoying the event replied, "You got a right lot of good going on down here Ma'am". She then she asked him if he was enjoying the champagne he replied "Nay M'am I likes a Jubilee Stout." Shortly after he was served with a Jubilee Stout!

He would sit in the corner oozing with satisfaction of his idyllic life and was never lost for a droll comment on any subject you could bother him with. Always dressed in an ancient boiler suit and cap, he was seemingly always lighting his pipe. He loved to tell tales about the past. He dispelled any hints of urgency with his ultra-relaxed approach to life. His boiler suit had innumerable patches on his chest area.

"When I'm on't tractor," he would explain with an air of self-mockery, "I like to smoke my pipe. When its not fully out it burns a hole in me pocket, an't wife patches it up from an old boiler suit." .

Once he wandered into the pub and announced to all and sundry. "Dost tha know what 'appened to me today?"

No response, though he gained undivided attention from everyone.

"Ah lost t'tractor."

Silence.

"I got off t'tractor for a smoke and ta fill up us pipe, and when I turned round tractor'd gone. I looked around an it were in't next field – all't way down to't stream and up t'next hill. Ee, ah were right glad to see it again."

He would then reach into his pocket, taking out his well worn wallet removing some tattered postcard – "Look here at t'whale stranded on Hayburn Wyke rocks when I were a lad."

Then with a glint of impish devilment he would whip out a postcard of naked ladies also on the same rocks.

"What were the women like when you were a lad?" I enquired once.

"Worse if 'owt!" he laughed. That simple phrase spoke volumes of dialogue.

A great character who would occasionally drop by was Geoff Bird, who had a farm half a mile away from the Shepherd's Arms. One morning, after he'd finished milking his large herd of Friesians, he heard a car crunching up the gravel drive and saw two men in suits with briefcases getting out. They came towards him across the yard, and inquired:

"Are you Mr Bird?"

"Aye, that I am."

"We're from the National Parks commission. Is this your caravan?"

"Aye, it is."

"We're sorry to have to tell you it has to go. Because your farm house is in the National Park, you cannot have a caravan outside here."

"Dost tha mean I can't have a caravan outside my own house, in my own stackyard, to put up my daughter and her husband to live in for a coupla months while she's pregnant?"

"I'm afraid so, sir."

"Just wait there a minute," he said and walked off into the house.

A moment later, he reappeared loading a double-barreled shotgun.

"I give thee thirty seconds to get off my land, then ahm gointa shoot tha," he offered calmly.

"That attitude will get you nowhere Mr Bird", they said.

"Fifteen" answered Geoff. They scrambled into the car and left, threatening: "We'll be back."

Several nights later, while he was in bed, a similar car pulled into the drive, having switched its engine off and doused its lights down the road. He reached for the shotgun, fired one barrel over the car roof, and watched it turn and speed away. He emptied the other barrel into the boot. They never returned.

Also a regular at the Shepherd's Arms was a man called Tony Jenkins who fell in love with Staintondale, selling his lucrative business to indulge in his passion for rearing Shire horses. He bought a farm overlooking the cliffs with sweeping, dramatic views over Hayburn Wyke. As the great poet Alexander Pope put it:

"Happy is the man whose wish and care a few paternal acres bound. Content to breathe the air in his native ground.

His farm is set in a patch the National Trust has called paradise. When he first arrived and moved into the farm, he said to his wife "I'm off love, to the Shepherd's Arms for a swift half". He returned home the next day, having indulged in several slow halves with his friends, and fallen asleep in the pub, and was to bear the nickname 'Swift Half Jenkins' locally from then on. To know Swift Half was to know a happy man.

Soon he would establish at Staintondale the Shire-horse Farm, which became a popular tourist attraction.

The pub was run by Dick Lockey and his gentle wife, Mary. Dick was known as Doctor Dick for the nourishing ale he dispensed. The pub overlooked glorious vistas of the North Sea, across Swift Half's charming farmland with its magnificent shire horses. Swift Half was having a long running battle with the powers that be, in trying to expand his shire horse visitors centre, which needed new amenities and improved road access etc. The National Parks were making life as difficult as possible for this gentleman, they submerged him with a plague of planning permissions and excessive demands, a conflict that went on for what seemed like an eternity.

Swift Half said "We offered to put a new farm track in, and we have done that at a cost of well over £4,000. They have come back to us over the passing places, and we have offered to do two of them. I think the County should meet me somewhere along the line. After all, I am providing an amenity to the area" (the park attracted 10,000 visitors to the area yearly). He ended up writing and publishing two books about the situation before he gained the permission he needed.

The Sons did more than drink at the Shepherd's. Fred especially has supported the local churches between Ravenscar and Cloughton, as they were under threat of closure. He had great affection for the local rural community. On one occasion we attached a low loader to the back of his Jeep,and lifted on an electric organ to be used for a wedding service. The Rev Harry Foyle had asked Fred if he could help, as the old church organ was out of action and the wedding of a popular young couple would have been marred without music. The sight of six blokes holding on to an electric organ as we whizzed through the countryside seemed out of context with the area. However this gave us a great sense of purpose, to deliver the instrument on time for the happy occasion. The Rev Harry and congregation were delighted and relieved on our arrival.

Our activities were to bear fruit as a result of the announcement in 1993 that Scarborough Council and Yorkshire Water were prepared to abandon dumping of untreated sewage at Scarborough and build a full treatment works round the corner of the North Bay, at Cowlam Hole, was greeted with joy by all who had been involved for over a decade in the fight against the filthy practice. But we later heard with amazement that despite the universal scientific evidence and new laws by the EEC against the practice Yorkshire Water had decided to pollute the sea with raw untreated sewage at – of all places – Robin Hood's Bay!

The Scarborough Evening News came out strongly against the YWA (Yorkshire Water) in a leading article headed "Another mess", in which it said: "Yorkshire Water seems to have learned nothing from the farcical sewage scheme at Scalby Mills . . . Now it has managed to push through another shameful outfall scheme – at Robin Hood's Bay, with effluent waste still being pumped out to sea . . . It is amazing that local planning officials have agreed to the scheme."

The Bay, as we called it, commanded deep affection from all members of the Sons because of its serene natural beauty, with its red-roofed houses and narrow enchanting streets sweeping down to the sea and the natural amphitheatre of the bay. Its continuing charm never failed to delight the eye and raise the spirits.

So the shocking news that, taking advantage of a gap in the regulations concerning areas of small population numbers, the YWA were preparing to launch a raw untreated sewage scheme for the villages of Robin Hood's Bay and neighbouring Fylingdales caused what can only be termed as a near-revolution. We learned that the scheme would feature a pumping station right in the middle of the scenic dock area, a slipway leading to the beach, where boats were pulled up after use. We had been alerted by Steve Mallalieu, who with his wife, Jean, ran the old marine laboratory at the Bay, which they had converted into a learning centre for the marine environment. The plan had to be fought, and although we were weary after our 10-year struggle we met at the Shepherd's Arms to prepare for the battle to stop the pollution of Robin Hood's Bay and fight against Yorkshire Water's outdated and obnoxious plan.

Steve, a skilled diver and fisherman, who had previously worked for Yorkshire Water and knew how they operated told us: "When at a preliminary meeting with Fylingdales councillors I saw a computer model they had done on tides I realised that it did not reflect or resemble in any way what was happening day-to-day in the sea. In my role as an inspector for them I was prosecuting poor old farmers on the coast for farm emissions, so when I told the YWA that their so-called water-treatment plants were the biggest polluters they immediately terminated my employment. They tried their cunning tricks on the locals in order to impress them with their computer models, which, as I said, had nothing to do with reality. They didn't even ask the fishermen who, of course made their daily livelihood from the sea in all conditions. The Sons helped to set up our protest group."

Once again, to hatch our battle plan we hiked up to the *Sacred Temple* (the Shepherd's Arms public house), and, around a glowing fire, decided that we should emphasise the new evidence of disease levels caused by the absurd outdated policy of dumping raw sewage into the sea and calling this a treatment. Now Robin Hood's Bay was under the same threat as Scarborough had been.

Before the official YW public presentation we were invited Robin Hoods Bay for the first local meeting. As we drove to the Bay we were still in a state of shock to think that they were going to put the pumping station right in the middle of the most picturesque part of this beautiful resort at the height of the tourist season.

The invitation came from Trevor Ford, a retired headmaster living in the Bay, who told us that the first preliminary meeting on the plan had been held at Fylingdales, without the involvement of people in the Bay.

Not everyone was glad to see the Sons and Captain Syd at the meeting. The water authority representatives had tried to stop us attending because of our massive exposure of their incompetence – in fact one Scarborough councillor had such prejudice against us that he requested a Police presence in case our eviction would be required! Fortunately the event had been advertised as a public meeting for those interested, and we had been invited by Robin Hood's Bay residents.

The meeting started with YWA representatives and Borough councillors on the stage, and impressive graphics, diagrams, and Disney-style visual proposals, while YWA chairman of the meeting Barry Truman pointed out what a large amount of money would be spent on the proposals, which had been formulated by experts. He asked for questions.

Freddie asked the chairman why the YWA were not doing a full treatment scheme for a beautiful area like Robin Hood's Bay that relied on tourism and family visitors for much of its livelihood, pointing out that the scheme would be illegal under EEC law before it was complete. I stood up and said that this community's reputation of peace, beauty, and tranquillity ideal for weekend breaks, was already marred due to their outdated habit of dumping raw, untreated sewage in the sea. Freddie pointed out that the their Bridlington scheme which had failed the EEC tests was proof that this scheme was indeed outdated and a waste of public money. The Yorkshire Water presentation of computer simulations was a similar misrepresentation to that which had occurred at Scarborough and elsewhere throughout the country, and had nothing to do with the reality of what actually happened within the sea.

Trevor Ford, chairman of 'Save the Bay' campaign, said: "I would like to remind everyone that the Titanic was built by experts. The Sons of Neptune marine conservation group have proved that the Bridlington scheme was disastrous and could not conform to EEC regulations, so surely we are entitled to an in-depth opinion."

Some residents, however, were not convinced. Parish councillor Alf Wedgewood was in ecstasy that something was to be done about the sewage problem and that the YWA were going to spend a considerable amount of money. We felt that such was his enthusiasm to get something done that he never really analysed what was being proposed.

The YWA bureaucrats' presentation had been once again a mix of patronising over-confidence and shambolic amateurism. It was weakly presented by PR men who were completely challenged in public, and left the village hall in a state of bewilderment. For me personally, the greatest moment came when the local people who are normally quite reserved and wary of strangers, came forward and thanked us personally for helping them to save the Bay. At that moment we became more determined than ever to continue with our fight for a clean sea - the life blood of the village.

After the meeting Trevor said: "We have decided to form our own committee as we don't trust the parish council or the YWA." The first communication they received was a letter from Yorkshire Water saying that the Sons of Neptune should not be allowed to attend meetings or to speak. He replied that they were invited as the meeting was open to the public and especially to those with an interest in the marine environment.

Over the next few days, we started to become preoccupied with where to take the campaign next. As we walked back along the cliffs at Rock's Lane a few days later, we had a brainwave. Freddie said: "Now that we have so much evidence of the disease levels from the outfall, we'll have to do some sort of demonstration at Robin Hood's Bay . . . "

Our first move was to get an ideal location, and recently the BBC had done a film about Robins Hood Bay which featured Steve Mallalieu teaching scuba diving to clients who attended his marine centre. A view across the Bay from Ravenscar would not be out of place in a David Lean movie so we decided to visit Raven Hall. The setting for the Raven Hall Hotel is on the site of an old Roman signal station with one of the most magnificent views in the country. It has a nine-hole golf course and garden surrounded by castle turrets, which also have great vistas of the Bay over the golf course and cliffs. The Hall, which stands looking majestically over the Bay, has a chequered history. King George III is said to have been held there during his so-called madness and was flogged with birch branches, the doctor in charge of his treatment drinking and gambling regularly with the Hall's owner. Tradition has it that when they had a drunken bet about which of two lice crawling across the table would reach the other edge first the landlord lost the Hall lock stock and barrel to the doctor. Bram Stoker had written part of his notorious book Dracula at the Hall and many modern-day stars, such as James Last and Lonnie Donegan, in the 1960s used it as a retreat to relax miles away up the coast in seclusion between summer appearances on Scarborough's busy seafront. In the early 20th Century Ravenscar was marked out as having great potential as a new holiday resort with its magnificent sea views and new raillink. It failed, however, to attract substantial investment as the promoters had overlooked that the only access to the rocky beach was by a very steep path down unstable cliffs - almost vertical in places with no hand rails! It became known as the Town That Never Was.

From the 1970's the Hotel was owned by the Gridley family and noted far and wide for its excellence. Mike Gridley was in charge and was the very definition of a gentleman with a touch of class and finesse. Following his death his elegant wife Doreen succeeded him in the running of the Hotel following a successful singing career. Indeed it was said that she would often serenade her guests at breakfast to the strains 'Oh what a beautiful morning' and other songs from the shows. Freddie had asked her if we could stage part of our protest in the Hotel gardens and the mention of a TV documentary very much appealed as good marketing for the Hotel. The lower gardens were protected by high walls and battlements throwing long shadows which were the perfect setting for an appearance of Dracula who was to play the leading part in our protest, symbolizing Yorkshire Water role. Feddie wisely advised not to mention Dracula or sewage, or our consent to use the Hotel were likely to be short-lived! These subjects were not likely to overload the Hotel with advance bookings in any marketing campaign! (To this day the Hotel remains excellent with its superb views and golf course.)

We approached Sir Alan Ayckbourn, who had previously helped us with the Richard III festival. Sir Alan was now appreciated on a world-wide scale as a famous playwright, director and master of drama. To his credit, Alan allowed his actor-director, Robin Herford, who directed the successful Westend play of Susan Hill's 'Woman in Black', to take a bit of time out to help us at a time when the theatre was at its busiest.

My job was to get the media interested and having Dennis Dobson's news agency above my surgery was invaluable. Dennis was a man of quiet dignity and a master of media communication. By now the Sons had acquired a reputation for good publicity stunts. Dennis would frequently ask "Are you Sons of Neptune up to anything soon?" with typical media-man curiosity. He had an inward imposed laugh but could always find time to moan. "What is Dennis really like?" a young visiting reporter asked me, "Well," I replied, "he is a really nice bloke but if you gave him a million quid in cash he would later complain that some of the notes were dirty."

We knew that undertaker Bert Bernard would again lend us some coffins, and we decided to poster them up with the names of all the diseases caused by untreated sewage such as cholera, dysentery, hepatitis, meningitis or polio to really catch people's attention.

Then I remembered a patient I had had in my chiropody practice that day, and said: "Lads you won't believe this, but after lunch I noticed my first patient's name was a Miss Stoker. I greeted her with the question: "Are you any relation to Bram Stoker?" The Dracula author wrote his iconic horror after a visit to Whitby, the next town up the coast from the Bay. Whitby enjoys many other claims to fame - not least as the home and base of Captain Cook - and it enjoys an equally dramatic coastline, which is pretty instrumental to the vampire classic.

Miss Stoker replied: "Yes I am - I am his great-niece and before you ask any more, whatever you do, please don't mention that one dreadful book of his. Have you read his other novels?"

I couldn't say I had.

When she settled down she got onto the subject of Dracula quite quickly, and proceeded to tell me that the book was mainly written in Raven Hall. The Whitby Abbey graveyard, which has an eerie feel, and pirates' gravestones, which create a sinister atmosphere, Stoker was also inspired by a Scottish castle, she said firmly, not Vlad the Impaler!

I laughed at the thought of depicting our opponents as a bunch of blood sucking bats as they were after all taking our money and leaving their droppings for us to worry about.

Why not portray the water authorities as Dracula so the battle could be "Neptune v. the Water Authorities" Captain Syd could play Neptune, defending the ocean against the evil of the polluters.

"That will certainly get the media here," agreed Freddie, and we chuckled at the idea.

For the next few weeks we worked intensely to make sure this was a success, contacting the media and hyping up the event. We decided to dress as Victorian undertakers, with black sideburns and moustaches, stovepipe hats, and long black tailcoats. We would collect the coffins from Bert Bernards Undertakers and wrap them in black plastic sacks with white warnings of sewage borne diseases.

We were lucky to have the support of Tony Jenkins of Staintondale Shire Horse Farm who not only had a horse big enough for the job but also a Farm Museum which had among its exhibits a cart which looked old enough to have collected the dead from a battlefield. Couldn't be better!

Tony agreed to pick up Dracula, David Lazenby a conveniently tall fellow, staunch conservationist, supporter of the Sons, and bring him to Robins Hood Bay marine laboratory where Robin

Herford was directing a group of school girls for their role in the demonstration on the beach. From the Primrose Hill Girls School, North London they were in fact on a course at the laboratory organised by their vibrant Head Mistress.

On the day of the event we were greeted with warm sun and clear blue skies. The media were due to arrive at the Raven Hall Hotel at eleven where David was practising take off positions on the battlements with his black cloak billowing in the breeze. At the last minute and perhaps fortunately for the early morning strollers in the Hotel gardens, word came through that the TV crews were delayed and would meet us at Robin Hood's Bay. The battlement sequence would be filmed later in the day.

By the time we got there Tony was already in the top car-park with Mascot the powerful shire and the antique cart. The TV crews were down at the shore and ready to film their arrival in twenty minutes. If there was to be a hitch at - and there was - could there have been a worse time! In getting all the gear together, the cart saddle had been overlooked! Without this there was no effective connection between Mascot and the cart!

Spasms of panic! Freddie chased off to the Farm for the saddle and I down to the shore to confront the media. When I got down there I was surprised to hear they had gone off to the Dolphin pub where he found them hitting the real ale! The reason for the delay or indeed length of it seemed of no great consequence to them leaving us with the worry that we were going to lose crucial TV coverage that same evening. But the real ale soon inspired practical solutions.

Mascot and the cart could wait and be filmed later and tacked on at the beginning later in the editing room! So off to the shore where Robin Herford was already rehearsing his part of the production with the children dressed up in the Victorian style. Neptune was standing in the background waist deep in the sea trident in hand. Dracula meanwhile was hovering beneath the sea wall in shadows as dark as his robes. El Foundo, black as a crow in his cassock looked less concerned than his part in the forth coming tragedy required!

"What's going on now?" came a shout from Pat O'Hara of BBC North.

"We're just rehearsing the main event" I said

"Well we'll film that now and the rest when it happens. You know where I am" replied Pat who returned for another pint leaving his cameraman, soundman and runner to get on with it.

We were still anxious that the main demo would be missed by the media since most of the TV crews were anxious to get it in time for their lunchtime bulletins.

Fortunately, it was a magnificent day, the scene could not have been more spectacularly lit, and we heard later that the TV crews' laissez-faire demeanour was due to the fact that their editors were so confident we would put on a cracking show that everyone had been sent out to cover it for the entire day.

Meanwhile, back at Swift Half's farm, Freddie quickly discovered that Mrs Jenkins had gone out shopping, and had locked up the shed where the belts were. About to break in he saw her driving back across the vale. Time was running out and they were running round like headless chickens.

Back at the Bay, we had already placed a number of store dummies wrapped in seaweed at the end of the rocks to represent dead bodies.

Captain Syd was lowered into a rock-pool as far as his waist. He made a splendid Neptune with his waders concealed under plenty of seaweed, more on his crowned head, and a huge trident and shield bearing the legend: "If you destroy me, you destroy yourselves" – Jacques Cousteau.

Robin Herford arranged the schoolgirls round a large rock pool, where they happily started looking for marine creatures.

Behind them, looming up, was our Dracula character, with Water Authorities emblazoned on his chest. He spread out his black cloak, and snarled very well for a man with a couple of huge protruding fangs, sending the schoolgirls screaming away.

El Foundo ran across the beach, black cassock flowing in his slipstream, ringing a bell to warn of the danger but it was too late for anything but the last rites. One old lady tried to stop him as he ran from the beach to the village morgue with a dummy under his arm and shouted after him:

"What are you doing with that naked lady Vicar?"

"I like to keep close to my parishioners," quipped El Foundo.

The piece de resistance arrived as Tony turned up with the prize-winning Shire horse, Mascot, pulling a wagon laden with coffins – and the six Sons of Neptune in their Victorian gear.

The media were delighted as Swift Half drove down the landing towards the beach, but as he approached the slipway down to the sand, Mascot sensed danger, and promptly sat down. Tony leaped off the wagon. "I've never had any experience like this in fifty years of handling horses – he can tell it's too slippery. Quick lads, get off and spread some sand over the slipway."

We hopped off and got scooping and throwing sand while Tony did his horse-whispering charms on Mascot, who soon stood up again, and this time pulled the Victorian wagon over the rough terrain with gentle dignity. The sight of the Victorian undertakers loading dead bodies into coffins in this divine scenery was awesome. It also got our message across.

And the TV coverage was just as we envisaged. Steve Mallalieu who had joined in as a Victorian undertaker, stated to the TV cameras: "In this beautiful village, we tip raw untreated sewage into the sea. The time has come to call a halt to this disgusting, dangerous practice, and invest in modern technology to make our beaches clean and safe."

Asked why the Sons were demonstrating, Freddie said: "We are trying to get the message across to people that we can get diseases from this system. And if we don't do something about it, this scenario of death and disease will intensify." I added, "It is really up to the Government and the water authorities to face up to their responsibilities. They are bound by European law not to dump raw sewage into the sea, but they continue to build outdated outfall plants that are destroying the environment and are obviously illegal. All we can do is make the public more aware of what they are doing to our rivers and seas. I don't believe they can go ahead with this now that the world's leading scientists have condemned this vile practice."

At the end of the Tyne Tees TV coverage of the demo, the presenter gasped, "Now there's a demonstration with a difference."

A reporter from a local newspaper, called Iain Meekley, was an excellent fellow, but had treated our campaign with an air of cynical condescension, which at the time had not fazed us. At the press conference on the beach, he indicated that he now thought we might have a credible point.

Just then, Dave Lazenby, dressed as Count Dracula – who was still standing menacingly on the cliff above us, was noticed by Meekers. "Who is playing Dracula?" he asked. "Dr. Seward from Heidelberg University," I replied. We all sniggered – unnoticed by Meekers – as he duly wrote this down in his notebook (Dr Seward of Heidelberg is one of the main characters from Dracula).

Later on, as we celebrated our success in the Bay Hotel with a few pints, Freddie once again observed that the Town would be better off with a bunch of baboons in the Town Hall than some of the Councillors who gave support to Yorkshire Water. We raised many a mirthful toast to various baboons over the course of the evening.

The media coverage of this event had many ramifications and made us determined to continue the fight. Residents in the Bay felt a sense of dismay and anger, but their tight new committee rallied round Jean Mallalieu. "We raised an enormous amount of money to fight the scheme," she said. "The support was tremendous, we held raffles, barbecues and a huge weekend festival which all intensified the feelings against the project."

Barbara Wright, a respected local lady who owned a superb Georgian house overlooking the Bay was chairman of her own industrial company in Leeds, and became an enthusiastic supporter of the Sons, who were by now frequent visitors to the Save the Bay meetings. Barbara, who often chaired and hosted the meetings, was at first a staunch ally, but the YW manager Barry Truman, a shrewd operator, befriended her and one evening when we attended, Barbara suddenly turned against us for no apparent reason. We were shocked and wondered why. Later we were told: "Nothing passes unnoticed by villagers".

There are many possible origins for the name Robin Hood's Bay, but there are indications which may show the connection between bay town and the hero of popular legend. The sources of these revelations are the Robin Hood collection of medieval ballads which were passed down from century to century. It is said that Robin Hood was attracted to Whitby, and especially the Abbey, perhaps as the area was wealthy at that time. However, the most likely explanation is that the bold outlaw was often pursued and found a safe haven in the isolated Bay where local folklore suggests he and his merry men had boats readied to make their escape. On the adjacent moor there are still two mounds known as Robin Hood's Butts, which it is said were used as targets when his men were practising with their longbows.

Robin Hood's Bay in recent times has been inhabited by some marvellously colourful characters who were attracted to the ambience of the place and its leisurely pace of life. The Dolphin, one of the three pubs in the village, was like a second home to me. It was run by Gerry, a small man with a flaming red beard and hair who would have had no trouble in being cast as a leprechaun in any production. He had been gifted with great humour and wit, and to visit the pub at any time of the day and night one felt instantly at home amongst the most friendly, eccentric people, to whom he was host. He ran a good ship, the food was excellent including the 'Sons of Neptune Soup'. A frequent performer, and friend of Gerry, Martin Carty (Probably the worlds leading folk singer his influence in this field is renowned, his knowledge of the history of song would not be out of place in the British Library, Bob Dylan praises him as a huge influence) says "I loved to hear Gerry performing 'Albert and the Lion' in Chaucerian dialogue." There was also Steve Phillips, a noted singer-song writer, guitarist, painter and maker of musical instruments a man who controls his own destiny, at his most content in the Bay surrounded by his monet like garden. His good friend Mark Knofler made use of a guitar Steve made on the cover of 'Brothers In Arms' by Dire Straits one of the first multimillion selling CDs, later Steve and Mark formed the Notting Hillbillies. He tours the world but performs weekly in the Bay

Regular David Riley, who had a small boarding house just opposite, had worked in the rag trade. His wife, Karen, often helped out in the pub. They remember Robin, a former pub landlord from Leeds, who had retired to the Bay and was a regular customer at the Dolphin.

David recalls: "Robin had two Jack Russell terriers called Jack and Jill who were completely ruined and undisciplined and they would bite people at the slightest whim. On each occasion this happened to visitors, Robin would say in a contrite voice: "Oh they have never done that before!". I met Robin on the beach one day with one of his Jack Russells, and knowing that it was a vicious little bastard, I stood behind the little dog as I was talking to Robin, I could see the terrier's face as it occasionally turned to face me, its lips quivering and its teeth flashing. As it leapt to bite me I drop-kicked it like a rugby ball over Robin's shoulder. Robin looked aghast at the dog flying through the air and came out with his usual quip "Oh, I've never seen him do that before".

Karen remembers that in time the dogs became more vicious and Robin became their victim, he came in one day for his usual pint with one bandaged finger. Soon several more were injured, and it was not long before one hand was completely bandaged up. Inevitably the day arrived when he came in with both hands completely bandaged. She said: "I had to laugh as he clutched his pint between two clenched hands and could hardly lift the glass."

Robin had some very tall stories about his time as a Leeds landlord. "This big bloke used to come in, his trick was to begin to drink his beer when Big Ben began to chime twelve, and he could sink twelve pints by the time Big Ben struck the introduction of the midnight news. He did this regularly for a bet." Robin would insist that this was gospel truth and would often embellish the story by saying the same man could drink five double whiskies in less than a minute. I asked him what is this character doing now and he replied "Oh, he's dead". He also had a story about the Bay house he lived in, which he said was haunted by a poltergeist.

"Apparently the house belonged to a sea captain, a widower, who when ashore would come home to his only daughter, and go down to the Dolphin and caress the shores of inebriation. On one occasion, after a particularly heavy drinking session, he went back to sea, forgetting that he had locked his daughter in the attic. She was later found dead, and to this day there is supernatural activity, rattling noises in the night and objects flying about. This has been confirmed by many visitors to the house," claimed Robin.

Gerry attracted another odd character who occasionally helped him out behind the bar. He was George David Fell-Place, brother of the poet Milner Place and was a master of impish devilment. He festooned the bar with poetic works entitled "Odes to Raw Sewage In The Bay". Placey, as he was known, behaved like a duke, oozing with self importence. His tall figure would peer down upon you as he twirled his moustache, opening each sentence with 'Dear Boy' in an upper-crust accent, although his background was nouveau-riche. - his father had been a timber merchant buying country estates from impoverished gentry after WW2. The family became very wealthy, and Placey was educated at the upper-class private school Stowe. He had a flair for business but was defeated by his own desire for merry irresponsibility. Before he arrived at The Bay he had made money from farming, inn-keeping, and various other investments. At one pub, the Blinking Owl, in Boroughbridge, he had a collection of antique plates. When in a fun mood, he would load his two shotguns and shoot the plates off the wall in front of the customers. This type of behaviour had started at his father's home where he was said to have destroyed one of the most valuable collections of porcelain statues. It was then that his father had to evict him out into the world. On one occasion entering The Dolphin he insisted on recreating a rugby match using a loaf of bread and the customers in the bar had to join in and play every move in detail in front of bewildered clients in the restaurant. Gerry accepted this, as he too lived in a mood of wild hysteria.

"Dear Boy," Placey told me one day "I wish you luck with this sewage campaign, but don't forget you are dealing with the brainless lower orders." Hearing one day that we had just been to York Races he remarked: "Dear boy, I took Mandy Rice-Davies to York Races and filled her hat with champagne. She later pissed into my hat. Dear boy, I must get my worthy steed and head up the hill." Outside of The Dolphin there was a cloud of blue smoke, sparks, and bangs as he rode off on his wreck of an autocycle.

One customer remarked: "There was a time when he could have afforded a fleet of Rolls-Royces! He arrived in the village owing over £100,000 in the Sixties, which was a lot of money," True or not, he raised the humour level of the population, which was his greatest wealth.

While Placey was serving at The Dolphin for Gerry, an American lady visitor came in and in a strong American drawl asked: "'Excuse me, could you tell me if the scampi here is battered or breaded?" In reply, Placey drawled: "Madam, I can assure you that the scampi in this establishment is very well bredded!"

John Gilbert, an expert furniture restorer described how the Bay's atmosphere captured him. "My first view was passing by thinking 'what's that fishing village with Edwardian houses on top of the hill?' It was a light spring evening as I came down into the village with smoke rising from the chimneys. It seemed to wrap its arms around me. At that moment I thought 'This is where I would like to live'."

"When the Sons of Neptune first came to the village to instigate the sewage campaign, a lot of people thought they were OTT and felt they were troublemakers by criticizing the village with its outdated sewage system. They thought that this would put off visitors coming to Robin Hood's Bay. There were a lot of people swimming in the sea and getting problems as a result, which was almost certainly due to them swimming in what was in the sea. Of that I am certain in my own mind. I was supportive of the Sons' campaign for clean seas, as I was aware of their protest in Scarborough and on TV and other media. I knew in the long run it would benefit Robin Hood's Bay. At the time there was an increase in the number of complaints of bad stomachs and other illnesses as a result of swimming in the Bay. I found at my meetings with Yorkshire Water, that they were a bunch of scallywags. We soon discovered that if we wanted well-informed information of what was going on, that the best information came from Freddie Drabble, the leader of the Sons Of Neptune."

Another character was Captain Cooper, nicknamed 'Cooperman' who was the youngest ever sea captain to command supertankers. First impressions were of a quiet, kind yet fierce kind of man. An odd character, he was exactly the opposite of what you imagined a sea captain would be like.

John Gilbert observed: "When the Captain sailed around the Bay in a simple fishing boat he would return saying 'I've lost an engine here, I've lost an engine over here' and he became known as 'the engineer'. I was in my workshop and I kept hearing this noise I had not heard before, it was Cooperman taking a short cut across the rocky scars rather than up the safe sandy creek used for centuries by Bay fishermen. I got familiar with it. It was 'chug, burr, pow, bawk'- I knew it was him just by the sound'. He took over the Post Office and having all the organisation of a runaway threshing-machine would often mislay the pension money. On one occasion I observed him furiously going through the black binbags at the local dump. "What are you up to Cooperman?" I enquired. "Piss off", he said. Hours later he found the money.

To be fair he seemed to support the Sons of Neptune campaign but may have found Captain Sydney Smith's marine knowledge dwarfed his opinions. Dave Hunter, a retired helicopter technician and property owner in the Bay, said: "I heard Cooperman was writing a book about how to start a small business, I suggested he should buy a big one first!"

Gerry and Captain Cooper would often have drinking and debating sessions at the Dolphin, on one occasion he teased the Captain asking him what part of the oil tanker was the 'spalursh'. For hours Cooperman who really did know his oil tanker from top to bottom went through the various engineering structures of the ship till almost unconscious with booze pleaded with Gerry to tell him. The spalursh he announced, with impish glee, was the sound of the anchor hitting the sea! Cooperman was left in a cloud of silence.

There was also a man called "Shorts Norman", a Scot who had worked for British Aerospace. A man of mystery, by all accounts, who wandered around in shorts in all weathers, he gave all kinds of different locations for his birth, but frequently South-West Lanarkshire. He said he had played for several professional football teams in his time under assumed names, and could be traced to at least three locations in Scotland - Wickton, Milngavie, and Lanark. In Yorkshire he played for Scarborough and Bradford Park. He was very much a part of life in Robin Hood's Bay frequently occupying bars and demolishing alcohol by the gallon, but nevertheless charming everyone with his jovial humour. Over the next few years, he deteriorated from an athletic figure with a sharp brain into a declining wreck of a human being, though he is fondly remembered as that of a fine frame of a man in the Bay. The booze isolated him from the community and it was said that in order to supplement his guest-house, he would nick milk cartons from the Dolphin Inn and vegetables from Captain Cooper's shop. The people were sympathetic to his plight, using only humour to counteract his behaviour - for example, deliberately sticking milk cartons and sugar on the counter at the pub, and putting vegetables beyond their sell-by date out for him to liberate.

The Sons received their inspiration from the wonderful cross-section of humanity in the Bay dependant as they were for their living from the sea and the beach. They are the ones that helped us to fight the battle of Robin Hood's Bay. They, like the Sons, were fired up by Freddie's inspirational and powerful determination and passionate dialogue: "I have a right to go in that sea, I have a right to clean sea water, I have a right not to be put at risk of infection, and I demand that right," he declared.

YWA were eventually forced to abandon their sea-polluting scheme and to pump the Bay sewage to a treatment works near Whitby. Trevor Ford, chairman of the Save the Bay campaign, exclaimed with delight, as he looked down from his home above the marine laboratory a couple of years after the opening of the Whitby sewage-treatment works: "Just look at how clean the sea is now – you can see little crabs dashing about on the pristine sand, and even the seaweed looks better. I never thought I'd see this, it's a wonderful, sight."

Alan Ayckbourn's director, Robin Herford, instructs girls from Primrose Hill School, N London, Taking part in the Sons Dracula protest at Robin Hood's Bay.

A session with a local reporter for Sons dressed as Victorian undertakers.

Count Dracula (Dave Lazenby) representing YW sea pollution, sneaks up on children playing in rock pools.

e Northern Echo

No. 36,602   FRIDAY, MAY 20, 1988   18p ★★★★ STILL ONLY 18p

Dead sea warning

IF
YOU KILL
ME
YOU KILL
YOURSELVES

Making waves: Neptune, alias Capt Sid Smith, rises in anger from the sea in yesterday's protest

Sewer demo shock

Captain Syd MBE at age 82 insists on representing Neptune as Yorkshire Water continues it 'Viking Settlement' plan of dumping raw sewerage sludge into the North Sea without full treatment.

Tony Jenkinson with Julia Bradbury of 'Country File' at his Shirehorse Farm in Staintondale near Scarborough, which they have featured on two occasions. He teased members of the Sons, we responded that we gave him the best role ever in the Robins Hood Bay demo.

Hawaii and the queens

Our love of the environment of Yorkshire intensified as we felt the powers that be would need constant observation, otherwise they would return to their efforts to destroy the environment and its beauty. One of our favourite spots for recreational walking near Scarborough was the delightful Dalby Forest, where we celebrated the gift of life at the Moorcock Inn after a hike. It was nearby that a farmer who kept bees and frequently won first prize at the local village agricultural shows of Sneaton, Rosedale and Burniston, usually greeted the Sons with the proud boast that his honey had won first prize. He loved to tease Freddie, who would enter these shows with various types of garden produce. Freddie had become fascinated with bees and had begun to keep hives on the large acreage behind his home, where he kept his favourite horse and a group of flowerbeds. One particular feature was an old hay cart, which had an array of flowerpots, radiating a host of colours that would make the average kaleidoscope seem dull. As a shrewd observer of the environment he had realised the importance of bees and developed a passion for beekeeping as a relief from the intense campaign that the Sons had conducted for clean seas. At the beginning Freddie's learning curves for beekeeping were steep but fun. He came around to our house very excited that his bees were producing red and even blue honey, something previously unknown in the beekeeping world. Freddie said:" It's amazing! I'm finding that the honey they are producing is the same colour as the flowers they got their nectar from – green, yellow, blue, red, and purple!" .At first we thought this was his impish sense of humour, then, on being told by his gurus in the beekeeping world that this was far from normal, alarm bells went off, and after much bewilderment the culprit for this unusual happening was located. A local farmer in Burniston had bought a batch of rejected boiled coloured sweets to feed his pigs, and had left them outside a barn. Scenting an unusual sugary feast, the bees had been consuming the sweets wholesale, and had absorbed the dye, which had coloured the honey.

My first encounter with the bees was not a pleasant one. One evening I was walking down the field at the back of Freddie's house towards the barn Evening Star, to meet Freddie, who was tending his beehives, when I heard a loud shout. It was Freddie, completely outfitted in beekeeping gear. "Get back!" he yelled. "The bees are heading towards you!" I stood there puzzled for a few seconds, then several bees came swooping fiercely at me, diving down like planes upon an enemy. As a young child I had had a bad experience with bees and was now naturally terrified of them. I ran towards the house and soon lost most of them, but three bees persisted and kept up the attack. I imagined their wings as having Nazi swastikas on them. Two flew into my eyes and stung me on both eyelids. Terrified, and half-blind, I ran to the back door of the house, praying it would be unlocked. As luck would have it, it was open, and I rushed in and slammed it shut and at last felt safe. Yvette, Freddie's wife, was home, and she kindly gave me boracic acid and applied it with warm water and cotton wool. What a relief that soothing balm was. Freddie came through and declared: "It's your tracksuit. It's so gaudy it scared the bees!".

It was not very long before Freddie was producing excellent honey from his hives, and being a generous fellow we all received ample amounts. Little did we realise that this would lead to a bee adventure across the world to Hawaii.

Our scientific contacts in the U.S.A. regularly sent us invitations to various seminars on environmental matters. Professor Grimes sent us information on some that were of interest; and a U.S marine experimental lab in Hawaii seemed to tick all the right boxes to help our campaign.. A visit to Hawaii was being seriously considered, but what swung the decision to go was compounded when Freddie met with his local honey mogul Steve Ryan. The idea elated him. "Did you know that Hawaii and the north island of New Zealand are the only parts of the world that are unaffected by the dangerous Varroa mite, which has infiltrated from Asia and feeds on bee larvae, decimating hives all over the world? Could you bring back some of their queens - it would rejuvenate our hives?" The bee enthusiasts explained how they wanted a set of Hawaiian queen bees, which can lay 2,600 eggs a day, to introduce into their bee colonies to help boost their ailing hives. So we had yet another environmental campaign – to save the British bee – which we were delighted to do, as the Sons had been warned by Nobel-prize-winner Prof Peter

Bullock during our campaign for clean seas that it was just a matter of time before the indiscriminate use of insecticides on the soil would contaminate the water table, affecting the plants and flowers and this cumulative build-up would affect the bees, which pollinate most of our food plants. Added to this the increase in the activities of electronic communications may also be a contributing factor.

Freddie and I set off for our Hawaiian adventure, which would include a visit to the US Government's National Energy Laboratory, where the most progressive experiments on the Pacific Ocean were being conducted. On boarding the American Airlines plane at Gatwick, bound for Hawaii via Los Angeles, we were in extremely good spirits and looking forward to seeing these beautiful islands in the Pacific. Soon after take-off we were both relaxed and in a jovial mood as Freddie looked at the flight path on the onboard monitor. After about fifteen minutes he said: "Hey! We are going towards Russia!"

"Don't worry," I said "they usually fly up to Scotland, across Iceland and down over Canada."

As I sat back, relaxed, loving the experience of flying, Freddie continued to look concerned and eventually exclaimed "Look at the screen!" Much to my amazement his fears were confirmed. The plane was flying eastwards.

Then over the intercom came a message from the captain "We have a slight problem. The door to the hold on the luggage compartment is not locking properly. This could affect cabin pressure, so we are returning to Heathrow. We have come out to sea to jettison fuel, a normal precaution in this situation."

"Heck," I said. "This means we might miss our LA connection to Hawaii." This was a real concern, as I had arranged to meet Maggie and Bill Lynch, my good friends in LA, as we were due to have a few hours with them before our flight continued. Some passengers were now getting alarmed and anxious; we could feel the tension in the air.

The captain spoke again: "This is not a serious problem. The light on the luggage hold door has not confirmed that it is locked

241

correctly so we cannot go to a higher altitude. This is standard procedure. We are safe now and will land shortly. Some years ago a similar plane ignored this warning and came down into the Pacific Ocean." The irony was not lost on us.

On landing back in the airport there was the most intense smell of aviation fuel, and several people, including the chap in the seat opposite us, rushed frantically to the doors to get off the aircraft. The captain spoke again: "Please don't be alarmed. Everything is fine now. As is usual in these situations we will refuel and a new crew will arrive shortly."

Most people remained calm. As we were waiting all the aircraft doors were opened to let fresh air into the cabin, the smell of aviation fuel eventually evaporated. Soon we were all relaxed again, and deciding to stretch our legs we walked up to the front exit of the first-class cabin, where everyone mixed and chatted to one another. We encountered a gentleman whose son played golf at the same club where Tiger Woods was a member, in California. He showed us a photo of his son with Tiger and invited us to the club anytime. As both Freddie and play fun golf, we found this amusing.

Before take-off I managed to call Bill and Maggie to inform them of the delay, and on arrival at Los Angeles they met us with their car and we got a quick tour of the city, Bill, a musician, knew every square inch of LA. I had met his wife, Maggie, when writing Little Richard's biography in LA, at the home of Little Richard's producer Robert "Bumps" Blackwell.

Freddie is not a city person, and the gaudy dementia of neon lights and freeways bubbling with traffic made little impression on him. Bill and Maggie took us to a nice restaurant near Venice Beach which is frequented by a multitude of LA's eccentrics. It gave me time to update my usual interest of music gossip with Bill.

Then it was back to LAX airport to catch the "Alloha" flight to Honolulu. The hotel we stayed at left us in no doubt that Elvis had done a sequence for his movie "Blue Hawaii" here, as an oil painting of him dominated the lounge. We met a very tall man with a huge Tom Mix stove-pipe hat, and when I told him I liked the hat he burst into enthusiastic dialogue about hats. Starting by saying: "I'm from Texas, and we like our hats there," he proceeded to tell us the history of his hat collection. Cowboy names swamped us - Roy Rodgers, John Wayne, Gene Autry etc. "I have even got a Clint Eastwood hat, but this is my favourite," he said proudly, "a genuine Tom Mix stove-pipe that cost 3,000 dollars".

"Are you guys here for the cattle ranch?" he asked. We were amazed to hear this, what on earth made him think that, we wondered, as this was the last thing we associated Hawaii with. Later we discovered some of the greatest cattle ranchers in the USA were actually in Hawaii, a revelation to us. Freddie said: "We are here to visit a bee farm."

"Goddammit," he said."I had a lot of beehives on my Texas cattle ranch. Now I have a cattle ranch here in Hawaii but I'm considering moving, The situation in Texas has gotten real bad. I can't wear my six-guns any more but in Montana I can!"

We had a few more beers with him and joined with him to sing "Honolulu Baby" a la Laurel and Hardy. Next morning we went straight to the airport to fly to the main island, Hawaii. Both Freddie and I took window seats for the spectacular views. In a matter of minutes Freddie met a scientist who worked at the US marine research laboratory on the island, and who was a colleague of our American friend, Professor Jay Grimes. When Freddie mentioned that we were involved in marine research, and had been for many years, he said: "What a coincidence! I have been working at the marine research laboratory in Hawaii." Freddie told him that we had had a lot of help from Professor Jay Grimes, he said: "Really? I have passed many scientific papers to Professor Jay, we communicate frequently." Freddie explained our interest in marine research from our role as sea bathers, our interest was in the survival of bugs in the marine environment and its effect on the safety of sea bathing waters, and then explained the involvement of Professor Jay and how he had helped us to change the UK and EEC laws about the dangers of sewage and sludge dumping.

"That's mighty good work" he said. "Professor Jay is a great guy."

Freddie said: "I then showed interest in the projects he was doing on the island of Hawaii. He told me about the projects he was involved in and gave me his card and told us that he was sure they would show us around the laboratory once we mentioned his name. He then gave us some of his papers as an insight into what he was doing. He was principally involved in the use of the Pacific Ocean in agricultural and climatic conditions." In Hawaii, he said, they were fortunate that it was a volcanic island - a huge volcano that comes out of the Pacific to a height 4,000-plus metres and plummets to an equal depth under the sea. This means that they can access extremely cold water very close to the coastline and can pump it through pipes on the land in Hawaii to transport it to the growing areas. The cold water then produces condensation and that becomes the water that is needed to produce a second cropping, and forms the atmosphere that is needed to produce crops of strawberries, tomatoes, potatoes, and much more. They were experimenting with all types of plants and crops.

When we visited this area we were greeted like long-lost friends and introduced to a bewildering number of experiments that were under way; an amazing experience which further solidified our strong belief in the marine environment and how important it can be for life and the human race.

We arrived at Konakulula airport. It was in the open air with a series of Hawaiian thatched huts. On landing we were greeted by ladies who put garlands of flowers around our necks, it was at this moment that we knew we had arrived at a beautiful exotic land. We hired a Jeep, checked into a hotel, then drove to the beach hut at Kona which was sandy with rocky outcrops. As we walked on the beach I said to Freddie "I would love to see a turtle."

"There's one over there!" said a fellow standing next to me. Sure enough there were two or three turtles nearby to me barely distinguishable from the rocks. "You can swim with them but there is a 10,000 dollar fine if you touch them," the fellow added. We put on our snorkels and flippers and entered the calm sea. As soon as we hit the water it was like swimming through the centre of the National Geographic magazine, the colours were magnificent and the variety of the species of fish was astounding.

As conservationists our spirits were given a high energy infusion leading into an exalted state. Our love of the marine environment was sealed by this awesome display of Mother Nature. We swam with turtles, parrot fish, reef sharks etc. It was like a super dream. On the surface the sea seemed just like Scarborough bay, but once you looked under the surface it was a marvellous vista. To experience the coral reefs, the colours, the variation, the flotation in such a marine environment was an encounter with paradise.

Unfortunately we missed the whales who come here to breed, but touring round the island never failed to excite the senses; the flowers, the colours, the plants, many as big as our native trees, and the volcanic areas. We drove right round the island in a day, the variety of scenery was staggering. As we drove up to the top of the island we passed a US base where the troops were out on manoeuvres. A senior officer parked in a Jeep waved at us. I said to him "We are just tourists!"

"That's fine" he replied.

"Do you know General Lynch?" I asked him "My good friend Bill Lynch is his son."

The officer adopted a military stance and stood to attention "Well that's fine. Boy! General Lynch is a four-star General. A great guy! Have yourselves a great tour!" He saluted us and waved us on.

As soon as we got further up into the mountains there were cattle everywhere for miles and miles. Yes, there is no doubt that there are cattle ranches in Hawaii! Further on we encountered rain and the scenery became very much like my beloved North Yorkshire Moors. The most dramatic scenery however was around the volcanic plateau. As we drove across there were huge fissures blowing steam hundreds of feet into the air, at first this was quite scary but we were encouraged as we saw locals driving by without a care in the world. Across the volcanic vista on the edge of inactive peaks interspersed between huge valleys where sulphur had gushed into the air at various points, this left us in a state of amazement. We arrived at the largest volcanic rim, ten miles across, and looking down into the crater we could see groups of people walking about like tiny ants hundreds of feet below.

As we recovered from our ten-hour trip around the island - Freddie did all the driving around the various climatic zones - we were kept alert by listening to a disk of "Round the Horne" the BBC radio programme which we had listened to many, many times.

The next morning we went to another beach, where the sea was enormous, as we approached it for a swim it seemed to roar at us like an enraged giant creature. The crash of the waves was terrifying. We were used to high seas but these waves were massive, yet the local kids on the beach leapt around like dolphins in the water. We remained hesitant until this tall American guy approached

"You have to time your entrance," he said. "I have been going in every morning for the last eleven years," he added confidently. "Just watch!" He ran out cockily as a huge wave approached, he dived under and in seconds was above the incoming waves. I thought to myself "I bet he wouldn't do that in the North Sea on a January morning in freezing temperatures." But not wishing to be out-done we followed. My heart sank as a massive wave approached, seeming as tall as a skyscraper. I dived into it and managed to come out the other side on the surface. The sound as it crashed behind me was like a storm in full force. As we swam further out it was calm, but the swell seemed gigantic - even though I was used to ocean swimming I felt nervous and at times like these my imagination fired up the theme song from "Jaws". Not wanting to seem a wimp I stayed floating on the swell for about five minutes, casually pretending not to be looking for the dreaded shark. I swam back in on the crest of another wave which whirled me towards the beach and dumped me onto the sands like a piece of seaweed. Freddie also came back in and we both gasped a kind of frightened laugh.

We got talking to some of the kids on the beach. "Are there any sharks out there?" I asked one youngster.

"Yeah sure, Cliff here has the scars from a shark attack" said this athletic youth.

"You are kidding me" I said

"Nope" he replied coolly. "Cliff - come over here and show these guys your shark bite!"

Cliff, a tall youth, approached, all to keen to show us his bite. He raised his arm and there on his abdomen in a huge semi-circle of zigzag scars from his armpit right down to his hip was the evidence of this bite for all to see. Terrifying.

"Yeah" he said casually. "There are loads of sharks out there. I know a lot of guys who have got bitten." He dived back into the sea unperturbed.

The next day we had arranged to drive to the bay where Captain Cook was killed, and we planned to snorkel and explore the reefs. Our guide was a local fisherman who said that for conservation reasons we were not allowed to enter the sea via the bay but could enter from the boat just outside. As we sailed out to sea, much to our delight we encountered a school of dolphins. Dolphins always seem to elate the human spirit and it certainly added to ours. On taking some photos I tripped and cut my heel and it started to bleed. The boatman quipped "You had better not go in the water, the sharks will get you!" My heart sank, here I was on the trip of my lifetime, about to dive into the most exotic environment in the world and he had to say that! I patched the wound up with some tissue and it seemed to stop bleeding so when we arrived it seemed fine. Getting ready to dive and putting on my flippers I put some sun cream over the area to quell any remaining smell of blood.

Soon we both dived in. It was unbelievable, like diving into the ceiling of huge cathedral looking down into a vast expanse of vivid colours, corals, fish, turtles, and - yes, several hundred feet below, sharks. The views were so spectacular that the sharks actually took a back seat in my mind. We swam to Captain Cook's memorial in the bay, with the Union Jack flying high. The volcanic rocks were slippery and sharp as we clambered up this little piece of Blighty on the other side of the world. We felt at home because Captain Cook sailed from Whitby, Scarborough's nearest neighbour.

On returning to the boat our next stop was to drive to one of the biggest beehive producers in the world, the Gus Queen Bee factory in Kona. "Sharks and bees in one day? Oh no!" I thought.

Apart from the incident with Freddie's bees I was badly stung as a young boy and still had an innate fear of these insects. On the way to the bee farm we called in at a plantation to buy some local coffee beans and to compose myself for the big bee encounter. As we drove to the bee colonies I could see thousands of beehives across acres of land and deep down I was terrified. The huge iron gates opened as we entered the complex. Within seconds the bees were all over the windows and windscreen. Freddie hopped out of the Jeep nonchalantly in his shorts and teeshirt to be greeted by the friendly owner. After a warm greeting he saw me still cowering with fear in the Jeep came around, and opened the door, and to my horror bees came into the car, but he took no notice and said: "Come on, come out man, they won't harm you! These are friendly Hawaiian bees - they just do the hula-hula! Just relax." I tried, and unbelievably they just crawled gently over me.

We went into the bee factory and a staff member showed us how the queen bees were to be packed for the trip home. Each queen was put into a special wooden box accompanied by six princesses to keep them calm so that we could carry them through customs, cafés, restaurants and even the plane. The boxes were about the length of a matchbox and needed to be sprayed with water every few hours. We had already had to receive permission from MAFF (Defra), the US government, and the state of Hawaii to transport the bees back to the UK and we had the appropriate documents.

When we arrived back at Los Angeles airport we seemed to cause absolute chaos when going through customs and immigration as the LA airport security insisted there was no information about our rescue mission and had never dealt with the transportation of queens before. The officer in charge pressed the red button as he had no information on his computer. I think they thought we were smuggling drugs or ammunition, soon we were surrounded by fully armed military police who were about to march us off to the nearest slammer when a voice cried: "I know these guys! They are okay. They are not terrorists!" The chief security officer said: "Who are you?"

"I am a US citizen and my dad happens to be Inspector-General of the US Army, General Lynch!"

The officer was taken aback and Bill persuaded them that we were just Limey conservationists, and a phone call to Hawaii confirmed our legitimacy. Thankfully we had such good friends as Bill and Maggie or we could have been in the jailhouse. We were grateful and we all went for a meal, including the bees. When we returned to the airport and boarded the aircraft we took our seats and just as we were about to take off there was an announcement from the purser. "I understand there is somebody on board with some queen bees can they please put their hands up!"

Freddie put his hands up, she came rushing down. "Where are they?" she exclaimed. Freddie reached up to the overhead luggage rack and she shouted in alarm "Don't let them out!"

Freddie was by now used to these reactions. We had to keep them with us all the time and I had to keep saying "Don't forget the queens" and people would turn around and do a double take. Normally the bees would be exported or go by special transport so this was for us very exciting and rewarding. These bees are such a powerful breed and probably the best in the world.

Freddie calmly replied: "They can't get out. They are having a nice little sleep in their boxes. They are with their princesses and all they need is a drop of water every three hours and that's that".

One passenger gasped: "That's really cute!" The hostess and our fellow passengers breathed a collective sigh of relief. She smiled and said "Enjoy your flight and have a nice day!" The flight continued with no problems except for an increase in the passengers' curiosity, several of them eventually becoming brave enough to ask questions about the state and wellbeing of the bees.

On our return to the UK Steve Ryan said that our trip to Hawaii had been a huge success, helping to preserve the UK bee population. We had enjoyed it, too.

Professor Peter Bullock, of the European Environmental Committee one of the world's leading soil scientists, winner of the Nobel Prize for his work with the International Committee on Global Warming. When showing me around Rothamstead Experimental Station, near Harpenden stated : "I believe that in the future, if there are wars, they will be over water, not oil. One person in every three on the planet has no access to fresh water – the results of chemicals and pesticides used by man have not impacted fully yet on the water table, but there is no doubt that this will affect plants and insects."

Dr Barbara Lee, Host scientist at the US National Energy Laboratories Hawaii, with Charles White and Freddie Drabble. Here we were shown the awesome power of sea water in producing food for mankind.

Kona Bee Factory, Hawaii. Where the bees remained unaffected by the veroa mite, which had decimated the bee population across the world.

A lady packs queen bees for transport to the UK. Their amazing ability to lay 2,500 eggs an hour in summer for seven years will reinvigorate English bees.

Victory at last

Freddie's tenacity, together with his immense affection for the environment, led him to exploit every opportunity to stop the horrific plan to build a sewage plant on the magnificent heritage coast. The appointment of a new chairman of Yorkshire Water looked like a breakthrough for the Sons after Sir Gordon Jones retired. The Sons had acquired the minimum shares to enable us to gain entry to the Company annual general meetings – often staging publicity stunts to make our points. Sir Gordon had to defend himself against newspaper reports that he had been awarded a £44,000 a year increase in salary, bringing him up to £119,000 in the year to the end of 1991.

The YWA were losing the public relations battle, Sir Gordon claiming that he was due to that amount because the structure of water companies was different to that of other companies, as chairmen were appointed on a part-time basis, which the salaries represented (Sir Gordon was only part-time, as he had other chairmanships, ie Hicksons Chemicals) This was the beginning of the tidal wave of greed to come – at the same time the chairman of another water company, Mr John Bellaz, saw his pay packet jump from £88,700 to £149,500. Sir Gordon, was, at that time chairman of all the Water Authorities Associations – appointed by Margaret Thatcher to administer these policies.

Sir Gordon retired, and the new chairman was Kevin Bond, a former police superintendent. At first he avoided any encounter with the Sons, and continued to pursue Government policy, even though our relentless criticism in the media was having a major impact on public opinion. The YWA's line was to imply, along with some aspects of the establishment, that we were protesting just for the sake of protesting, and that we would oppose any plans. Freddie took the bull by the horns and phoned Bond directly, inviting him to come to Scarborough to get a first-hand account of our concerns. Meeting him near the Heritage Coast path, Freddie took him for a walk and emphasised his obvious love of the coastline. His common sense and practical approach to the best position to place the plant - underground so that it did not blemish the Heritage Coast, and in a natural valley, where it would be out of sight and well away from the population - impressed the new chairman who at last saw the Sons in their true colours.

Freddie said: "I invited Mr Bond to Scarborough, took him on the cliffs and showed him the magnificent scenery of the Heritage Coast, and told him that this was our equivalent of the Lake District - the natural beauty that attracts people to Scarborough. To destroy this would betray not only this generation, but future generations. As I spoke I felt that for the first time this was somebody who understood what our campaign was about."

It was this meeting that set in motion the plan to move from Scalby to near the Cowlam Hole location first suggested by Captain Syd and the Sons. Kevin Bond was superseded by a new chairman, John Napier, who began to communicate with the Sons in a spirit of understanding and good will. Freddie's years of incredible diplomacy in dealing with the board had at last borne fruit. He felt that John Napier was a man of in-depth knowledge in dealing with corporate matters with a wider vision. Freddie had a thorough insight into the structure of the YW, as well as his own business acumen and ability as a lawyer, and it seemed to register favourably with Napier.

My own first meeting with John Napier was at the opening of the Whitby sewage treatment plant, on the outskirts of Whitby. Freddie was unable to make it and so I had to represent the Sons. I nearly missed the event when my Jeep slid down the steep hill from Boggle Hole, as a freak snowstorm had created an ice sheet. On my arrival at the plant I felt that while the atmosphere was friendly there was an air of apprehension, and when I was introduced as the representative of the Sons there was a slight chill to the atmosphere. Our reputation with Yorkshire Water had given us the image as vociferous opponents; whilst their public relations arm of the company only came into being when we began our campaign. Once again, the expert for the company was confidently showing the group around the plant referring only to bacteria. I interrupted "What about viruses? They are often more pathogenic than bacteria?" There was a puzzled silence. Our trip to the US had given us the confidence and knowledge to demand the best possible system for clean beaches and a clean sea, safe enough for bathers. I was introduced to John Napier and instantly liked him. He had a great sense of flair and style, was well informed about our group, and Freddie had sensed that at last the Yorkshire Water had a man with a panoramic view of the industry and the vision to bring it up to date. Freddie and John developed a good relationship and shared an understanding of what was needed to solve the problems of sea pollution.

Freddie said : "I first encountered John Napier at the Yorkshire Water AGM when he was appointed chairman. I was asking him questions and I asked him to come over to Scarborough to meet the Sons and play bowls or golf and have a meal with us. He instantly struck me as "one of the lads". He seemed a very likeable chap and very easy to get along with. In fact, I thought to myself, if he lived in Scarborough I would have invited him to join the Sons of Neptune. We knew he had worked in Australia, the Gobi desert, and various other parts of the world. He struck me as somebody we could do business with. He talked our language and from then on we were able to work very closely with him. If we had any problems we could discuss them clearly. We explained our position to him and what we were trying to achieve. The big difference was that he was someone who was able to listen and willing to listen to our position, where we had come from and where we intended to go. He realised that we were going to go there (ie get full treatment) and if he was not able to go along with us we would remain friends and we would respect each others position, but that we would not stop. We would carry on. We realised that he was someone who did not stand on his position as Chairman of Yorkshire Water. He had no airs or graces and blessed with the common touch.

"He could see that we were not out to get publicity for ourselves and that we were extremely busy in our own rights, professions and businesses, and that actually we did not want to spend a lot of our own time writing letters and attending meetings. We had our own life and pressures and we resented wasting our time arguing with people. The other thing is that we simply wanted a decent life for ourselves in the environment and we did not want a polluted environment. We wanted clean seas for ourselves and our children, and we were not going to sacrifice something as essential as that to life and that we were going to carry on with our campaign even though it was arduous and time consuming. Nevertheless we were going to carry on with it.

If he was prepared to see our point of view and if they were prepared to listen and to go along with what was considered to be reasonable, not to be excessive - to achieve what we considered to be common sense and scientifically proven to be necessary. Then we would be more than happy to work with them and not to cause trouble if they would do what was scientifically proved to be necessary. We developed a close and friendly relationship as a result of this understanding".

The time had come when Yorkshire Water consulted with the Sons rather than remaining in conflict.

During the building work and necessary modernisation of these plants we were invited to observe the work in progress in February 2001. A great moment was when, on Freddie's birthday, were we were asked, with local MP Laurie Quinn and senior Yorkshire Water management to see the completion of the plant for Scarborough, at Cowlam Hole. It was something for which we had fought for 15 years. Freddie said: "It was a great birthday present. I feel very satisfied with the way it's constructed and the way it's blending in with the environment. There was an atmosphere of co-operation, and Yorkshire Water were interested in taking all views on board. They were quite different from the Yorkshire Water of the past – this could never have happened but for the work that we put in over years. We see this as a real jewel for Scarborough. I told the media I felt proud that Scarborough had this scheme at last, after the Sons had for so long been treated as outlaws, even though as business men we had spent our own time and money while being ridiculed by those whose duty it was to take care of the town. The Victorians left us a beautiful town, and it will be nice to leave future generations clean bathing water, the essential asset of Scarborough's tourist industry."

Freddie's knowledge of the most progressive treatment plants worldwide, the coastline, and business in general cemented our friendship with John Napier. We had several meetings with him, typical of these was John arriving in his chauffeur driven Mercedes at our isolated rustic headquarters - an old barn well down a field at the back of Freddie's house. This had served as our meeting place for many years. An early Victorian mahogany bar which we had rescued from one of Scarborough's oldest coaching inns complemented the swinging sign 'Evening Star' which had been painted by one of our supporters - local signwriter Ken Middleton. Matters of the environment and life in general were more amicably resolved in front of a log fire accompanied by fine food and a few bottles of wine! Most Thursdays the meeting would be preceded by a game of golf or bowls or a hike along the cliffs.

Freddie said: "On the morning of the opening of the new plant, a cold and frosty February morning John Napier joined us for a sea bathe in the North Bay. John had organised a superb breakfast at the Royal Hotel, the full monty, with silver service, black pudding, kedgeree, mushrooms, sausages etc, a complete range of everything you could desire for breakfast. Nothing could be more rewarding than this after our chilly dip in the North Sea. As soon as we sat down glasses of the finest malt whisky were served at 09:30 in the morning. A merry atmosphere ensued and laughter echoed through the salubrious dining room of the Royal Hotel. John seemed perfectly happy and relaxed as the waiters delivered super service. He was in his element, totally delighted with the events. So much so that after several whiskies apiece and several helpings of this excellent breakfast Chairman John reached to pass more whisky around."

I asked Cec the Gent what time it was, as John had to open the new plant with Baroness Young at 11am.

"10:30," said Cecil. I turned to Chairman John and asked him if he knew what time it was. He replied "no" casually, as if he had no cares in the world. I don't think he was aware of the time and if I hadn't reminded him he would still be enjoying the breakfast until late in the afternoon. I told him the time.

"Goodness" he exclaimed "we had better be going. I will get my car sorted out." So he got going and so did we.

"On arrival at the plant I couldn't believe how he had got freshened up so quickly, and we sat at a table surrounded by Town Hall officials, Councillors, and Yorkshire Water bigwigs. The officials completely ignored us and declined to recognise our role in bringing this event about.

"John introduced us to Baroness Young, Chief Executive of the Environment Agency. She had worthy credentials for her role - Green Globe Task Force, vice president of Flora and Fauna International, Birdlife International, and various wildlife trusts - and she had worked at Cranfield University, where Professor Bullock, who was one of the Sons' scientific advisers and a Nobel prize winner in 2008, did his research. Then John gave a hearty speech in which he praised the Sons for their work. This could not have happened without the Sons of Neptune, he said, and Baroness Young spoke and also praised our contribution. The Town Hall contingent had a disapproving look. It was one hell of a climax to mark the end of fifteen years of hard campaigning. Yorkshire Water were now co-operating fully with us, they had taken fully on-board all that we asked to protect our marine environment. They fully understood the science, the dangers and their need to respond to them and they realised that they could not have achieved this without us and so this was also why we had a great sense of elation.

They thanked us the best way they could. We were invited to every opening of every sewage works on the east coast as recognition for the contribution of our campaign. A sponsored wintry dip in the sea with John Napier a few hours before the official opening of the Scarborough plant not only raised £11,000 for the worthy Macmillan Nurses but sent out a powerful message from the Chairman of Yorkshire Water that the sea was now clean for swimming! The Sons took the opportunity of releasing a casket of white doves to celebrate the peace which now existed between us after a campaign of almost fifteen years and its successful outcome!

The battle between the Sons and Yorkshire Water was over at last. They had installed the latest ultra-violet radiation to kill off residual bacteria and viruses. The targets of our campaign had been achieved and the right of every man woman and child to go into the sea without fear of infection was assured.

Freddie's tenacity continued with constant communications

with John Napier, who had become a close friend to him and the Sons. He also kept in touch with Professor Bruce Denness, who was continually monitoring our seas, while we were always aware that there was more work to be done. At one meeting at the Yorkshire Water chairman's office we now spotted a group photograph of the Sons above his desk - an indication of the complete turnaround, as we were previously considered the enemy of the organisation.

Then at the end of 2010 the EEC put further pressure on the UK. This stated that by 2015 all coastal areas would be graded – from "Excellent" to "Poor", the average, we were told, would aim for "Sufficient". Yorkshire Water announced that their target was to be "excellent", leading the field in sea-water cleanliness, etc. In 2010 a new and more-informed group of experts had emerged at Yorkshire Water. They communicated with Freddie and the Sons to arrange a meeting so that we could join together to achieve this excellence.

The first meeting took place at Freddie's law office in December 2010 with YWA's representatives Lee Pitcher and Ed Bramley. Professor Denness travelled from The Isle of Wight to attend. An in-depth discussion took place on the state of our seas and beaches, and as a result of this there were exchanges of valuable data and proposed new plans. This was to lead to a meeting of the leading experts in the field of ocean pollution in the UK and Europe. Then in March 2011 Yorkshire Water arranged for a conference at the old Sitwell mansion (now the Scarborough Business Centre) to discuss and proceed on working to achieve excellence in the field of science and marine engineering.

The Sons were represented by Chris Found, Cecil Ridley, Freddie Drabble, Charles White, and Dr Bruce Denness, plus our supporter, Stuart Carlisle. The YWA had Lee Pitcher, Ed Bramley, and their scientific experts, Professor David Kay – from the Centre for Research into Environmental Health, University of Wales – plus Richard Dannat, associate director of Interek Metoc.

This was a zenith moment in marine conservation. The Sons' work had been recognised in this field. Professor Kay, a world leading expert is this field, said that we would achieve our goal of excellence in clean seas, and complimented the Sons, saying:

"You were the first to observe this happening, and the first to take action."

John Napier, Chairman of Yorkshire Water 2002 became the first chairman to accept the Sons of Neptune scientific research and fully supported the Sons' campaign for clean seas in the face of political opposition. We regard him as a true professional who pursued excellence for the enviroment.

The Sons celebrate the awarding of an EEC Blue Flag with a celebratory dip in the wintry North Sea 1 February 2002. YWA chairman John Napier is second right. The event raised £11,000 for Macmillan nurses.

Chief Executive of the Environment Agency Baroness Young with John Napier, chairman of Yorkshire Water, plus Freddie Drabble and Charles White at the official opening of the new treatment works, on 2 February 2002.

John Napier, chairman of Yorkshire Water, plus Freddie Drabble, Cecil Ridley, Charles White and Chris Found release 12 doves of peace to celebrate achieving the best bathing water quality via the new £30 million waste water treatment works built as a result of the Sons Campaign.

Chris Found, Charles White, Richard Dannet, associate director of Interek Metoc, Cec Ridley, Stuart Carlisle, Ed Bramley, from Yorkshire Water, Freddie Drabble, Bryan Dew, Professor David Kay, Centre for Research into Environment and Health, University of Wales. Seated, Dr Bruce Denness, formerly Professor of ocean engineering at Newcastle University and Lee Pitcher, from Yorkshire Water.

Approaching Christmas 2007 a few red and green lights on the boats in Scarborough's new Marina reflecting in the Harbour inspired a splendid way of commemorating the late Capt Sydney Smith and Bill Sheader. If there was beauty in a few lights imagine the effect of the boats being illuminated for Christmas! The Sons would award Challenge Cups and prizes to the yacht and fishing boat with the best Christmas decorations. This has now become an annual event with the Mayor and Mayoress invited to judge and award the prizes. As the photo shows, the Marina is now a very exciting place to be at Christmas time as daylight fades and the lights come on sending colours rippling in the waters. A magical place for young and old alike.

Neptune talks to the earth

If I had gone to a fortune teller forty years ago and he or she had told me that I would spend twenty years of my life fighting a campaign to prevent raw sewage and other pollutants from being poured into the bays of a beautiful seaside resort I would have thought it was hilarious and asked for my money back. When I studied geography at school in Roscommon in Ireland, Yorkshire was portrayed as a bleak industrial landscape with fierce combustion and black smoke emerging from dark satanic mills. At least the photos of steel factories in Sheffield gave that impression. The dark moors were impressed upon my mind as such by the Bronte sisters and David Storry's "Sporting Life" seemed to confirm this desolate barren view. I had vowed never to visit the North of England.

A complete change of opinion occurred upon meeting my wife-to-be, who was from Yorkshire. I came north from London to Scarborough and was enraptured by the variation, magnificence and beauty of the County. All my plans to travel to Canada and the U.S.A. evaporated instantly.

The force that drove the Sons to protect the environment was inexplicable, especially to Freddie and me, yet the support of all the Sons was essential. We often said that if there had only been one or two of us then we would not have had a chance but when there were six of us from a range of business and professions that foundation was much more difficult for others to shake.

Our all year round sea bathing had instilled an exalted state of indestructibility. But if the sea had cast that spell on us it had asked for something in return for such exhilaration. The sea which gave life to living things seemed to have spoken to us in a spiritual way. No amount of mockery or ridicule could deter us from our duty.

Freddie said "It was the sea literally telling us to wake up and do something!" We had been going in the sea and had seen the changes. The disappearance of the eels and crabs which had once been wriggling under our feet. The breaking waves had lost their sparkling white. Grey was the colour which now greeted us! At times we could only gasp in despair. But the sea had cast its spell on us. Walking away was not an option in the face of a crime against creation."

The Sea seemed to speak to us, saying: "I have existed for billions and billions of years. Man appeared just an instant ago yet is beginning to destroy me. Over the billions of years my atmosphere has changed to the most extreme temperatures and conditions, a multitude of living creatures have evolved from me and various life-forms have evolved and existed for various times and conditions to suit my purpose.

"Mankind has proved the most precious but is now emerging as a self destructive being. Mankind, you have produced great art, civilisations, religions, politicians and intellectuals yet you have failed to protect the very environment that gave you life. Blinded by greed, arrogance and egotism you have entered a retrogressive phase and seem unable to evolve to greater levels.

"The use of war as a solution for any human activity is no longer acceptable, as it is simply insane. Global warming is normally a natural phenomenon in evolution not the product of the work of a single selfish species. In the past man had little impact, but now man's activity exacerbates the annihilation of known existence and deviates wildly from the natural course, and if this continues this would destroy the oceans, the land and the atmosphere, which has now reached levels of toxicity that could destroy me. Thus the life of all creatures could disappear in this state of putridity.

"Greenhouse gas continues to increase, accelerating at a faster pace than previously believed. Mankind has pulverised my oceans with exceptionally deadly acids and chemicals, such as caesium. However, it is the increase in the amount of $Co2$ which creates carbonic acid, now at a level of 30 per cent, which by the end of the next generation, will reach a level of 150 per cent. Recent suggestions by the power industries indicate that they would like to bury compressed carbon in my sea. This was previously tried by the US, German, and Japanese, who thought it would be a great idea to put compressed emissions of carbon to marinate as waste in the sea. The result was that shellfish and molluscs melted and disintegrated and all other living creatures were destroyed by the level of acidity. The atmospheric chemistry of life and the life-forming DNA was obliterated, and the food-chain of all living creatures was destroyed. In recent times a change of 30 per cent in CO_2, is more than we have seen in 20 million years, and it is likely that the oceans, which are already the source of life's amazing diversity, will change into nothing more than a lifeless holding tank for toxic trash. Coral reefs are withered to boneyard levels across the oceans of the planet. Those who are environmentally aware are mostly ignored as mankind continues to be propelled by greed, self-interest, and an extreme false sense of indestructibility, blinded by materialism and pseudo self-importance.

The earth has a geological cycle of death and renewal, when magma at the earth's core erupts new oceans are formed. It is a ceaseless activity which has been going on since the formation of the planet. Just as what happens to mankind is irrelevant to the world of geology, what happens to world geology is not irrelevant to the human race. It is a manifestation of the infinitely little changes over the infinitely great. The unending flow of energy from unstable atoms wrecking the stability of the world, the molecular structure of the earth changes, and so too will life-forms. Man's activity exacerbates the natural change, so the ocean acidification is apocalyptic in its impact.

Mankind's role would become obsolete, and so would all known life-forms. After all, 300million years is just the blink of an eye in the time of the earth's life of 10billion years.

The most important conservationist of modern times, Sir David Attenborough, has warned mankind that the effects of over-population would lead to mass starvation, as we are already unable to feed our starving nations.

I have often thought that man is too insignificant to comprehend his own existence. Our senses should concentrate on caring for the realistic creation that is God – the planet and all we see here and feel. As Albert Einstein said: Religion without science is blind", and Stephen Hawking said: "God is the name people give to the reason we are here." My own observation is that faith is an ability to believe that which we know to be untrue .

At this stage the majority of the human race does not seem to care what happens to the very source which gave them life on this wonderful planet.

Does such a species deserve such a diverse universe in which they live? Can they save themselves from obliteration? Yes! Where there is life there is hope, but mankind must change to save the environment which sustains him.

Man's binding to the multitude of religious and political ideologies is retrogressive and divisive, and has led to the glorification of war and man's annihilation of his fellow man.

This point was emotively imparted by Harry Patch, the last surviving soldier of the Great War (the war to end all wars), who died at the age of 111. Describing as "organised murder", he condemned war, saying: "It was not worth one life, let alone all the millions."

Various religious interpretations have been important and have had a beneficial effect on social cultural and family activities, though many of these contribute to fractious impressions which are divisive in racial and territorial harmony. Science and religion should be in harmony, but unfortunately they have drifted apart. Thus man's interpretation of the God of all creation seems to have no rational explanation. This world, this planet, its solar system and the galaxies are the only tangible reality. The vanishing shapes of this rich and elegant world may never be known by future generations, but we still have time to save this wonderful world - if life can regulate the atmosphere it can regulate the climate.

Man in communion with Nature is endowed with the power of truth, which transcends mere politics and philosophies. The Sons of Neptune were gifted a portion of that communion. It comes with great energy, much fun and an amazing insight!

The Sons of Neptune list of members

The author: Charles White, chiropodist (podiatrist), musicologist, broadcaster, and conservationist.

Freddie Drabble, lawyer, athlete, and conservationist. With his friend, Charles White, a co-founder of the Sons of Neptune, and is leader of the group.

Capt. Sydney Smith (1907 - 19th November 2000), master mariner, and world leading authority on tidal matters. Decorated by Winston Churchill and His Majesty King George for his bravery during World War Two, he became President of Trinity House in 1982, and was elevated to the position of Honorary Brother in 1992. His unique knowledge of the sea made a crucial contribution to the success of the campaign.

Chris Found, a chartered accountant and a man of unique ability and a superb athlete, noted for his rugby, tennis, golf, bowls, and hiking, as well as his sharp-witted humour. Nickname 'El Foundo the Magnificent' because of his admiration of the Spanish heroic figure El Cid. His support was significant in organising hikes and events, and taking control of the group's finances.

Cecil Ridley, known as 'Cecil the Gentleman' because of his old-world charm and humour. A respected Scarborough turf accountant, he had a great sense of self-mockery, and his communication skills were a great help to the campaign. His philosophy produced a certain amount of comfort for clients who lost by gambling with his business. His dialogue would produce such phrases as: "You don't get everything in this world", "Better luck next time", "You can't go very far wrong by backing second favourites", "If you don't bet you cannot win". And : "Someone's got to win"

Bryan Dew, who was Pilkington's marketing man in the area, a former member of the Diplomatic Corps, and model English gentleman, who radiated charm at all times. He started his professional career in London, mixing with high society, such as the

Terry family, famed for their chocolate empire, and the Simpsons of Piccadilly, where he socialised, sipping champagne before Wimbledon. His experiences were often told with great humour, much to our delight, and later led to his talent as a cartoonist in the company magazine, titled "Dew for a laugh ". The story of how he once took several dozen Victoria Crosses – the ultimate war decoration, inscribed "For Valour" – to the RAF college Cranwell for an exhibition at the behest of a jolly eccentric Air Vice-Marshal. He was so nervous on the train that he continually took them from his briefcase to count them in case he had lost any, to the amazement of fellow passengers. He referred to his four children, three boys and a girl, as "The Dewdrops". His wife Lady Pamela, is a great supporter of the Sons, noted for her splendid hospitality, beautiful garden – and delicious elderflower wine, which captured the flavours and bouquet of summer in a bottle.

Geoff Nunn, public school master, a gentle giant with a vivacious sense of humour. He braved the criticism and condescension of the local establishment to support the group, and his strong character proved unshakable.

The Sons of Neptune list of supporters

Barry Hampshire, journalist and musician, charity fundraiser. As a news editor and friend he encouraged me to write over the years. Also a great supporter of the Sons. His proof reading and editing skills remain unsurpassed.

Patrick Argent, college lecturer and former editor of Graphic Design Magazine, noted expert on the worlds leading designers, Paul Rand, Milton Glazier, John Southerland, Richard Seymore, Michael Johnson etc. His help and advice is greatly appreciated.

David Lazenby, who provided practical help with many of the Sons demonstrations, spiritual and scientific one with the aid of his trusty bible the other with his hours of research on environmental matters.

Jennie Parvin, whose brilliant management kept Freddie's law practice in the very best of health throughout the campaign.

Chris Coole, whose background support in matters technical could always be relied on.

Professor Peter Bullock, Nobel Prize winning scientist, affectionately known as Professor Pete, a man of quiet dignity and extraordinary achievement, internationally renowned for his wide understanding of eco-systems that support life on Earth . He was the world's leading soil scientist, with particular significance to the production of food, fibre, and medicines, soil-carbon storage, the processing of waste, water purification, and regulation of flooding and erosion, He showed how soil-science provides the central keystone in the understanding the full impacts of climate change. His presidencies included the International Commission of Soil Micromorphology and the Council of the British Society of Soil Science of the European Union. Peter was a shy man, a typical English gentleman, and would never show any indication of his status on the world stage. He loved cricket and beer and was always charming. He advised me on the state of the European Commission on the environment, and it was only later that I realised how crucial this advice was.

Stuart Carlisle, who gallantly stepped in to keep the Sons up to six when Geoff moved to Keswick.

The Sons' wives, Anne, Yvette, Pam, Dee and Heather who were carried along with the tide.

My thanks to many multi-media sources:

Special thanks to Scarborough Evening News, Yorkshire Post, Yorkshire Evening News, Harry Mead, of the Northern Echo, Sunday Times, Observer, The Guardian, The Independent, etc. BBC Tv Newsnight, BBC North "Against All Odds", BBC Radio York, BBC Radio Four, Calendar, Tyne-Tees Tv, etc.

Reporters Nick Wood, Gerard Tubbs, Michael Buerk, Grant Mansfield, James Hogg, Graeme Thompson, Susannah York, Ned Thacker, Pat O'Hara, Martin Wainwright, etc.

Supporters of the Sons of Neptune: Herbert Temple, chairman of Trinity House, Frances Sutherland (Captain Syd film), and David Lazenby.

To Sir Alan Ayckbourn and Sir David Attenborough who inspired a greater love of the environment.

The staff at Newby and Scalby Library for their help.

To Paul and Sharon at the Hayburn Wyke Hotel, for their help with the history of Rob in Hood's Bay and their beer, good food, and company, and the proprietors of the Raven Hall Hotel for great views and magnificent golf.

Photographs

The majority of photographs are from the Sons of Neptune Archives and copyright of Charles White.

All efforts have been made to locate and gain permission for use of other images and media sources and are credited where information is available.

Neptune Letters

During our battle for clean seas, we had to use multi-media to get our case across. We literally sent thousands of letters all over the UK, Europe and USA. Here are a sample of the more significant letters and replies, which are the result of ultimate tenacity.

STATEMENT TO SCARBOROUGH EVENING NEWS

Referring to the recent Statement from the Yorkshire Water Authority concerning the stability of the 200' Castle Hill cliff towering above and behind the site of the proposed sewage-treatment works and pumping station on the Marine Drive, a professional geologist has now inspected the cliff face and carried out research on the strata generally for the Sons of Neptune Group who have frequently drawn attention over their 1½ years' campaign to the frequent rockfalls and "Beware Dangerous Cliffs" notices at the site.

The geologist concerned is Mr. John Dunlevey who lived in Scarborough for many years and is now in the employment of the National Building Research Institute and Council for Scientific and Industrial Research in Pretoria, South Africa. He holds B.Sc. Honours and Masters Degrees in Geology and is likely to be awarded a Doctorate shortly.

His Report is that the Castle Hill is a faulted structure and that construction carried out at the site proposed would almost certainly cause severe instability in the cliff face.

The Sons of Neptune are further advised by Mr. Dunlevey that the instability which would be caused by carrying out the works would be quite likely to affect vital parts of the ancient monument including the remains of the Roman Signal Station and St. Mary's Chapel on top of the Headland. In view of this the Sons of Neptune Group call for independent experts in slope stability to be brought in immediately to prepare a Report comparing the stability of the strata at the Castle Hill situation with that at Cowlam Hole so that the matter can be resolved without any more delay.

The initial appraisal by Mr. Dunlevey indicates that the cost of stabilising the Castle Hill cliffs, if it could be accomplished at all, would be a vast amount of money making the whole Scheme far more expensive than the Cowlam Hole alternative. In addition, the retaining wall, extending to a considerable height at the back of the screening plant, would be a horrendous structure and a hideous disfigurement of the glorious Marine Drive Scenery.

Senior South African geologist Professor John Dunlevey condemns S.B.C. and Y.W.A. for their insane plan to build a sewage plant underneath the castle headland, with offices and carparks etc for Y.W.A. staff. This would have brought the Castle headland down across Marine Drive into the sea!

From the Press Office of Tyne Tees Television Limited
City Road, Newcastle upon Tyne NE1 2AL
Telephone: 091-261-0181

FIRST EDITION

SCARBOROUGH: A Suitable Case For Treatment

On Thursday, 3rd December, 1987, at 10.32 p.m.

What do a solicitor, a turf accountant, a teacher, a business executive,
and a chiropodist have in common? They all belong to "The Sons of Neptune"
an unlikely group of conservationists who for the last 5 years have been
having a running battle with the Yorkshire Water Authority and Scarborough
Council. The row is over what to do with the state of Scarborough's
beaches, which attract £80 million a year in tourist revenue. The problem
is, they are dirty. There are things being discharged from the crumbling
Victorian sewage system which you wouldn't want your Granny to see.

Yorkshire Water are intending to spend £21 million to build a new long sea
outfall ...ich will bring Scarborough's two beaches up to EEC standards.
The Sons of Neptune say the new system won't work because the bugs will be
washed straight back to shore. They use scientific evidence to back them.
Yorkshire Water say the new system will work. They too claim scientific
evidence supports them.

The people of Scarborough have been bombarded with argument and counter
argument for the past five years. Work has now started on the new scheme,
and still the row continues.

"The people of Scarborough are victims of misinformation and I think when
this scheme is put into action the people of Scarborough will see for
themselves that this is what we need."

                                        Councillor Mrs. Eileen Harbron.

"The pro·sal to dump raw untreated human waste when the leading scientists
in the world say this will activate viruses and bacteria and cause disease...
for a tourist town to do that - it is like a lethal, vile enemy coming in
our town and imposing this upon us."

                                        Charles White, Sons of Neptune.

"It does us no good as a tourist town, as a resort authority, for a group
like the Sons of Neptune to continue to put forward specious arguments."

                                        John Trabble
                                        Chief Executive, Scarborough Council

"I am one hundred per cent happy that we have all the evidence that we need that
proves that Yorkshire Water's scheme for Scarborough is not only farcical, it's
disgraceful."

                                        Freddie Drabble, Sons of Neptune.

RESEARCHER: BRIAN HOLLAND
DIRECTOR·   BERNARD PRESTON
PRODUCER.   GEORGE COURTICE

A TYNE TEES TELEVISION PRODUCTION. Further enquiries to Laurie Taylor, Chief Press Officer

Dirty work

Sir, — As a regular subscriber to the Yorkshire Post and as a conservationist, may I firstly congratulate you on your excellent coverage of hazardous waste in the last few months. It is a magnificent public service which exposes a criminal act against this generation and future generations.

However, on the subject of the environment, I cannot agree with your editorial on July 11. A day by the sea, in which you blame dogs for the fact that not a single beach in the North of England won a blue flag.

This is a gross distortion of the truth and is rather like blaming German umpha umpha bands for the Second World War. Britain is the only European country sludge-dumping and dumping raw untreated human waste into the sea and, as you reported on the previous Saturday, July 9, "the EC flag is given to beaches with

unpolluted sea water and where no untreated sewage is pumped into the sea".

Absolutely correct, so why tell us it is dogs on the beaches that are the cause of pollution? Because the UK water authorities do not wish the Great British public to realise the truth about their floundering miasma of red tape and bureaucratic bungling, but most of all their misrepresentation on the disease-carrying waste they pump daily into our sea.

As a conservationist I have travelled

to the US and Canada where sewage treatment is 60 times stricter than the UK. Our group, the Sons of Neptune, have been advised by the world's leading professors in oceanography and marine microbiology, who condemn the YWA outfall system as dangerous and outdated.

Yet the YWA fail to admit that the Bridlington scheme has failed the EC preliminary tests and that they want to build a similar outdated and potentially-dangerous outfall screening plant at Scarborough. I say dangerous

because scientific evidence now confirms that the microbial die-off does not occur but that they (the bacteria and viruses) remain virulent in the sea for long periods of time.

No wonder the YWA are desperately trying to keep us in the dark on this matter. The reason no less is to whizz through privatisation of the water authorities so the public will bear the burden of updating archaic retrogressive industry.

To blame dog dirt on beaches for failure of any resort in the North of England for not getting a blue EC flag is as outrageous as any minister of truth in a George Orwell novel and is contributing to the destruction of our precious environment. — Yours faithfully,

CHARLES WHITE
Sons of Neptune Ltd, Scarborough.

At this stage the Sons had scientific evidence that this would create a micro biological time bomb which the parties concerned were more than aware. But privatisation ruled, money before people and the environment.

278

YORKSHIRE POST

FRIDAY AUGUST 12 1988

LETTERS TO THE EDITOR

The terrors of the deep

Sir, — Mr J.M. Taylor, general manager of Yorkshire Water's North and East division, opens his letter to you (July 29) with the statement that he likes to think of himself as a conservationist. Unfortunately, it is an outfall pipe-dream on his part.

Yorkshire Water believe that adequate coastal sewage treatment is simply an outfall pipe which reaches the sea beyond low water mark but of minimum distance beyond that. Down that pipe goes everything which leaves the domestic toilet, except perhaps pet alligators, and anything else which, after chopping or mulching, cannot be forced through a pea-size mesh.

Mr Taylor clearly believes in the conservation of dangerous bacteria and viruses. These could easily be removed with the sludge and by disinfection of the remaining effluent. However, under Mr Taylor's system they are released into the sea where the dangerous viruses live for a year or more. Bacteria can survive for weeks, and even after apparent death many enter into a state of dormancy but continued virulence for an indefinite period. Is this the conservation Mr Taylor has in mind?

Does Mr Taylor believe in the conservation of seals? Their population in the North Sea has been decimated in recent weeks by *Picornaviruses*. These are present in domestic sewage and cause such diseases as hepatitis, meningitis and polio.

As Mr Taylor says, the results of bacterial tests along the Yorkshire coast are on a publicly available register. They are not, however, on display at the Scalby Mills public information centre which Mr Taylor proudly announces has been visited by 5,000 people. Why not?

Perhaps it is because out of Yorkshire Water's 23 monitored beaches only one passed the EEC guideline tests. And this was no EEC mandatory limits in 1983 and 1984. Hardly satisfactory results for a public exhibition.

Perhaps this may help to explain why Yorkshire Water have £70m cash reserves pending privatisation. In our opinion, it would have been bankrupt many times over if Yorkshire's seas and rivers were unpolluted.

These are facts which will not be on display at Scalby Mills. Perhaps they will be on the list of contingent liabilities when the accounts are ready for the shares in pollution to be marketed to the public

— Yours faithfully,
CHARLES J. WHITE
Sons of Neptune Limited
Scarborough.

Y.W.A. continued to support untreated sewage dumping into our beautiful bays with displays that do not mention that the scheme is already obsolete by E.C. Laws and will literally waste millions of pounds and pollute the bathing waters.

THE
NORTH
SEA

Mr C White
███████████
███████████
███████

3 October 1988

Dear Charles

Thank you for your contribution to the North Sea Series.
The transmission dates for the programmes are as follows:-

7 October	THE NORTH SEA	- Everything Connects
14 October		- Neptune's Children
21 October		- The Rhine - Romance & Rubbish
28 October		- ... And Man Created Holland
4 November		- Denmark's Fishy Business
11 November		- Norway - Our Common Future

The programmes will be broadcast on the above Fridays
at 8.00pm on BBC2 in the Newcastle, Leeds and Norwich
Regions. For your interest the series is also being
shown in Denmark, Norway and The Netherlands.

It is expected that the series will be shown throughout
the whole country early in the New Year. When we have
a date and time for this we will contact you again.

Yours sincerely

Mark Scrimshaw
Producer

UNIVERSITY OF NEW HAMPSHIRE

Office of the Director
Sea Grant College Program
85 Adams Point Road
Durham, New Hampshire 03824-3406
PHONE: (603) 862-2175
FAX: (603) 862-1101

May 17, 1990

Mr. Freddie Drabble, Esq.
Sons of Neptune Ltd.
1 Cromwell Parade
Scarborough, YO11 2DP
UNITED KINGDOM

Dear Freddie:

I was delighted to receive your telephone call earlier this week with the good news about North West and South West Water Authorities. Send me the details, when you get a chance.

Enclosed is a recent article concerning the collaboration between the New England Sea Grant programs and the Republic of Ireland and Northern Ireland. Most of that effort is occurring on the western shores of Ireland, so the information may not be of much help to you. However, I telephoned my fellow Sea Grant Director in Connecticut, Dr. Ed Monahan (see photo on p. 19), explained the situation, and he suggested that you contact Dr. James (Jim) Wilson, Dept. of Environmental Sciences, Trinity College, Dublin, Ireland. Apparently, he is very interested in pollution of the Irish Sea and might be of some help.

I look forward to learning of more good news from the UK!

Sincerely yours,

D. Jay Grimes
Professor and Director

Prof. Jay Grimes will be forever in our debt as it was he who scientifically proved that bugs do not die in the sea but in fact can become super bugs.

FD/LG   28th March 1990

Dear Mrs. Rumley,

re:- The Scarborough £28m Raw Sewage Scheme

We would invite Scarborough Hotels Association to urgently review their whole-
hearted support for the above Scheme in view of the world wide scientific concern
over the discharge of raw sewage into the sea. The concern of this campaign expressed
many years ago is now fully supported by the United Nations Environment Programme,
EEC and House of Commons Committee on Beach Pollution.

You may also be interested to note the reaction of the St. Ives Hotels Association
in connection with a similar scheme to the Scarborough scheme proposed for St.
Ives Bay. Out of a voting population of 15,000 people, 7,874 people voted. 99%
of those people voted against the long sea outfall raw sewage Scheme proposed.

We find it astonishing that Scarborough Hotels Association should continue to support
the Scarborough Raw Sewage Outfall Scheme and, in view of world opinion, we
now ask you to give it your immediate condemnation demanding its immediate
suspension as it cannot be upgraded to treatment. Yorkshire Water have already
accepted that the site at Scalby Mills is too small. They were, of course, fully aware
of this before Contracts were ever signed for the scheme. In addition, as you may
well be aware, the Scheme incorporates storm water overflows of raw sewage
at low water mark at Peasholm Gap and also directly off the Marine Drive near
the existing short outfall.

We request your immediate consideration on this matter vital to Scarborough's
tourist and fishing industries. We should be grateful if you would circulate a copy
of this letter to the Committee Members of the Association.

Yours sincerely,

Mrs. E. Rumley,
Scarborough Hotels Association,
Granby Hotel,
Queen Street,
SCARBOROUGH.

We had delivered scientific data to the S.B.H.A. which was
discarded on delivery. The general attitude was not to go against
the Scarborough Borough Council.

Lancashire
County
Council

COUNTY HALL,

PRESTON,

LANCASHIRE.

County Councillor Mrs. Louise J. Ellman
Leader of the County Council

11th May, 1990.

Dear Freddie,

I thought you might be interested to see the enclosed
statements. The pipe line application has been rejected
by the Department of the Environment and North West Water
have been asked to go back to the drawing board!

We must now ensure that we get the best solution to the
problem. Many thanks for all your help. This is a great
victory but the battle is not yet over!

Best wishes.

Yours sincerely,

L. ᴅ Le

F. Drabble, Esq.,
Sons of Neptune,
1 Cromwell Parade,
SCARBOROUGH,
YO11 2DP.

The Sons published The Denness Report based on Prof.
Jay's U.S. Report to Congress. Louise Ellman was delighted with
the report which condemned the outdated practice dumping raw
untreated sewage. Yorkshire Water and Scarborough Council chose
the Viking settlement plan which was to waste millions. Lancashire
chose the proper treatment plan and saved millions whilst making
bathing and fishing in coastal waters a healthier situation.

CARLO RIPA DI MEANA
Member of the Commission of the European Communities

Brussels 17 Febr. 1992
10199

Dear Mr Drabble,

Thank you for your letters of 4 and 17 October 1991. I would like to inform you that your complaints about the Scarborough raw sewage scheme were registered under file numbers P 910/90 and P 666/91 within the scope of Directive 76/464/EEC.

The Commission has sent a letter of formal notice to the Government of the United Kingdom as provided for in article 169 of the EEC Treaty giving the opportunity to submit its observations on the pollution problems associated with the long sea outfall in Scarborough.

Concerning Directive 76/160/EEC, the results from the 1991 bathing season are not yet available to the Commission and compliance can therefore not be assessed at present.

Yours sincerely,

[signature]

Mr F. Drabble
SONS OF NEPTUNE LTD.
1 Cromwell Parade
UK-SCARBOROUGH, YO11 2DP

The Sons delighted that Carlo Ripa Di Meana, a leader of the European Communities accepted that our complaints would be observed.

285

BEI♦EIB

DEN EUROPÆISKE INVESTERINGSBANK
EUROPÄISCHE INVESTITIONSBANK
ΕΥΡΩΠΑΙΚΗ ΤΡΑΠΕΖΑ ΕΠΕΝΔΥΣΕΩΝ
EUROPEAN INVESTMENT BANK
BANCO EUROPEO DE INVERSIONES
BANQUE EUROPEENNE D'INVESTISSEMENT
BANCA EUROPEA PER GLI INVESTIMENTI
EUROPESE INVESTERINGSBANK
BANCO EUROPEU DE INVESTIMENTO

SONS OF NEPTUNE LIMITED
1 Cromwell Parade

GB - SCARBOROUGH YO11 2DP

Luxembourg, 5 March 1992   Ref. PM2/JVK/mf   02703

Dear Sirs,

Ref.:   Scarborough wastewater disposal

        We thank you for you letter dated 2 March 1992 and we have noted your
comments.

                    Yours sincerely,

                EUROPEAN INVESTMENT BANK

            J. van Kaam   F. Bargagli-Petrucci

Freddie wrote to the European Investment Bank and asked
them not to fund Yorkshire Waters outfall schemes particularly the
Scarborough one. This was to lead to the UK being pressured into
cleaning up it's act as 'The Dirty Old Man of Europe'

LONDON SWIA IBS

17th November 1992

From: The Private Secretary to H.R.H. The Prince of Wales

Dear Mr. Drabble,

Thank you very much for your letters of 23rd September and 21st October. I do apologise for the long delay in replying.

The Prince of Wales has asked me to explain that, whilst he has looked at the new papers which you enclosed, it is simply not possible for His Royal Highness to become involved in the kind of detailed discussions which are now taking place.

His Royal Highness has asked me to explain that he has every sympathy for the way in which you are tackling matters of significance to your local environment but, quite apart from the fact that His Royal Highness does not possess the resources which would be necessary to carry out any detailed investigation, it would simply not be appropriate for him to attempt to intervene in matters such as this. His Royal Highness's position makes it possible for him to make his views known on matters of principle, but he cannot become a kind of ombudsman, intervening in local planning matters - however tempting that might sometimes be.

His Royal Highness has asked me to send you his best wishes.

Yours sincerely,

Commander Richard Aylard, RN

Freddie Drabble Esq.,
Sons of Neptune Ltd.,
1 Cromwell Parade,
Scarborough,
Yorkshire YO11 2DP.

SCARBOROUGH

Evening News
COMMENT

Another mess

YORKSHIRE Water seems to have learned nothing from the farcical sewage outfall scheme at Scalby Mills in Scarborough.

After many objections and at much additional cost, Yorkshire Water finally bowed to the inevitable and put forward plans for a proper treatment plant.

But now the company has managed to push through another shameful outfall scheme – at Robin Hood's Bay, with effluent waste still being pumped out to sea.

It is amazing that the North York Moors planning committee agreed to the scheme when it normally operates a strict veto over plans that will spoil the area's reputation.

Even short-sighted Yorkshire Water officials and local planning chiefs must know by now that the public does not want any more un-treated sewage dumped at sea. The new scheme will be an improvement on what exists at the moment but it is no longer acceptable to merely run the effluent through screens and mesh.

Environmentalists the Sons of Neptune are right to back residents who are furious over approval for another Yorkshire Water outrage.

SCARBOROUGH

Evening News
**17-23 Aberdeen Walk, Scarborough
North Yorkshire, YO11 1BB**
Tel (0723) 363636. Fax (0723) 354092

EUROPEAN COMMISSION
DIRECTORATE-GENERAL XI
ENVIRONMENT, NUCLEAR SAFETY AND CIVIL PROTECTION

Legal affairs and application of Community law

26.07.94 /XI/017745

Brussels,
XI.1 D(94)

Sons of Neptune Limited
Mr. Freddie Drabble

United Kingdom

Dear Mr. Drabble,

I write to inform you that as a result of yours and others complaints relating to discharges of raw sewage and, in one case, the discharge of industrial effluents directly into the aquatic environment the Commission has started action against the United Kingdom for non compliance with Directive 76/464/EEC - pollution caused by certain dangerous substances discharged into the aquatic environment of the Community.

Yours sincerely,

L. Krämer
Head of Unit

Rue de la Loi 200, B-1049 Brussels, Belgium - Office: 5, avenue de Beaulieu, 4/11.
Telephone: direct line (+32-2)299.22.65, exchange 299.11.11. Fax: 299.10.70.
Telex: COMEU B 21877. Telegraphic address: COMEUR Brussels.

Robens Institute
University of Surrey
Guildford, Surrey
GU2 5XH United Kingdom

Telephone 01483 259203
Facsimile 01483 503517
Telex 859331

Direct Line:

R O B E N S
Institute

23 September 1994

Mr F. Drabble
Drabble and Co.,

Dear Freddy

Thank you for the full copy of the WS Atkins' report, which I received today. I have read the
microbiology section and was quite astonished by the naïvety of the methods, data interpretation
and conclusions. I should be surprised if this section was written by a microbiologist.

Of more immediate concern to you is the toxicity data for the chemicals isolated from the stack
emissions. I enclose copies of the BDH hazard data sheets for each of the major components of
the emission gas, listed in the Ceram Research Report, and for Chloroform and Benzene, listed
as trace components. It is very interesting that most of these chemicals are known irritants and
that the toxicity of one or two is enhanced in the presence of benzene. I am sure Scarborough
Council will delight in this information.

I shall read the WS Atkins' Report, in depth, this weekend. If the quality of the microbiology
section is a reflection of the general quality of the report it will make interesting reading.

Yours sincerely

Stephen Pedley

Printed on recycled paper

The S.B.C. Atkins report was at first cherry picked by
Scarborough Council as favourable to them and the YWA. Later
other interpretations such as the Robens Report exposed the
dangers of the chemical applications of various acids to quell the
smells, vapours etc. Eventually the SBC were forced to take legal
action against the YWA

EUROPEAN PARLIAMENT

<small>MEMBER OF THE EUROPEAN PARLIAMENT</small>

Tel:
Fax:

5th February 1996

Mr Freddie Drabble
Sons of Neptune Ltd
1 Cromwell Parade
Scarborough
YO11 2DP

Dear Freddie,

Thank you very much for your letter of 26th January regarding the Urban Waste Water Directive. I have taken the correspondence to Brussels with me and my office will be raising the matter with the official responsible within the Commission.

Thank you for keeping me informed and I will be in touch as soon as I have some news for you.

Yours sincerely,

Ken Collins MEP

(Dictated by Ken Collins and signed in his absence)

Sir Ken Collins was very supportive of the Sons. Former MEP and Chairman of the European Parliament's Environment Committee at the time of our campaign. He deserves great credit as an environmentalist.

Scarborough Diary

with Mick Jefferson.

YOU can e-mail Mick Jefferson via editorial@scarboroughevening news.co.uk or direct at mick.jefferson@amserve.net, or send him a fax on 01723 383825.

Sons were right

HOW times change.

The final vindication of the stand that the Sons of Neptune made over sewage came when the minister of trade and two colleagues toured Scarborough's new £30 million treatment works.

One of the party, Helen Jackson, a former parliamentary secretary to Mo Mowlam, paid tribute to persistent campaigners for the works, naming the Sons in particular.

What a change from the days when the Sons were frequently vilified by figures in authority and accused of harming the tourist trade.

Attitudes have changed since then. We are all greener and environmentally aware, and clean bathing waters have become a big plus for resorts.

It turns out that the Sons, who from an early stage were pressing for the works we now have, were years ahead in their thinking than many of the rest of us.

Fighting for the beaches

Yorkshire tops the league

IT is all too easy for the environmentalists to hog the headlines. Whenever an oil tanker runs aground or a chemical firm spills pollutants into a river, the stories are rightly front-page news. But when private industry, in this case the privatised water companies, make improvements in the environment, it is rare to find a green campaigner or a journalist giving the good news the same treatment as the bad receives.

Yet the fact that three of Yorkshire's main beaches are now ranked among the best in the country is testimony to the efforts of firms like the much-maligned Yorkshire Water in cleaning up our coastal reaches through a massive investment in treatment works. Without this money being spent, it is unlikely that Scarborough, Bridlington and Filey would be flying the Seaside Award flags as they will be doing so proudly this Easter.

But it is also a tribute to the citizens, councillors and traders of these seaside family favourites that their beaches have scored so highly in a league table drawn up by the organisers of the Keep Britain Tidy campaign. By doing the simple things well, such as ensuring the beaches are clean from early morning, towns such as Scarborough have become role models for other seaside resorts who want to clean up their own act. Indeed, it is this combination of clean, safe waters (it is a tribute to Yorkshire Water's efforts that one of the most vociferous East Coast environmental groups, the Sons of Neptune, is now championing its case) and neat, tidy beaches which is winning plaudits from surfers, Greens and holidaymakers alike.

All this bodes well for a good Easter, even if the weather is playing its familiar fickle game. For, although many people will take to southern Spain and warmer climes at this time of year, Yorkshire's coast, with its bracing airs and its breathtaking sweeps of sea and sand, is impossible to beat on a good day. As the Sons of Neptune rather dramatically put it, the fight to clean up the beaches has been worth it for the seas are the Champagne of life. Many will toast to that.

Letters to the Editor

Group scores victory after the dark ages of coastal sewage

From: Patrick Argent, Fulford Road, Scarborough.

IN reading your front page lead story ("Small resorts miss £110m tide of investment on water quality", *Yorkshire Post*, November 5) it is crucially important, however, to remember that the whole basis of the modern enlightened approach to the clean and safe treatment of sewage off the UK's coastal waters is a direct result of the pioneering work of the Yorkshire marine conservation group, the Sons of Neptune.

The group's initial campaign centred on the objection to a wholly inadequate long sea outfall scheme at Scarborough, before they brought the whole issue of coastal sewage pollution into the national and international political arena.

Since their resounding victory in their 15-year campaign for EU legislation outlawing the dumping of raw untreated sewage and toxic waste off the UK coasts, the Scarborough-based Neptune group has been virtually ignored by the media.

The group's commissioning of a comprehensive scientific report by Professor Bruce Denness was the defining moment which unequivocally condemned the pollution of UK and European beaches.

The report irrefutably proved the dumping of raw, untreated sewage via long sea outfalls was pathogenically dangerous to both human and marine life.

Despite receiving initial copies of the findings, the regional water company (Yorkshire Water Authority) still considered their then Viking-age settlement solution for the Yorkshire coast, a viable one.

Roman civil engineers 2,000 years ago would have been capable of building a far more sophisticated and effective system of dealing with the interminable problem of sewage disposal. They at least fundamentally understood the critical importance of the separation of people from raw sewage.

The Sons of Neptune tireless campaign was in effect, a modern-day development of the ground-breaking work in the 19th century of Sir Joseph Bazalgette, in alerting society to the wholesale irresponsibility and inherent dangers of discharging unregulated human waste into coastal waters.

The group's ensuing vigorous and tenacious campaign forced the YWA to eventually update their antiquated and wholly obsolete system, which by then had invariably wasted millions of pounds.

The safe and effective treatment of human sewage has been one of the very cornerstones of any ordered and advanced civilisation, yet this easily understood concept completely escaped the attention of both the water authority and Scarborough Borough Council at the time.

The latest development announcing the upgrade of waste-treatments works by Yorkshire Water in partnership with other organisations in a bid to achieve EU Blue Flag designated beaches, is a situation that could hardly be ever imagined during the water industry's entrenched dark ages of the 1980s and 1990s.

MAIN EVENTS OF SONS OF NEPTUNE CAMPAIGN

During 10 Years from 9th January 1983 to 9th January 1993

1983

Towards the end of 1982 confidential discussions took place between Yorkshire Water and certain local organisations including local fishermen concerning the possibility of a new Raw Sewage Outfall pipe discharging from the Marine Drive into the sea. Such rumours reached the ears of the Sons of Neptune at the beginning of January 1983 who reacted with shock and disbelief at the proposals for the following reasons:-

(a) The Marine Drive, being an historic local scenic beauty spot was obviously totally environmentally unsuitable for desecration by a sewage works.

(b) The site itself was incapable of development for the purpose proposed due to unstable cliffs directly at the rear.

(c) Raw sewage discharge, as proposed, only 600 metres from the Marine Drive would guarantee that raw sewage would be returned to both bays.

A few days later Sir Meredith Whittaker, Proprietor of Scarborough and District Newspapers wrote letter to the Evening News in which the rumours were confirmed. This was quickly followed by other letters expressing shock and disbelief at the proposals including one from the Sons of Neptune. On the day that our letter was published Maggie Mainprize, leader of the Fisherman's Association made a public statement condemning the proposals. The Sons made contact with her to press for a public meeting and this was held a few weeks later at Castle Community Centre. It was at this meeting that the Sons came into contact with Capt. Sydney Smith (UK Tidal Expert) born in Scarborough and with notable family seafaring ancestors dating back to the 17th Century. We found that all his experience backed our own convictions concerning the scheme and, in particular, it would lead to the pollution of both Bays.

As a representative of Yorkshire Water did not attend the meeting at Castle Community Centre, a further meeting was arranged within weeks at which they were requested to attend and this meeting took place at St Mary's Parish House. Yorkshire Water were questioned by the Sons of Neptune and Captain Smith, and their answers left the public total dissatisfied.

7/3/83   Scarborough Council gave outline Planning Consent to Yorkshire Water's Marine Drive Raw Sewage Works. The voting 32-8.

Capt. Sydney Smith's formal report stated that the scheme would be "disastrous".

6/4/83   Sons of Neptune formal complaint to Ombudsman that Yorkshire Water's decision had been taken without consideration being given to a full treatment scheme. This was denied by Yorkshire Water who alleged that a treatment scheme would cost an additional £3.5m/5m and such additional expenditure was not justified.

7/6/83   Scarborough coble fishermen backed the Sons of Neptune.

September – December '83
          Consultations between Sons of Neptune with Capt. Smith and Yorkshire Water. Sons of Neptune produced pictures of Castle Headland years ago proving the extent of subsequent subsidence in the very place where the sewage works was proposed.

          Sons of Neptune, with Captain Sydney Smith and local coblemen, investigate and identify Cowlam Hole as the site most suitable to take advantage of favourable currents for discharge of the sewage into the sea to the north of Scarborough.

1984

27/3/84   Sons challenge cost of cliff stabilisation on Marine Drive.

Summer '84 Continuation of Marine Survey work by Sons of Neptune with Capt. Smith off the Marine Drive and also at Cowlam Hole to establish depth at various tides and complete such works started in the summer of 1983.

26/7/84   Sons of Neptune Consultant Geologist confirms that Castle Head Cliff behind the proposed site for the sewage works is unstable and incapable of being stabilised. Such reports were sent to the Press and Yorkshire Water. This fully backed the evidence from the old pictures produced late in 1983 to Yorkshire Water.

28/8/84   Yorkshire Water announce cancellation of Marine Drive Scheme. Sons celebrate this victory in the best possible way by a dip in the sea to mark the successful conclusion of the campaign to prevent raw sewage being discharged from the Marine Drive where it would have destroyed both the North & South Bays with pollution.

1985

Little was heard from Yorkshire Water for most of this year and, as they had already costed due to pressure from the Sons of Neptune, two alternative Cowlam Hole schemes it was assumed that they would now be putting together a Cowlam scheme for outline planning consent.

However, this was proved wrong when late in the year the Sons heard that Yorkshire Water, instead of going to Cowlam, were in fact planning a sewage works at Scalby Mills.

1986

6/1/86   A Press Statement was released in which the Sons leaked to Scarborough Evening news what Yorkshire Water were planning for Scalby Mills. It turned out that this had all been discussed in confidence with various parties earlier in 1985 unknown to the Sons of Neptune.

21/2/86   Sons of Neptune complained to Ombudsman that Yorkshire Water were seeking to obtain approval of the scheme without consulting all interest parties, ie, no consultation with Sons of Neptune. The Ombudsman later rejected this complaint.

25/4/86   Sons of Neptune complained to EEC against UK in respect of the Scarborough Scheme registered as official.

June/July/August 1986
    Regular contact with Dr Bruce Denness, former Professor of Ocean Engineering at Newcastle Upon Tyne University and Capt Smith to discuss tidal information and local conditions led to subsequent instructions for the preparation of the Denness Report which it was agreed would be published as soon as possible by the Sons of Neptune and be authored by Dr Denness.

16/8/86   Contact with Professor D J Grimes of Maryland University, USA, Professor of Microbiology with research papers published on the survival of bacteria in the sea and report to the US House of Congress on waste disposal to the sea and its health impact.

1987

14/5/87   London Press Launch of Denness Report.

23/6/87   BBC Newsnight Special Edition devoted to the Sons campaign and includes interviews with Dr Denness and Professor Grimes.

17/7/87   Registration by EC of Sons of Neptune formal complaints that the ability of bacteria and viruses to survive in the sea for longer than believed made the Scarborough Raw Sewage Scheme not only obsolete but unable to comply with the bathing Water Directive and constitute a danger to human health and the Marine Environment.

24/8/87   Awareness of Prince of Wales and his expressed interest to be kept informed.

12/11/87   Visit to US by Sons of Neptune for discussions with Professor Grimes relating to research of survival of pathogens in the sea the whole of his published research paper having been made available to us including his report to US congress on waste disposal to the Oceans and human health impacts in 1986.

24/11/87   Formal objection of Yorkshire Water's Planning Application for the Scalby Mills Raw Sewage Works.

3/12/87   Tyne Tees documentary "A Suitable Case For Treatment" examines the issues raised by the Sons.

1988

29th/30th June '88
"The Neptune Project'. Yorkshire Water, having argued that whilst bacteria in the sea might live longer elsewhere, (eg, USA) they did not do so in the North Sea at Scarborough. Sons of Neptune in conjunction with Robens Institute carried out the "Neptune Project" whereby work was carried out continually for 24 hours on bacteria in sea water samples taken in the vicinity of the outfall position, brought to the shore and then sampled hourly to prove that the bacteria did not die quickly enough to enable the outfall scheme to comply with EC safety laws.

June '88   Help to Lancashire with research results as they were fighting similar battle against North West Water to protect Blackpool, Morecambe Bay and the whole of the Fylde Coast from sewage pollution. The Son's research enabled the campaigns to be established by Lancashire County Council and the Fleetwood 'Save Our Bay' campaign. These campaigns were ultimately successful in avoiding a raw sewage scheme there.

September '88
Similar help to campaigns in Cornwall, Wales, Scotland, Tyneside, Lytham, Robin Hood's Bay, Yorkshire and Southend.

1989

5/1/89   BBC North East "The North Sea" series begins narrated by Susannah York. One of the parts, in which the Sons are involved, named after then "Neptune's Children".

2/3/89   Margaret Thatcher interviewed by Michael Buerk on BBC's "Nature" states that all sewage discharged into the sea in the UK is "treated sewage". Sons launch immediate protest and Michael Buerk is obliged to correct the matter nationally on the next issue of the "Nature" programme following a National Campaign on 6th March organised by the Sons of Neptune to draw attention to the Thatcher Government's Raw Sewage in the Sea policies. The highlight of this campaign was the sons launch of the "Thatcherloo" on the River Thames which was sailed under the Tower Bridge towards the Houses of Parliament. The inscription "Thatcherloo proves Thatcherlie".

26/4/89   Confirmation from EC that they are now considering measures to control the use of Long Sea Outfalls.

9/6/89   Letter from Euro MP McMillan Scot confirms our complaints with the ED have contributed to such moves.

27/9/89   Sons submit, by invitation, a memorandum of evidence on beach pollution to the House of Commons environmental committee.

13/11/89   Publication of EC Proposals for a Community Directive covering waste water treatment. Sons of Neptune comment on such draft.

1990

10/5/90   The news that the Penzance Scheme is to be a Treatment Scheme.

24/7/90   Publication of House of Commons Environment Committee Report on Beach Pollution. Incorporates evidence from Sons of Neptune. The Report concludes that full treatment of sewage is necessary for all discharges.

23/10/90   Letter from Ken Collins Euro MP for Strathclyde, chairman for the European Environmental Committee,

9/5/90   News of success at Blackpool. Evidence provided has lead to the Raw Sewage Scheme wanted by North West Water being rejected by the Department of the Environment. Morecambe, Blackpool and the rest of the Fylde coast has been saved from sewage pollution.

October '90 Input to draft EC Waste Water Directive.

1991

18/3/91   Campaign against peracetic acid being used for overflow discharges into Scalby Beck. Objection against this lodged with National Rivers Authority. Eventual withdrawal of the proposal by Yorkshire Water.

April '91   "Yorkshire Water in the Dock". See Evening News Report.

May '91   Discovery of sewage sludge deposits on Scarborough's North Bay beach. Bacterial analysis by the Sons of such sledge reveal heavy contamination by sewage bacteria. Subsequent sampling and analysis by Robens Institute and Pat Gowen of Norfolk Friends of the Earth confirm the nature of the sludge.

July '91   Invitation to county Hall Truro at the request of Cornwall County Council to advise the Council on the extent of treatment required for effective long-term compliance with the Bathing Water Directive. Sons flown to Cornwall.

July '91   Provision of sewage sludge samples to National Rivers Authority and meeting with them in Scarborough.

14/8/91   "Holiday Which" survey of Resort Bathing Water provides Scarborough second most contaminated after Blackpool. Evening News headline "Scarborough in a Sea of Shame". Both Bays exceed legal limits.

12/9/91	David Trippier, Minister of State for the Environment opens officially the Scalby Mills sewage scheme. Samples of sewage sludge from the beach are shown to him.
April '91	EC Urban Waste Water Directive comes into force.
1/11/91	Yorkshire Water withdraw their proposal to use peracetic acid. National Rivers Authority which had been carrying out an investigation into the safety of the chemical refused to say whether they considered it to be safe for use in the sea.

1992

	Campaign to prevent sighting of proposed new sewage treatment plant firstly in Donkey Field directly to the north of Scalby Beck opposite Scholes Park road and also against the proposed site at the corner of Field Lane/Burniston Road, Scarborough.
February '92	Campaign against the building of four large sewage tanks at Newby/Scalby which would discharge into the Beck during times of heavy rain. The NRA had said the tanks would reduce the overflow into Scalby Beck once every two years. This has already proved to be false to prove the Son's statement that such tanks were not simply storm water overflows but a substitute for proper and effective drainage during normal rain conditions. Formal objections raised with the NRA.
	Personal letter from Carlo Ripa De Meana confirming that the Sons of Neptune complaints about the Scarborough Raw Sewage Scheme have been registered within the scope of Directive 76/464EEC and that the Commission had given formal notice to the UK Government as provided for in Article 169 of the EEC Treaty giving the opportunity to submit its observations on the pollution problems associated with the Long Sea Outfall in Scarborough.
March '92	Contact with Election Candidates with regard to obtaining their pledges that, if elected, they would fight for clean seas and beaches and campaign for Full Sewage Treatment in their constituency to comply with the 1991 ED Urban Waste Water Directive.
July '92	The stench from Scalby Mills is so bad that residents call on the Chairman of Yorkshire Water, Sir Gordon Jones to meet them or resign.
August '92	Sons of Neptune attend Yorkshire Water AGM at Harrogate in an attempt to get two of the directors voted off the Board and replaced by representatives of the Sons of Neptune as Directors.

September '92

Sons of Neptune address meeting at Scalby and Newby Parish council and also subsequent Public Meeting called by the Council to oppose the sighting of the Sewage Works and Sludge processing Works at Field Lane/Burniston Road corner. The proposal to do so was subsequently withdrawn by Yorkshire Water.

September '92

NRA disclosed 1992 salmonella and enterovirus results confirming both Scarborough's North & South Beach had failed the enterovirus tests meaning effective failure of the bathing water directive.

Scarborough Evening News - transcribed cuttings & quotes *1983-1993*

8/3/83   Council Approves Marine Drive Scheme 900M outfall Scarborough Hotels Association send the council a letter:

"The plant is a setback in our efforts to keep us at the top of the resorts league."

Councillor Don Dalton agrees, "It will stick out like a sore thumb on our glorious marine Drive."

Russell Bradley, Chief Executive of Scarborough Council, says:

"I have been advised by Mr Ayrton that the possibility of nuisance and smell is almost negligible."

7/3/83   A group calling itself the Sons of Neptune are planning a three pronged attack on the Marine Drive Scheme: a protest to the DoE; canvass Shaw MP potential voting campaign on what Shaw does

13/3/83   Sons protest to Ombudsman

16/6/83   JR Lewis a doctor of philosophy and former director of Leeds Wellcome Marine Lab at Robin Hood's Bay writes a feature on sewage disposal to the sea for the SEN. He compares it favourably with dumping chemicals at sea:

"sewage in the sea poses fewer problems... because it is organic and easily decomposed." CJW writes to SEN: "Philosophy is concerned with two things...

28/6/83   Local ombudsman decides not to pursue claim saying YWA "extensive consultation" with main bodies, inc government departments and local fishing associations

5/7/83   Moving one survey team to Cowlam Hole "a waste of public funds" Bob Bedford, Chair, Development Services Committee

Cllr Greenan urges YWA to press ahead ASAP

7/8/83   SEN Leader:

"Despite what the Sons of Neptune say, we believe the vast majority of ratepayers are happy to have screened sewage pumped into the sea and accept the YWA case that it will not come back on the beach. But does the pumping and screening station really have to be on Marine Drive?"

9/8/83   Sons take YWA Area Manager Ken Eley on a boat trip to Cowlam. There has been confusion about exactly which part of Jackson's Bay is Cowlam Hole. Sons mean a gulley 1100 metres north of Scalby Mills, YWA understood one 650 metres further than that. Both sides describe the meeting as cordial and pleasant.

6/9/83   Pitts: "If we dilly-dally, the YWA will spend the money elsewhere, and then we will lose our clean beach status."

28/9/83   Council agrees plan to close the bulk of the North Beach while the sewage plant is being built

26/10/83 A big concrete and steel pile which was to have supported the construction collapses.

1/10/84   Sons celebrate announcement of the end of planning of the Marine Drive scheme. YWA claim five years worth of preparation and survey work is "not wasted"

10/6/85   We'll Fight Scalby Mills Scheme SoN - SoN delighted YWA considering Cowlam

3/2/86   SEN Leader: "Does £3.5M Matter?"

Three and a half million pounds is the difference between the Cowlam and Scalby Mills Schemes. SoN were right last time. Is £3.5M anything at all to avoid any possibility of their being right again?"

5/2/86   SEN Leader:

"We do not wish to further embarrass Councillors Jean Greenan, Michael Pitts, ? Jenkinson and Mr Ken Hull over their April 1983 statement explaining why the YWA scheme was such a very good thing and how the Sons of Neptune did not know what they were talking about. (It turned out that the Sons Of Neptune did know better than then Mayor Greenan...)"

25/3/86   Scarborough Council Environmental Committee votes for Scalby Mills Scheme to go ahead ASAP.

Councillor (Dr) George McIntyre says: "Sewage disposal to the sea ecologically, these proposals would cause no problems and could prove a positive benefit."

Roy Ayrton: The sea is an extremely hostile environment for sewage bacteria. Sewage released well out to sea... a clean and simple operation."

16/4/86   Development Services Committee approve scheme at Scalby Mills

21/4/86   Nineteen senior fishermen averaging over forty years experience at sea each sign a statement backing Syd and the Sons and condemning the scheme

23/4/86   "Some Fishermen Have Changed Their Minds YWA" Mr RI Crease, YWA North and East Divisional Operations Manager said representatives of all fishing interests in Scarborough attended a meeting at which the scheme was accepted.

24/4/86	Sons make repeated call for a public enquiry
1986	One councillor calls on the town to boycott the Sons' respective businesses
25/4/86	FD replies to exMayor Jean Greenan's attack on the Sons as "scientific illiterates" and "mad hatters": "We have never been invited to present to the council... "
2/5/86	"Computer Challenge to Sons" Fisherman Stuart Ogden, skipper of the Valhalla
29/5/86	"Shaw Hits Back At Sons" like being savaged by a dead sheep "I have always taken the view that, subject to full consideration of the facts, the YWA long sea outfall scheme should be proceeded with just as fast as possible, in the interests of everyone." "You informed me that you had additional expert evidence that would rule out the present proposals and favour your own Cowlam Hole proposals. "I pressed your group to make it available to the council and 1 ensured a copy was sent to the Department of the Environment."
25/9/86	DoE Approves Scalby Mills decision rules out public enquiry.
28/3/87	Ten more beaches in Scarborough Borough are designated as bathing beaches by the EC. They will also be tested from now on; whereas up to now, only the North and South bays have.
14/5/87	The Sons go to London to launch the Denness report at a press conference. Professor Denness claims the 1450metre outfall will put more people at risk of disease than at present.
21/5/87	YW does some "market research", paying members of the public six pounds a time to attend a session to discuss the scheme
20/7/87	Sons petition EC to ban sewage disposal to the sea as the 1975 Directive is inadequate does not cover viruses
31/7/87	Scheme building to start in October
14/10/87	Maff says burning toxic waste at sea mostly organochloride waste from the pharmaceutical industry is "the best practical environmentally acceptable option" for getting rid of the stuff. Waste produced includes hydrochloric acid which is pumped into the sea, and what Maff describes as a "micro film" on the water surface
25/11/87	Prince Charles describes the North Sea as "an enormous rubbish dump"

26/11/87   Environment Secretary Nick Ridley says the government will:

End the dumping of toxic waste at sea

Prohibit rubbish dumping in the sea by end of 1989

Control river pollution more

That announcement must have stuck in his throat. The son of a Viscount, Nick Ridley was very much to the right of even Thatcher's Conservative party at its zenith. In his diaries, Alan Clark W described Ridley's thinking as "pure Adam Smith Institute." This [abominable abuse of the great Scottish economist's name] describes a loony-right lobby group who believe there should be no public sector at all, and that big business should be absolutely free to do whatever it wants. This was indeed Ridley's belief, and he placed no value on the environment whatsoever.

His arrogance was so immense he never had anything but contempt for anyone who ever disagreed with him. Throughout his Ministerial career, he was regularly burned in effigy a distinction only earned by the PM herself during the miners' strike. Putting such a man in charge of the department was the clearest possible demonstration of Thatcher's attitude towards environmental issues.

1/8/88   Lancashire County Council calls for a public inquiry into Blackpool's £50M sewage scheme

30/8/89   Sons stage another mock funeral at Scalby Mills

1/11/89   Champagne on the beach: the Sons celebrate Commissioner Carlo Ripa de Meana's announcement of plans to ban sewage disposal to the sea Europewide. "The proposal is designed to bring to an end an intolerable situation which is worthy of the middle ages direct dumping into our rivers, lakes and seas of filthy water." CRM

13/11/89   YW says the scheme's cost will at least double if the EC bans sewage disposal to the sea.

21/11/89   DoE officials admit to the House of Commons select Committee that they do not know how long bacteria and viruses from sewage survive at sea. The committee points out that this is at odds with the Department's official position that sea bathing is perfectly safe. The Sons comment that their position has always been that long outfalls are cosmetic only sewage must be treated.

5/3/90   Environment Secretary Chris Patten announces that the disposal of raw sewage to the sea is to be banned. Brussels has forced the government's hand and the EC regulations must become UK law.

29/5/90   Roy Ayrton says that the outfall, to be completed by the following May, will bring "radical and comprehensive improvement. "There are presently 500 sea outfalls for sewage around UK shores. Only a minute percentage of these are designed to anywhere near the standards of the long sea outfall which will serve Scarborough. The system could be among the best, if not the best, in the country."

26/7/90   The Commons Environment Committee reports and backs the Sons. It says outfalls are not the answer and agrees there is a real risk of infection from sea bathing.

7/4/91   Roy Ayrton assures Councillors that Oxymaster, based on peracetic acid, is suitable for use.

3/6/91   Sons claim YW disinfectant Oxymaster damages sea life

2nd week   Which? Reports on the state of Britain's beaches. Only Blackpool is
August 91   worse than Scarborough, both breach EC tests according to Which? Tests, by the Robens Institute at Surrey University

14/8/91   Mavis Don, Mayor, says the new Which? Report will cost the town millions of pounds in lost tourist revenue. The council may need to go cap in hand to central government.

15/8/91   David Jones, council tourism chief is furious with Which? "If they are putting out this scientific report in the interests of the public and it has its merits, then it should be discussed on a scientific basis, and not in the confrontational way this has been released." Separately, Roy Ayrton comments on the EC looking at including virus tests in its bathing water quality standards: "It may support the traditional reliance on bacterial indicator standards which have for decades provided an effective measure. Any assertion that there are health risks associated with bathing in good quality water, such as that found along Scarborough coastline is unfounded."

17/8/91   NRA says North Bay passes its test, "It's looking good for the last two weeks the best results on record, seasonally." If the beach fails another test for the year, it fails the standard. It failed one soon after the plant opened.

28/8/91   ICI wants YW to try its "Coastguard" product instead of Oxymaster. NRA says, "It's bleach. It might kill 99% of viruses, but it will also kill an awful lot of other things as well."

30/8/91   YW could face prosecution by the council over the smells plaguing residents of Scalby Mills. Complaints still coming in thick and fast.

4/9/91   NRA chiefs test sludge sent by SEN from a slick on the beach. Editor Neil Speight describes it as "a foul and slimy sight that stretched across the sand." Tests revealed the liquid around the sludge contained 3500 E Coli / 100 ml seawater and total coliform count of 25,500 /100ml. EC limits are 2000 and 10000 respectively. Graham Tate NRA pollution control area manager said the tests showed it was not a danger to public health. Ayrton says it is quite wrong to compare the sludge results to bathing water quality standards. "There is no foundation at all that it is connected with sewage sludge." In fact, E Coli is only naturally found in faeces. He continues: "I continue to be satisfied that the outfall is doing an excellent job. The water quality test results have been consistently excellent.

10/9/91   YW says Scarborough will get treatment as part of "hundreds of millions" to be spent on the Yorkshire Coast.

11/9/91   New sewage plans announced for Scalby Mills farmland. The newly required treatment plant is to be built north west of the outfall.

13/9/91   David Trippler W, environment minister, visits the scheme and is publicly harangued by the Sons as assembled crowds applaud.

10/10/91   Ayrton claims the brown slick spotted off Scarborough coast throughout the summer was a natural phenomenon. Samples sent to Plymouth for testing revealed it was caused by cytoplankton. "The appearance of these plankton fluctuates. It appears to be related to the weather and sea conditions. But it is absolutely natural and there is nothing to be concerned about.

25/10/91   Ayrton's boss, Public health Chief Kaetrin Camegie Smith says, "I speak to GP's regularly and there is no evidence of cases of illness being caused by swimming in the sea. 1 don't want to be seen taking sides for or against the Sons, but 1 don't think they are being very helpful."

26/10/91   Ayrton on the sludge: "These natural sediments attract bacteria the sludges in the North Bay are not a new phenomenon. They have been present for many years. This year's bathing water sample results show the outfall scheme achieving high quality water standards in the North Bay. There is clear evidence of the great environmental benefits which the outfall is achieving."

28/10/91   Barry Truman, YW area manager says work is to begin on a £2 m scheme to prevent storm sewage overflows these occurred 14 times in the previous year.

5/11/91   Sons demand NRA position on peracetic acid

12/11/91   Roy Ayrton praises new scheme: North Bay bacteria count down by 80% on 1990 South Bay down 50 60%

30/11/91   Freddie Drabble writes to SEN:

"Yorkshire Water accept the Robens report, but deny this substance comes from the outfall. The other parts of the report which they accept include: that a "large area" of the North Bay has been affected, some it heavily, by the sludge. That rock pool water tested at eleven times over the EC safety limit for bathing water. That there are very high levels of bacteria in the sludge 1000 times more than nearby sand and 100 times the limit for bathing water.

FD is responding to a previous letter from B Truman YWA Malton Area

Manager of 22 November which claimed the sludge was still there from the previous scheme

NEXT to FD's letter is one from Allan ? 23 North Cliff Ave, pointing out:

- Peracetic acid causes cancer related mutations

- Marine biologist @ Sea Life Centre complained to NRA that the local marine environment was "killing things"

- Slicks occurring - exactly as predicted by STS

- Stench - people's washing comes in stinking

- heavy deposits of smelly black sludge - residents of 20 years never saw it before

YW states the scheme was built to comply with the 1975 directive. August 1991 saw Which? Test fail the North and South Bays in tests for viruses. They were the second most virus-infected bathing waters surveyed - the worst being Blackpool's, here a new scheme to sort it out was already underway.

10/12/91	1st Gowen report in SEN. Freddie Drabble says: "Our next step must be Europe in order to get this sorted out."
11/12/91	NRA claims all organic content found in sludgey sand from North Bay "algal material" no sewage bacteria present
13/12/91	Sons reply to Hull University report for NRA - of no sewage in bay. Sons reports: Robens Institute at the University of Surrey found a "high level of faecal contamination" in the sludge. Retired microbiology lecturer Dr Pat Gowen of Norwich finds traces of urine, hair and a nail cutting which could only have come from sewage.
13/2/92	Councillors to seek legal advice over YW plans to build four large underground sewage tanks for storm overflows in Scalby
Nov 92	Yorkshire Water fined £8000 over emissions.
9/3/93	Peter Tidd, Vice Chairman of Burniston Parish Council, accuses residents who have complained of smells of, "stirring the pot"
1/7/93	Cayton Bay seawater registers bacterial levels 1000 times EC guide levels. Ayrton says, "this is a very odd result because previously the bathing water quality at Cayton has been consistently of top quality."
3/7/93	[Yorkshire Post] Don Robinson: "I'm a shareholder in Yorkshire Water, and there will be a lot of questions to answer at the shareholder's meeting this year. The way the customers have been treated is appalling."

This list ends here but the fight continued and still continues. The protection of the environment is priority simply because if we destroy it, we destroy ourselves.